LORNA MACKINNON is an award-winning coach with over a decade's experience of life coaching and has an international client base. She developed the technique used in *Your Star Sign Life Coach* after she discovered that giving clients an astrological reading, prior to coaching them, made the coaching process far more effective.

Currently financial independence coach for *Woman Abroad* magazine, career management columnist for *Pharmaceutical Field* and astrologer and relationship coach for www.soyouvebeendumped.com, Lorna has a long-standing interest (spanning some twenty years) in astrology, metaphysics and personal development, all of which she draws upon when working with clients. She can be visited on the web at www.cosmiccoaching.com.

LORNA MacKINNON

USE LIFE COACHING TECHNIQUES
TO MAXIMIZE YOUR STAR SIGN'S
POTENTIAL AND CREATE
THE LIFE YOU WANT

YOUR
STAR SIGN
LIFE COACH

MARLOWE & COMPANY • NEW YORK

YOUR STAR SIGN LIFE COACH:
Use Life Coaching Techniques to Maximize
Your Star Sign's Potential and Create the Life You Want

Copyright © 2002 by Lorna MacKinnon

Published by
Marlowe & Company
An Imprint of Avalon Publishing Group Incorporated
161 William Street, 16th Floor
New York, NY 10038

First published in the United Kingdom in 2002 by Rider,
an imprint of Ebury Press.
This edition published by arrangement.

Library of Congress Cataloging-in-Publication Data
MacKinnon, Lorna.
[Cosmic coaching]
Your star sign life coach : use life coaching techniques to maximize your star sign's
potential and create the life you want / by Lorna MacKinnon.
p. cm.
Originally published: Cosmic coaching. U.K. : Rider, 2002.
Includes bibliographical references and index.
ISBN 1-56924-559-2 (trade paper)
1. Astrology. 2. Success—Miscellanea. I. Title.
BF1729.S88 M33 2002
133.5—dc21   2002141412

9 8 7 6 5 4 3 2 1

DESIGNED BY PAULINE NEUWIRTH, NEUWIRTH & ASSOCIATES, INC.

Printed in the United States of America
Distributed by Publishers Group West

To all my clients—past, present, and future—who grant me the privilege of partnering with them to shape their lives and careers. To my parents for bringing me up with a healthy sense of self-worth and belief in myself. To Zen, my Aries Samoyed, for ensuring that I get plenty of play and healthy exercise. To my husband, Paul, for love and support.

CONTENTS

ACKNOWLEDGMENTS

To my friends, clients, colleagues, and family who have supported me throughout this project, thank you.

To my agent, Teresa Chris, thank you for believing in *Cosmic Coaching* and finding me a publisher. Thank you for your belief in me and your support.

To Julia McCutchen and colleagues at Random House, for all your work, support, and dedication to making this book happen.

To Suzanne McCloskey at Marlowe & Company for transforming the text, and thanks to everyone else at Marlowe who was involved with the American edition of the book.

To Joanna Carreras, for enabling me to bring my voice to the page and for bringing out my best. Thank you for your generosity in allowing me the freedom to make some (much needed) last-minute alterations.

To my fellow coaches, for providing a supportive community within which to explore new ideas.

To Thomas Leonard, founder of Coach University and Coachville, for inspiring me to become a coach.

To my parents, for inspiring me to believe in myself.

To my husband, for inspiring me to keep going when frustration had threatened to overwhelm me, and for listening to me uncomplainingly when I've "talked shop."

PREFACE

YOUR Star Sign Life Coach was written with one objective in mind: to provide you with the information you need to be more successful in your career, business, and personal life. Being more successful can often mean a larger home, a bigger income, getting a job, getting promoted, your own successful business, happier and more fulfilling relationships, a greater sense of well-being, and more respect from others, to name but a few. I am assuming that you are reading this book because you want some of these treasures for yourself.

These are all-powerful motivators and certainly on most people's wish list. However, wishing is not enough—we need to believe that we can attain our heart's desires and we need to take concerted action to manifest those desires. In short, we need to develop the goals, the belief, the guts, and an achievement plan. The life we aim to create and our way of going about this are unique to us. Through working on myself and with my clients I have come to the conclusion that one of the most effective ways to make changes is to ensure that those changes arise naturally from who you are. It is also a great deal easier to make changes if you enjoy the method by which you bring them about. For example, I find repeating affirmations ad infinitum a real drag and used to give up before accomplishing anything worthwhile. I then decided to turn this lust for a quick result into a powerful, unique method of subconscious programming called 911 Affirmations (see page 7), which was perfect for my personality type. I needed to develop a system for personal development that worked for me rather than trying to make an off-the-shelf solution fit my needs. I also found that the only way to get lasting, meaningful results for my clients was to work with them on a regular one-to-one basis and to develop a different coaching program for each and every one of them. Fortunately, I could streamline the process by developing different coaching exercises for different personality types. A concept that I bring to you through the medium of this book.

Your Star Sign Life Coach uses a system of personal development tailored to different star signs (or personality types, for those of you who are not into astrology). It has been developed and refined over the years and has transformed many lives, some of which you will read about in this book. Some of the clients' case details have been changed to protect the client's privacy. It is designed to make attaining your goals an easier and more enjoyable experience than fighting against who you are. Whether or not you believe in astrology, look for the sun sign temperament most similar to yours and start to work with the exercises in that chapter to create the life you want.

Whatever your experience with personal development may be, I hope that, whichever stage you've reached in your own journey through life, you'll find this book interesting and helpful.

INTRODUCTION

WE all want to make the best of ourselves using our natural and acquired talents, so that we can achieve the maximum success, happiness, and fulfillment that we are capable of in this lifetime. Yet we are also unique individuals, so the right approach for one person may be completely wrong for someone else. What works for me, a Leo, who likes to get maximum results for minimum effort, is unlikely to work for Capricorn, who likes to take the path of most resistance. By using astrology to understand who you uniquely are and what you are working on in this life, you arm yourself with the self-knowledge that is essential for success. Your star chart reveals your strengths and weaknesses, how you get in your own way, your life lessons, and life purpose. Sounds great, doesn't it?

Now how do you make the most of this information? Through the use of life coaching, which is about translating self-knowledge into a road map for success. The object of life coaching is to find out exactly what you need to move forward and achieve your goals, and to make sure that you keep taking the focused action necessary to attain them. Coaching takes an inside out approach to your life in order to get the circumstances of your life to change. We'll unlock your potential and invest in your ability to achieve. We'll usher in a new era of sustainable success built upon strong foundations. You'll learn how to make the right choices in life for the person you uniquely are. By making right choices we learn how to create and enjoy the life we truly desire. Achieving self-mastery in relationships, work, and life delivers to us lasting joy, energy, balance, and prosperity.

When you think of a coach, what do you think of? A fitness coach who gets you out of bed one morning and takes you for a daily run in the park? A sports coach who works with you on a one-on-one basis to perfect your sporting technique? In both cases the one-to-one approach succeeds because your coach works out precisely where you need to focus to achieve the results you desire. This is exactly what I do with my clients by phone, E-mail, or face-to-face. This is what I am paid for and this is why they achieve results far more quickly than if they were not getting that one-on-one attention. If I were working with a class of forty people I would have to attend to everybody's strengths and weaknesses, thereby lessening the effectiveness of the teaching for each individual.

Coaching works because each session is uniquely tailored to each client. *Your Star Sign Life Coach* is the closest I can get to this through the medium of writing. The coaching process, tips, exercises, and success stories are uniquely tailored to each sun sign. The one thing this book can't do is provide you with the structure to assimilate the coaching concepts as working with a coach would do. You'll have to create this for yourself, possibly by working through the book with a friend or committing yourself to working through one section a day. To get the most out of this book, work it! Read it, do the exercises, and apply them immediately. Don't just put the book on the shelf to gather dust. Keep revisiting it, keep working with it and let it coach you. Spend some time designing and working on your life; create it rather than just drifting along from day to day. When you take the time to plan, the doing becomes much easier. This is the idea that underpins client coaching. Whatever you are trying to achieve, working weekly with a coach allows you the time and framework to work on your life as opposed to merely being in it.

Your Star Sign Life Coach looks at your sun sign (often called "birth sign" or "star sign") and how you can work with it to maximize your potential and ensure that you make the right choices in life. As an astrologer and coach, I like to think of a client's sun sign as representing the "present them," the individual they are now. Your sun sign also represents your role in life. It represents the part of you that you are striving to express and honor, the characteristics for which you wish to be recognized.

While it is essential that anyone using astrology for personal and spiritual growth looks beyond their sun sign and has a proper natal chart done, most people, when asked what they want to do (or not do) with their lives and how they want to be seen, will describe themselves in terms of their sun sign. An individual with the sun in Aries might say that they want to be seen as a pioneer, while I (sun in Leo) would talk about wanting to be seen as a leader and authority in my field. For most of us, our sun sign represents those parts of us that are we proud to own.

The sun sign serves as an accessible starting point for anyone wishing to learn about themselves through astrology. Those of you who want to take your interest in astrology further should get a natal chart done. This can be done by a professional astrologer.

NATAL ASTROLOGY

YOUR NATAL CHART is a snapshot picture of the universe at your moment of birth. This powerful tool is your foundation for life. It is your blueprint and road map. The natal chart tells the astrologer where you have come from in childhood and past lives—this is called patterns or momentums of behavior. Your natal chart reveals your psychology (how you think), your spirituality (what you believe), and your life mission (what service you have come to render to the planet). Your natal astrology expresses your talents, potential attainments, abilities, and special God-given gifts. Everything happening in your life today goes back to this original chart. It is your personal and unique story. Natal astrology reveals both challenges and abilities you have brought into this life and is most helpful in finding passion in your life, career, and relationships. The natal chart is the key to unlocking the mystery behind karmic lessons in love and life purpose. We are here to master our karma (astrology) and stepping into the light (knowledge and understanding) is empowerment.

This book will show you how to use your positive sun sign traits to your advantage and how to enhance them. You will also be shown powerful techniques for making the most of the negative characteristics of your sun sign. For example, a Pisces who feels that they are oversensitive could turn this trait into a major positive by using it to anticipate and satisfy the needs of clients. By using this book you are not surrendering to some notion that the planets control your destiny—they don't. You are merely arming yourself with the awareness that because your sun sign determines your personality it also increases, or decreases, the probability of you following a particular path in life.

In effect, astrology predicts the probability of certain events happening. By being aware of this you can choose to take those actions that either increase or decrease the probability of an event happening to you. So, for example, if you've been told that June is going to be a great month for romance, you can either go out and meet lots of new people (increasing your chances of finding romance) or stay indoors (decreasing your chances of finding romance). In order to create the life you want, you need to give the cosmos a helping hand.

In order to get the most out of this book, I would recommend that you read it through once to familiarize yourself with the self-coaching process. If you are going to be using this book without the motivational support of a personal coach, I would recommend that you find a supportive group of friends, who won't be threatened by your growing success, to keep you motivated and moving forward.

Next, I would strongly recommend that you commit to working through each chapter that you feel is relevant to you, so you might decide to work through those chapters that cover your ascendant and moon signs. You may also want to look at the characteristics given for each sun sign to see whether you have similar characteristics to those of a sun sign other than your own. If this is the case, then work with the exercises in the chapters that are appropriate to your situation. All the chapters that you choose to work with will need regular revisiting in order to keep up the momentum and consolidate your successes. Each chapter contains advice, case studies, exercises, resources, and action plans.

By combining astrology with coaching you will be able to understand yourself better and start making far-reaching and positive changes to your life. All that is required is a decision on your part to put the necessary work in to make yourself into one of life's winners. Coaching is similar to joining a gym. You can pay your money, but if you don't show up and do the work you won't get the results.

It's the same with reading this book. If you skim through it and don't do any of the exercises, nothing will happen. To get the most out of this book, you need to read it, do the exercises, and apply them immediately. Don't let this be another book full of great ideas that you do nothing about. Value yourself enough to take action—now.

CHAPTER 1

ARIES

March 21–April 19

THE FIRST SIGN OF THE ZODIAC, ARIES IS CONCERNED WITH:

- INITIATION, NEW BEGINNINGS, PIONEERING
- ACTION, DARING, CHALLENGES, ADVENTURE
- EXPLORATION, CREATIVITY, DISCOVERING
- WINNING, AGGRESSION, PERSONAL GOALS
- BEING IN CONTROL, SELF-INTEREST
- COURAGE, OPENNESS, DIRECTNESS, HONESTY, NOBILITY

ARIES, the first sign of the zodiac, is the sign of new beginnings. The dynamic ram is a pioneer in body and spirit, embracing new ideas and personal freedom with incredible gusto. Ariens thrive on challenges and will not be thrown off course, except by their own impatience. Arien energy is motivated by inspiration and aspiration—you crave freedom and opportunity, and demand to be stimulated and stretched by new experiences.

Aries is the most outgoing and impulsive, not to mention willful, of the fire signs—try coaching an Aries and you'll see what I mean! Ruled by the planet Mars (the Roman god of war), Aries is the most restless fire sign—don't expect Aries to stick around for the long haul (leave that to an earth sign).

The sign of the ram is the cardinal fire sign of the zodiac. If you were to use one word to describe Aries, it would have to be heat.

Prone to explosive outbursts of passion or rage, this determined childlike sign makes for a life that is never boring.

Fire signs are usually competitive, ambitious, assertive, dominant, and full of confidence for the future. Ariens living to their fullest potential are likely to be energetic, enthusiastic, upbeat, and warm. Spontaneous and fiery, they can find themselves in trouble if they fail to "look before they leap." Both as a coach and an executive search consultant, I've had plenty of Aries clients needing help after having ignored the details and small print. Another area where Aries can trip up is in the arena of office politics. Aries can be so busy looking forward that he or she fails to notice the backstabbing Machiavelli sneaking up behind.

As the first sign of the zodiac, Aries, your destiny is to initiate things and lead the way. Consolidation and being a follower are not for you. Take one of my clients, Josh, for example, who joined a small software company as director of marketing. Josh could not get enthusiastic about his new role. The company was a conservative one with plans for slow and steady growth. Josh, however, believed that they should be pushing forward aggressively and aiming for rapid growth—so that he could make his 30 percent equity worth enough for him to give up work.

A true Aries, Josh pushed and pushed to get his way, with the result that his earth sign colleagues left and set up their own company, leaving Josh to run things on his own. This would have been fine had Josh not found himself with a sleeping partner who owned 50 percent of the company. Josh came to me to find a solution to this dilemma.

We established that Dan, the sleeping partner, was not going to give up his stake. Josh wasn't prepared to be pragmatic and accept that Dan would be entitled to a share of the proceeds of Josh's labors, but that it was still worth building up the company—and thus Josh's net worth. We had to look at how Josh could negotiate the best severance deal possible. Not easy for an Aries who wants everything sorted out quickly, coaching Josh to stay put until he was offered an acceptable deal took some doing, believe me.

While this was going on, Josh and I looked at his employment options and, having considered his strengths, weaknesses, enthusiasms, and desired lifestyle, it was decided that becoming a full-time private investor was his best option. Since turning his favorite hobby into a full-time occupation, Josh has never looked back.

STRENGTHS TO FOCUS ON

▶ **Energetic leader, Inspirational**
▶ **Embraces change and challenges**
▶ **Risk taker**
▶ **Believes the best of others**
▶ **Will help others achieve their dreams**
▶ **Keeps on going when others would give up**
▶ **Fearlessness**
▶ **Defends others**
▶ **Openness and honesty**
▶ **Brings out the best in others**
▶ **Spontaneousness**
▶ **Pioneering**
▶ **Takes action**

EXERCISE ONE

S.M.A.R.T.est Goals for Aries

I KNOW that you're busy, Aries, and that you expect results fast, so let's move on to accelerated goal setting. Let's forget S.M.A.R.T. goals and go for S.M.A.R.T.er goals—for human dynamos.

Those of you who read personal development books will be familiar with the exhortation to make our goals S.M.A.R.T.—Specific, Measurable, Action-oriented, Realistic, and Timed. The only problem is, realistic goals don't inspire us. These realistic goals are of course set by our analytical, cautious left brain and are skewed by any self-limiting beliefs that we may have. No wonder they don't excite us!

I want you to apply some right-brain or creative thinking to your current goals.

Are you ready? Then let's begin.

1. Think of a goal you are currently trying to achieve. What time frame are you currently trying to achieve it in? For example, to get five dates in the next month.

2. What have you already tried that hasn't worked yet? For, example, sitting around thinking about it, asking a couple of friends to set you up on a blind date, joining a dating agency.

3. Now, ask yourself this question: What would I do differently if I had to achieve double my goal in half the time? For example, if I had to get ten dates in two weeks, I would join more than one dating agency; I would go out of my way to strike up conversations with people; I would look at placing a personal ad; I would use an Internet dating service; I would tell my friends that I was looking to widen my circle of acquaintances and ask them if there were any fun, single people they could introduce me to; I would be more courageous about asking people out (not harassing them though—remember, people have the right to say no). It goes without saying, however, that I would not under any circumstances put my personal safety at risk by giving out my address, going to a stranger's house, inviting them to mine, or meeting them anywhere other than a public place.

I sent Alan, a fellow coach, this exercise to stretch him. As a trainee looking to make the transition to coaching full-time, his S.M.A.R.T. goal had been to attract five clients in one month. Coaching is not the easiest thing to sell in the UK, so this was a perfectly realistic goal, if a little uninspiring. To attain it, Alan was going to place an ad, ask colleagues for referrals, and join a networking group.

I challenged Alan to get fifteen clients in two weeks, with the promise that if he did that I would buy him a bottle of champagne. Guess what? He rose to the occasion spectacularly, gaining his fifteen clients within the allotted time. He threw himself into asking for referrals, phoning contacts with a vision of signing them up or getting referrals; he arranged a personal development talk at his local bookstore, netting five clients; he attended a couple of networking meetings; he offered to coach colleagues; and he lined himself up a coaching slot on his local radio station.

Can you see how setting bigger goals raises your game and transforms your thinking? This is one of the main reasons that my clients engage a coach.

COACH'S TIP

If you're a fire sign, a perfect approach to goal setting might just be the G.S.O.G. (Get Some Other Guy to do it) approach to goal setting. It certainly works for me when it comes to administrative and company finances! Just remember that when you delegate, you need to specify what you want and when you want it by. Leave the other person to decide how they'll accomplish the task you've set them.

WEAKNESSES THAT CAN TRIP YOU UP

▶ **Appalling judge of character**
▶ **Disagreeability, ill-manneredness**
▶ **Brashness**
▶ **Determination to be the boss**
▶ **Egotisticalness**
▶ **Impulsiveness and willfulness**
▶ **Intolerance**
▶ **Jealousy**
▶ **Hates being told what to do**
▶ **Rarely listens**
▶ **Selfishness**
▶ **Totally oblivious to his or her effect on others, insensitivity**

So how do you turn these so-called negatives into powerful tools for personal growth? Well, first of all you're going to forget trying to improve on them.

I want to you to look at what you consider to be your greatest flaw and make peace with it—no more expending energy wrestling with yourself, denying who you are. I want you to look at this weakness and ask yourself what it is telling you about where you need to go next or focus upon in your life. For example, if you're insensitive, it's probably because you are mixing with the wrong type of people, so move on. Weaknesses are fabulous signs; they point to the goals we should be aiming for.

EXERCISE TWO

Love Your Weaknesses

FOR THIS exercise I want you to write down all the ways in which your greatest weakness has helped you get to where you are now. Give it credit. For example, as a Leo, I can be rather indolent and impatient; however, by honoring this and accepting that I'm not going to change, I now find ways of working smarter and faster. This weakness is now one of my greatest strengths.

Take the path of least resistance and focus on your greatest strengths—do what you do superbly well and delegate the rest. For example, like most fire signs, I hate administrative duties, so I delegate tham, leaving me free to do what I do well and enjoy. By doing this I have far more energy to focus on getting where I want to be.

COACH'S TIP

Life often runs more smoothly if you educate people about your weaknesses. For example, if you get bored easily, educate people to keep their conversations short, relevant, and stimulating. For those of you who are turned on by the idea of maximum results for minimum efforts, try this lazy Leo's approach to getting what you want.

---

9 1 1 Affirmations

TRADITIONAL affirmations work on repetition. Many personal development books will instruct you to stand up straight, grin into the mirror, and repeat, "I am rich, I am attractive," ad infinitum.

This takes far too long and, if you are a fire sign like me, is far too boring. If you have a conscious mind that just loves to answer back, you run the risk of neutralizing the effects of your hard work (not to mention potential embarrassment if someone walks in). I'm now going to introduce you to a high-performance, kick-start, instant gratification technique that can be used as an alternative. It is based upon the fact that with sufficient levels of arousal, ideas and patterns imprint into your mind and behavior in as little as one repetition, an effect referred to as "one-stop learning." The technique is described in the following stages:

1. Create a list of things that get you excited, frightened, grief-stricken, or enraged. For example, sex, roller coasters, driving fast, getting intensely angry, exercise, remembering the breakup of a close, intense relationship, public speaking, etc. Don't hold back. Work out what really affects you at a strong, emotional level.
2. Create a list of affirmations—positive, plausible, powerful, and dynamic statements that you want to imprint on your psyche. Nothing succeeds like excess here. For example:

   ♦ I am a millionaire—I live in a constant state of fabulous wealth and enjoy abundance.
   ♦ I have all the resources and talents I need to become absolutely, fantastically rich.
   ♦ I am super sexy—people adore me. I have charm and charisma in abundance.

   Ensure that you get as many over-the-top adjectives like fantastic, stupendous, fabulous as you can into the sentence. Do not hold back on these—half measures give mediocre results.
3. Get yourself into a heightened state of autonomic arousal, using

some of your favorites from step one (above). Once your heart is pumping and your breathing has quickened, begin repeating your affirmation in the most dramatic, empowered, and memorable way you can think of. See it, feel it, live it, experience it using all five senses.

Other ways to enhance the effectiveness of affirmations are to clap as you say them; dance as you say them; make your affirmations rhyme, and sing or chant them; put them onto tape, repeating each one 20–30 times, and play them as you sleep or go out jogging. When recording affirmations, use powerful language (lots of words like fabulous, fantastic, marvelous, etc.) and record them when you're feeling good.

ARIES MAN

UNLESS THERE are influences in his birth chart that are stronger than his Aries sun sign, the typical Aries male will have some or all of the following characteristics:

- Impulsive
- Has an abundance of energy and enthusiasm
- Has a domineering sex appeal
- Has strong opinions
- Is a meticulous dresser who wears clothes appropriate to the current challenge
- Is honest, sometimes tactless
- Is fiercely competitive
- Appears to be totally self-assured and can play "hard to get"
- Takes initiative and expects others to follow
- Is enterprising
- Has very clear goals
- Puts his partner on a pedestal
- Needs to win
- Uses wit and brains to get what he wants

◆ **Is terrified of becoming incapacitated or dependent in any way**

He will be blessed with a lean and strong body, long bones, strong shoulders, and a thick, long neck. Aries usually has a piercing, challenging gaze, which dominates a long face. The Arien face often sports a scar gained from a fight (in the case of my dog) or an accident (in the case of my husband).

ARIES WOMAN

IN ADDITION to the personality and behavior traits exhibited by the Aries male, the Aries woman is:

◆ **Optimistic and enthusiastic**
◆ **Dresses according to what she wants to achieve that day**
◆ **Direct and speaks her mind (she can suffer because of this)**
◆ **Is warm, vital, and lively**
◆ **Lives in the mind**
◆ **Can be domineering**
◆ **Is open and honest**
◆ **Has an ambitious career or, if not, has plenty of interests outside the home**
◆ **Demands loyalty**
◆ **Can achieve the impossible, gets frustratded when unsuccessful**
◆ **Makes a defensive and loving parent**

COACH'S TIP

Aries, be aware of your strengths and use them. Never disregard your pioneering spirit; by embracing it, you will enjoy life more. Your innate nature is to push and push against barriers, obstacles and, often, other people. People can find this objectionable at times, but you find that in order not to self-destruct, you must act instead of just thinking about acting. Have the courage to be forceful—it is the unreasonable woman who changes the world. (A word of advice here, Aries, sometimes you will attain your goals more easily by "going with the flow" and having the ability to know what you can and cannot change. For example, you cannot change a bear market into a bull market—the battle you can win is picking the stocks that rise.)

As an Arien, you adore a challenge of the magnitude to propel you into action. This challenge may just be frustration or, at a more calculated level, you may be fighting to implement an action plan that is close to your heart. If neither of these scenarios is the case and you find that your direction is not clear and your energies have dissipated, then listen to the guidance of your inner voice. An answer will be forthcoming. An Aries without direction or without a cause is not a rampant ram, merely a sorry sheep!

Avoid negative emotions like regret and self-pity, as they prevent you from capitalizing on one of your most valuable assets—straightforwardness.

You love extremes, Aries, and grow personally and professionally by experiencing them. However, if your extremes go beyond accepted norms, you may find yourself ostracized.

EXERCISE FOUR

Decision making: Cultivating Your Inner Voice

WE ALL have our inner voice (sometimes referred to as intuition or gut feeling), which when listened to guides us to make decisions that are always in our best interest. This inner voice is invaluable when you have critical decisions to make. To cultivate this inner voice, follow the instructions below.

Begin with a small test. During the day, stop and ask your inner voice for guidance on a specific decision. Make the request a small one, such as the right outfit to wear or book to choose. Images will appear, you may hear a voice or feel a gut reaction—all offering you the right choice to make. Pay attention to the signals and act on them.

Another way of asking your inner voice is to ask out loud, "What should I do?" Note what comes into your head—this is the answer.

For larger decisions, it is always wise to add time to the decision-making process. So sleep on it, but before you go to bed, ask your inner voice for guidance on the issue. Your wisdom will appear during sleep and may even wake you up, so make sure that you have a pen and paper by your bed. It goes without saying that you should hone your ability to tune into your inner voice before making a life-changing decision.

THE HIDDEN (OR NOT-SO-HIDDEN) ARIES

INSIDE ANYONE with strong Aries tendencies is a person convinced that they are far more interesting than anyone else, which can lead Ariens to bemoan the fact that they never meet anyone interesting. This was certainly the case for Kate, an Aries client of mine who was proud of her ambitious career and ability to "fight her corner," but who felt that there were no interesting people with whom to form relationships. A couple of coaching exercises that helped to get Kate unstuck can be found in the Love, Romance, and Sex Life section of Aries (page 30).

Aries makes it patently obvious that all that matters to the ram is winning—whomever or whatever the prize. Fighting, verbal sparring, competing, and finding new ways to do things are what make Aries tick. This is not surprising, as the planet Mars rules Aries—the planet of aggressive energy and creative action. Aries is a true visionary and originator who must be first in every aspect of their life. Failure does not enter the typical Arien's mind, which is why they can miss clear warnings of impending disaster—this is a sign that reframes every outcome as part of the winning process.

The only fear that a typical Aries has is that they won't be valued or liked, even though they are one of life's winners.

ARIES LIKES

▶ **Action**
▶ **Coming first**
▶ **Challenges**
▶ **Spontaneity**
▶ **Having their own way**

ARIES DISLIKES

▶ **Delays or waiting**
▶ **Admitting failure**
▶ **Being unopposed**
▶ **Tyranny**
▶ **Taking advice or being told what to do**

POSSIBLE PROBLEM AREAS FOR ARIES, AND SOLUTIONS

EACH SUN SIGN bestows upon us certain personality traits; when these traits are suppressed, problems will arise. However, with the winning combination of astrology and coaching we can examine the problem and assess the proper solution based on sun sign characteristics. If, as an Aries, you see things below that really strike home, try the solution. You may be amazed at the results.

PROBLEM: Projects that go wrong, relations with coworkers degenerating into conflict.

SOLUTION: See your role as "ideas person" and visionary; focus on inspiring others to implement your vision. Learn to listen rather than always being the one to speak. (See Listening Skills on page 14)

PROBLEM: Lacking true confidence (and direction). Failing to know what you want, just jumping in with both feet and pretending to be decisive.

SOLUTION: Sit down and work out what your true needs and values are—then decisions will become easier to make (see Decision Making for Libra Bosses, page 198). For exercises on goal setting and values, see the Define Your Values exercise on page 20 of this chapter.

PROBLEM: Always finding yourself on the receiving end of conflict and harsh treatment.

SOLUTION: Find out what it is you really want to achieve—then act accordingly.

PROBLEM: Being deserted by others because you do not appear to notice their existence.

SOLUTION: Wake up, Aries, and show a little sense. If you want to keep lovers and others sweet, try a little empathy—that means try putting yourself in their shoes.

EXERCISE FIVE

Heartfelt Listening

A FANTASTIC exercise, developed by the Heartmath Institute in California, is Deep Heart Listening, which can be used whenever you want to leave behind purely left-brain, analytical thinking, or to bring emotional intelligence to a difficult conversation.

Choose a specific conversation today where you will feel comfortable trying this technique, or if you're feeling bold, try it throughout the day.

Become aware of your heart and focus on it. Take three deep breaths while continuing to focus on your heart. Continue to focus on your heart as you listen to the other person speak.

Reflect back to the other person what you have been hearing. This ensures that you keep focused on the message that they are giving you and lets them feel heard. It also allows them to clarify their thoughts and gives them the opportunity to clarify the points they feel that you've missed.

Before beginning to speak focus on your heart. You will be amazed at the insights this style of listening provides you with.

EXERCISE SIX

Listening Skills for Aries

CAN YOU say that you truly listen to people? That you can empathize with them, allowing them to talk, identifying the source of their problem and letting them know that they have been "heard?" The following exercise is an introduction to listening in this way. It takes some practice but is invaluable once mastered.

Select a person to whom you have not really talked before. Now approach this person with the specific aim of starting a conversation with them. Your task is to focus on listening to them.

I can imagine you reading this book and thinking, What will I talk to a complete stranger about? Well, Aries, you don't talk, you listen. A suggested conversation opener might be: "What beautiful weather, how long do you think it will last?" Use something that is friendly, genuine, and relevant.

Next you will need to ask open questions—those that cannot be answered by just saying yes or no—to find out what the other person enjoys doing. Keep asking lighthearted questions about something they seem interested in. When you have asked a question, be quiet and let them speak; continue to ask questions and to listen; don't attempt to interject with anecdotes or advice—just let them talk and you listen.

You may feel foolish at first; you may not be remotely interested in the subject, but will find that the other person's passion soon draws you in.

This style of asking intelligent questions about another person's interests will make them feel "heard." Show that you're listening by summarizing what they've said to you, "Am I right in thinking that . . ."

By incorporating this technique of listening into your life—at work, at home, with friends—you will be training other people on a subconscious level to mirror the technique back to you, i.e., they will copy your new style. This should result in you being "heard," too.

Advanced Communication Skills for Aries: Developing Empathy

THE FOLLOWING process is called the "Meta-Mirror" and was developed by Robert Dilts and Todd Epstein. It's based on the principle that our relationship with someone is heavily influenced by our view of him or her. In fact, you could say that we don't have problems with a person, but with our internal representation of them.

This process will allow you to get some new information about a "problem" person and how they see you. Every time I have helped clients through this process, they have experienced improvements, often dramatic ones, in their relationship with the "problem" person.

1. Think of a person you currently find it difficult to deal with. It can be a partner, a boss, a colleague, a friend . . . anyone.

   Imagine you can see them in front of you across the room. You can put them anywhere in the room you like. From this first position (as yourself) notice your feelings and what you are saying to yourself as you see them—just as if they were there in reality. Now—and this is very important—let go of the feelings and thoughts from the first position. To shake them off, try reciting your phone number backwards, or imagining something arresting or unusual—anything that helps you to let them go.

2. Now go into a second position, as the problem person—as if you were becoming that person. In your imagination, physically walk over and stand in their shoes so you can see things from their point of view and make sense of things from their perspective. As you look back at the first-position you, how do you view him or her? What do you think and feel about him or her?

3. When you have all the information you need from that perspective, once again break your state to let go of those thoughts and feelings. Now go to a third position—a different standpoint where you can see both yourself and the other person from a detached position, as if you were making a fly-on-the-wall documentary. If you need to get even more detachment from the situation, you could stand on a chair to view it from above. From

here you can see the process of relationship between the two people and how each is reacting to the things the other does and says. What do you learn from this perspective? In what ways do you feel more resourceful when you are outside the problem?

4. Now move to a fourth position where you can see your first-position self and the third-position observer. Now swap their places. Let the first-position you have a rest, and let the more resourceful observer take over. You can move them over in any way you like—you can physically pick them up and carry them into place, you can mark the movement with the noise of a mechanical crane, or see them walking over to swap places. Now, in the shoes of the observer and standing where you used to be in position one, look at the person you were having a problem with. How do they seem different now? How do you feel differently about the situation?

5. Step over and become the "problem" person again. Experience what they feel and think about the new, more resourceful you, and notice how you are different now. Finally, leave the exercise and return to yourself, bringing everything that you've learned back with you.

CAREER/BUSINESS

ARIES is a true trailblazer, forging ahead and leaving chaos in his or her wake. While your chaotic desk, files, and office are easily navigable to you, Aries, your whirlwind working style can cause havoc for those trying to follow in your slipstream (or even picking up where you left off). Although you are a worthy team player (as long as you are team leader), you are unlikely to be suited to the procedure-driven corporate life. You can play the game for a while, but, before long, your need for freedom to carry out your duties your way will surface. The classic song "My Way" could have been penned for Ariens.

Although Ariens prefer a leadership role, they shine when given clear direction. They tend to excel in the armed forces. As long as they are not bogged down with the trivial, such as organizing your affairs or your environment, they do not mind structure. They are happiest when given plenty of variety and opportunities to prove themselves. They tend to do best in settings where they are set specific goals and given the autonomy to attain them in their own way. Hands-on managers really get their goat.

While Ariens enjoy initiating ventures and new projects, they are not into detail or consolidation. You are usually more than happy for others to be involved in laying the groundwork for a new venture, providing you with a solid foundation from which to launch yourself.

Ariens are often outspoken, opinionated, aggressive, and extremely competitive. If these character traits apply to you, then you need to find a work environment that will foster your strong will and independent spirit. Consequently, many Ariens fair best in smaller corporations or autonomous teams where they can be involved in all aspects of the business and where they can work with the corporate power players.

Okay, Aries, now for another exercise.

EXERCISE EIGHT

Create a Political Map of Your Organization

IN ORDER to make your career happen for you and to avoid being the unsung and unheard hero of your organization, you are going to need to identify the power players within your company. A few minutes spent pinpointing these movers and shakers and finding out how to align with them will pay off handsomely in terms of career development. For Aries, who wants to directly influence the power players in an organization—prior to taking over from them, of course—there is an even greater payoff in terms of ego gratification. You don't want to waste your time on deadbeats, do you? You're into fast-tracking, surely? As an added bonus, this exercise will help you to begin to hone those (almost nonexistent) political skills.

1. Get a copy of your company's organizational chart and carry out the following steps to work out who are the real power players in your office.

2. Start by identifying the people who could influence your career progression.

3. Write down this person's job title and also what that title actually means within your company.

4. Work out who this person reports to and who can review and veto this person's decisions.

5. Who consults this person on key decisions? Do they do so out of necessity or voluntarily?

6. How many and what kind of people report to this person? Check whether the person is in a line or staff position. Line positions are income-generating jobs whereas staff positions are overheads. Line positions usually carry more political clout than staff positions.

7. What is their management style? Is it one that you are comfortable with or do you need to modify your communication style to connect with this person?

8. How much does the overall success of the company depend on this person's decisions?

9. Is this person successful within the company? How often have they been promoted? Are they regarded as "on the way up" or "on the way out"?

10. Final question, who does this person network with personally and professionally? Is it the power players within your company or yesterday's men? This will tell you whether it is worth networking with them or whether you should focus your efforts elsewhere.

Ariens are not keen on being made into corporate clones, and any attempts to compartmentalize this feisty creature will lead to a swift head butting. Aries may just choose to charge off through the nearest exit without even deigning to give notice.

It should be clear to the career-loving Aries that the company in whom you invest your talents must be chosen with care, particularly as the power associated with large corporations intoxicates you. If you decide to work for a major corporation you will charge to the top as quickly as possible—for there is a greater degree of freedom at the top of an organization. Provided that you are given control of your particular specialty or product, there is no reason why you should not thrive and excel in a multinational, corporate powerhouse. Just be aware of what questions to ask. To help you with this, I've set you the following exercise.

EXERCISE NINE

Decisions, Decisions

ARIES IS one of the least diplomatic and empathetic signs of the zodiac. As a result of these characteristics, Aries has to be very careful to find a company that values employees with a strong will and unorthodox working style.

If you want to say good-bye to that sinking feeling you get when you know you've just landed yourself the job from hell, try this exercise.

When choosing a career or employer, it is essential to take into account the type of lifestyle you currently have or aspire to. Consider what is important to you. For example:

- ♦ What type of balance between personal/family and professional life is optimal for you?
- ♦ What impact will your chosen lifestyle have on your promotion prospects and finances?
- ♦ What type of career are you looking for and what price in terms of time, commitments, etc. are you prepared to pay?

Company culture also has a huge impact on your working life, so it is worth establishing what is important to you in terms of company culture and benefits.

Take a few minutes to assign an A, B, or C ranking to the statements below in terms of importance to you.

- ◆ Working for a meritocracy
- ◆ Working for a company that allows you a high degree of autonomy
- ◆ Working for a company that allows you to be creative
- ◆ Working for a company that expects you to show initiative
- ◆ Working for a company where you can influence, and have access to, the major power players
- ◆ Knowing that your job is important
- ◆ The opportunity to work part-time
- ◆ Programs for stress management
- ◆ Formalized opportunities for socializing with colleagues
- ◆ Childcare facilities
- ◆ Ongoing training
- ◆ Job-sharing schemes
- ◆ A formalized route for career progression and hierarchical structure
- ◆ A 9–5 culture
- ◆ The opportunity to be at the center of corporate activity

Now assess your values (some examples of values are given on page 21), interests, strengths, weaknesses, accomplishments, personal resources, and goals up front. Then you can begin to look for organizations that would value what you have to offer and for whom you would be a good cultural fit.

EXERCISE TEN

Define Your Values

These are the absolute "must haves" in our lives. They are what we are naturally drawn to and what we need in order to be authentically us.

Write down a list of your ten most important life values. If you come up with more than ten, then feel free to add them—the important thing is that you write down everything significant in your life.

Some common values my clients list are:

Responsibility	Variety	Respect
Creativity	Power	Achievements
Health	Autonomy	Acceptance
Happiness	Integrity	Humor
Money	Success	Kindness
Adventure	Freedom	Independence
Travel	Understanding	Excitement
Honesty	Compassion	Intimacy
Children	Trust	

Place your values in order of importance. This will help you to prioritize your goals and get to work immediately on what you need to bring into your life.

Now reconsider your current career goals. Are they appropriate to your value system? It is important for Aries to be aware of their values as many of my Arien clients find that they are too strong minded to align their values or goals with those of their company. Aries often find that if personal and corporate values and goals are misaligned, they cannot motivate themselves to perform. It is therefore extremely important that Aries finds or starts a company whose values align with their own.

One of my clients, Sarah, found that when she listed and prioritized her values, paying particular attention to those that influenced her decision-making process, she came up with the following:

- ◆ Respect for self and others
- ◆ Responsibility for self and actions
- ◆ Never being in debt
- ◆ Paying bills on time
- ◆ Balancing work and personal commitments
- ◆ Empowering others
- ◆ Making money
- ◆ Being connected to others

Is it any surprise that Sarah is thinking of becoming a financial independence coach or debt counselor?

The Aries office is likely to be minimalist, with a few trophies or talismans of success to spur the ram onto greater valor. It will have people or machines to take care of the oh, so boring details and will be positioned somewhere exciting if at all possible. My husband and I had office premises next to a deserted graveyard, frequented by aggressive drunks and drug addicts. Running the gamut of these threatening individuals was great fun for him, an Aries. As a Leo, I was less keen and relocated my company as soon as suitable premises became available.

The Aries office must be stimulating and allow plenty of movement—if my clients are the standard, then rock music and video games are musts. The Aries office will be impressive or, if not, the small enterprise-owning Aries will rent impressive-seeming premises to meet clients and the media. The office also needs to be accessible at all times.

ARIES CAREER GUIDE

Here are some occupations that an Aries might consider:

Advertising	Entrepreneur	Optometrist
Ambulance driver	Firefighter	Producer
Athlete	Hairdresser	Police officer
Butcher	Jockey	Politics
Coach	Journalism	PR executive
Computer- or video-	Landlord	Salesperson
game designer	Lawyer	Sportsperson
Courier	Leader	Stagehand
Dentist	Makeup artist	Stockbroker
Director	Metal worker	Stuntman/woman
EMT	Military officer	Surgeon
Entertainer	Neurologist	Valet

ARIES BOSS

LEADERS AT HEART, Ariens take bold business initiatives and expect others to follow in their wake. Aries really pays very little attention to the needs and motivations of his or her loyal foot soldiers. You are far too busy creating Aries's world to bother about controlling or monitoring the moves of those under you. Employees who need support and direction need not look to you, Aries! All you care about is results, you have no time for office politics, and you often are downright negligent when it comes to monitoring others' performance.

Your lack of patience can cause you to muscle in and to do others' jobs if they're not acting promptly enough for you. You also have a tendency to dive in and take charge of any situation and run the risk of executive burnout unless you learn to delegate.

The "hero manager syndrome" is a classic Arien trait. Look at Susan, an Arien client in her mid-forties. Susan, a middle manager in a retail outlet, felt totally overwhelmed and ineffective as a manager. When she first came for coaching, she had just had a poor performance review. She felt that other staff hampered or took no notice of her.

As a coach, one of the first things I do is to get a client to look at their role in a given situation. In Susan's case, we found that her problems mostly stemmed from being too nice and wanting to solve everyone's problems for him or her. Like many Aries, she was a great champion of what she believed to be the underdog. Far from making her staff like her, this style of management made them disrespect her. Why should they bother to solve a problem when she'd jump in and do it? What a boring role for them with no problems to contend with? Not only did she lose their respect in this way, but she compounded the situation by not being able to deliver on any of her promises. She had promised to solve too many problems.

We worked together to address these issues, evolving a new and more appropriate style of management for her to adopt, which she announced at a briefing for her department. She held a meeting with each member of her staff to explain exactly what she expected from them. She also began to coach her staff to solve their own problems. This freed her to find out exactly what was going on within the organization as a whole and where her department could impact on this. She started giving more feedback on strategic issues, thereby positioning herself for promotion when the opportunity arises.

Now that she has taken a coaching approach to management, she is far more able to make use of her subordinates' abilities, knowing which one to place where and making each feel valued. A year later, she has just received an excellent appraisal and is generally regarded as a great person to work for.

Of course Ariens, with their pathological dislike of routine, are not the greatest middle managers. They are often not remotely interested in holding peoples' hands and showing them the ropes, and are far too focused on their own agenda to want to manage the affairs of others. However, the payoff for Susan was being able to get involved in moving the company forward and breaking new ground.

Once they get above the level of middle management, Ariens make superb executives, because of their strength and leadership style. Only Saturn-ruled ultra-ambitious Capricorn joins the ranks of leaders as consistently, though not as fast, as Aries. You have optimism and drive in abundance. You are idealistic, hardworking, and know that you can make the future a success. Hell, you can even pull a business back from bankruptcy and can mobilize everybody in a crisis. You are inspirational at your best, and colleagues can usually see how loyal you are (when you buy into the corporate vision or, better still, shape it). You truly walk your talk, Aries, for although you are a demanding employer, the demands you place on others are only a fraction of those that you make of yourself. You are also extremely good at giving out rewards for work well done.

One area where you may need to do a little work is developing negotiating skills. You can have a tendency to leave others feeling resentful as you steamroller over them to get your own way. Your favored negotiating strategy appears to be that of attrition, and you tend to enjoy a fight so much that you will argue over points that are irrelevant. Learn to fight for what matters, Aries; let the rest ride and allow the other guy to win a few points. Negotiation is about winning the war, and sometimes you have to lose a battle in order to do so.

EXERCISE ELEVEN

Preparing for Negotiation

THERE are two key pieces of information that you need to effectively prepare for a negotiation. The first is your ideal plausible outcome (IPO); the second is what you will do if negotiation fails.

STEP ONE: *Defining Your Ideal Plausible Outcome*
In order to establish your ideal plausible outcome, there are two questions to ask:
  1. What do I really want?
  2. Why is it plausible that I should get it?

For example:
  1. I want a 30 percent pay increase
  2. When I started this job, I was learning my trade. Now I am one of the best people in the company, and I produce more than double what I produced when I started.

STEP TWO: *Work Out What You Will Do*
If You Can't Reach Agreement
Decide what you will do if you cannot or will not make a deal—this is your "second choice" option. At any point, you can compare what is being offered with what you will do if you do not reach agreement, and make a simple decision as to whether to walk away or continue negotiating. This is your ultimate leverage; the better your "second choice option," the easier it is to walk away from a deal—and the more willing you are to walk away, the more inflexibly you can hold out for what you want. For example, if you have job offers from six other firms and are prepared to take one of those offers, you can hold out for what you really want.

When the time to negotiate is upon you, calm yourself and take a moment to choose your state (how you want to feel), review your "second choice" option, rejoice in the strength it gives you, and focus on your ideal plausible outcome.

COACH'S TIP

People who genuinely believe that their desired outcome is achievable (what I am calling "believable") tend to fight harder and longer for their initial goals than those who have chosen an unrealistically optimistic outcome. Of course, the only person who needs to find your goals realistic is you. As in most areas of life, belief + expectancy = results.

ARIES EMPLOYEE

THE ARIES EMPLOYEE is either heaven-sent or a complete nightmare, depending on how their supervisor relates to them. Rams are not natural followers. However, if Aries's employer is appreciative and recognizes Aries's true talents, then the ram can be a loyal, supportive employee. You have an unorthodox work style, often preferring to arrive and work late, so you need to find an employer who is capable of believing in your ability to get the job done irrespective of the hours you keep.

You need a job that provides you with responsibility, decision-making powers, and variety. You cannot bear repetition or close supervision. Once you have mastered a job, it is time to move on or, at the very least, experiment with different ways of doing things. You also need a lot of praise and the assurance that your job is important.

You demand to work in the activity center of any business and need to interact with others. Taking orders is anathema to you, so the person giving them had better be recognizably senior to you, if not, they can bug off! Given your short fuse and hatred of routine, you are likely to walk out, get fired, or self-sabotage if you become disheartened by routine. Job security is not usually a priority for Aries, and you will blithely leave a job that no longer holds any challenges or opportunities. The eternal optimist, you can make your way under the most difficult of circumstances.

You tend to work best when answerable only to the boss, and are always looking for opportunities to learn and progress. You are confident and know that you do well. You seek success and respect rather than cash, and a wise employer will give you praise and titles to motivate you. You want to be a hero and will work long and hard to become indispensable to your organization if you are appreciated.

As long as your employers see your healthy ambition and ego as an asset rather than a threat, you will excel beyond their wildest dreams. You cannot stand working for an employer who belittles you or begrudges you your fiery, take-charge dynamism. To find an employer this psychologically mature will take some doing, but in terms of your sanity, not to mention your personal and professional growth, it is well worth it.

FINANCES AND WEALTH

FAME OR FORTUNE, Aries? Definitely the former for you heroic, glory-seeking rams. If you do get rich, which you frequently do, it is likely that your fortune will be made as a result of your incredible will to succeed.

You are brave and bold—the zodiac's go-getter. You love to be in charge and you like to take action. I have had a couple of Aries clients who have become very successful private investors once they learned to curb their natural Arien impulsiveness. It can take Aries a while to get in the habit of researching the companies and markets in which they want to invest, so Ariens need to make their vision of future rewards extremely compelling. One of my Arien clients loves the sheer adrenaline of spread betting, and while I don't advocate living on the edge all of the time, his chosen lifestyle works for him.

Getting rich is not usually a key motivator for the ram; certainly Aries doesn't spend a great deal of time planning to get rich; he or she simply gets moving and enjoys the journey. However, if an Aries does commit him- or herself to financial independence, results usually come very quickly, as rams have fewer blocks to action than most signs. For many Aries, however, money is only the "currency" that allows them to buy what they want. Rams live very much in the present and so are unlikely to build up a financial cushion. A need for immediate gratification is not always balanced with building up a financial reserve. Although for most signs a lack of a "nest egg" might curtail their freedom to take risks or walk out of a job, no such limitations apply to Aries.

Aries loves to take risks, so becoming a private investor or entre-preneur is likely to appeal to you. Entrepreneurship and trading both give you plenty of opportunity to go to war, enable you to be your own boss, and allow for freedom of movement. No matter what financial hardships you endure, you remain driven in your quest to be your own boss. Saving is hard for you during the start-up phase of an enterprise, so set up a retirement plan as soon as possible and for goodness sake don't be tempted to dip in and buy that shiny red Porsche. You may just live to a ripe old age.

COACH'S TIP

Aries tends to have bursts of energy. Either choose a pro-fession where this is an asset or aim for consistency of out-put. Try to curb your impulse to continually abandon ideas in the search for better ones.

Bear in mind that it takes most entrepreneurs several ven-tures to become successful, so make sure that you have enough money to tide you over during the bad times. Your partner may not appreciate being evicted. While we're on the subject of caution, you really should take out life and health insurance. I know you think you're invincible but, unfortu-nately, germs and other car drivers know different!

EXERCISE TWELVE

Building Up a Rainy-Day Fund

EVERY MONTH, put some money aside, either in a glass jar or a separate bank account labeled "The Rainy-Day Fund." Then, whenever you're hit with an unexpected bill or natural disaster, you can pay for it (at least partially) from the fund. Kick off your Rainy-Day Fund by taking the following steps:

◆ Decide on an ideal amount to place into the fund, based on past history and present income.

- No raiding the fund for an "emergency" treat—you need to build up enough of a resource to buy you some peace of mind.
- Don't go overboard—unless you want to. The Rainy-Day Fund is just there to ease the burden, not to replace traditional insurance. (It is there to cover those small emergencies where you just want to get something fixed, pay quickly, and avoid the hassle of red tape and dealing with third parties.)

If you decide to become a private investor you are likely to be attracted to fast-moving markets and to aim for the quick buck; long-term conservative ventures are unlikely to turn you on. Your desire to initiate and win usually enables you to get into speculative investments ahead of the herd, and you find this a great turn-on. But whereas you are ready to eat, breathe, and sleep your investment while it's preparing to rocket upwards, you are unlikely to be able to keep watch over it for more than a few weeks.

You are usually great on timing your investment activity, getting in just after the market hits rock bottom, and dipping out again just before it peaks. Is this intuition, war skills, or just good luck?

EXERCISE THIRTEEN

Getting the Universe to Write You a Check

THIS IS an exercise that seems to work for me, and for 90 percent of my clients who've tried it. It's simple and quick to do.

1. Decide on a sum of money, for example $10,000.
2. Decide when you want it by, for example, December 31, 2004.
3. Write yourself a check for that sum and post-date it with the date by which you want the money.

4. Place the check where you can see it.

That's all. If your belief is strong enough and you take the actions required to manifest your money, you should start to see an upturn in your finances.

Other easy and quick-to-do exercises can be found in the Finances and Wealth section for Leo (page 140).

LOVE, ROMANCE, AND SEX LIFE

FOR Aries, love is all about excitement, action, and conquest. This sign loves the thrill of the chase—the male advances with fiery ardor while the female ram hunts more subtly. People born under the sign of Aries positively smolder with red-hot energy; life with an Aries is never dull—occasionally stressful (I speak from experience here) but never, ever dull. If you become bored with an Aries you are probably just letting hidden anger and resentment build up to tarnish the relationship.

Aries of both sexes like to initiate relationships, and the role of seducer comes easily to the ram. Just be careful not to overwhelm your lover and drive them away, Aries. Worse still, don't sweep them off their feet and then leave them standing alone. Romance with an Aries will only work if you're fit and full of stamina, as this sign is never still and hates to be alone. Trying to have time out during an argument with an Aries is impossible unless you barricade the door or leave the house, and my, does this sign love to argue!

Aries always wants its own way and will usually put its wants and needs above those of a partner or relationship. Still, what can one expect from the brat of the zodiac? The argumentative ram rarely holds a grudge and ten minutes after delivering a verbal onslaught will come up looking for fun (or sex). In order to have long-lasting, satisfying relationships, the ram needs to respect others' needs and learn to allow relationships to unfold naturally rather than forcing the pace.

COACH'S TIP

Due to your impulsiveness and belief in courtly love, Aries, make sure that you are falling for the person as they really are, not as you imagine them. Try to find out early on what your partner is really like in terms of availability, hopes, aspirations, and values. That way you'll avoid finding yourself with the booby prize.

There is no doubt that Aries is a passionate and seductive character who will prove hard to resist. Aries will tend to opt for a successful partner, so sparks will fly in this competitive tango, and that thrills the ram. A mental attraction is often the first step for the feisty ram, though strong physical attraction is essential too. For the relationship to last, a deep mental connection is paramount.

We all go through periods when we find our partners exceedingly dull. Before writing your partner off and tossing the relationship in the garbage, try doing new things with your partner or forcing yourself to acknowledge what is interesting about them.

Look at what you need from a relationship to feel happy, for example, love, appreciation, great sex, stimulating conversation. Does your partner/relationship satisfy these needs? If this is the case, then stick with the relationship; if not, then move on. You need relationships that energize you rather than drain you.

EXERCISE FOURTEEN

Other People Are Interesting—Honest!

HERE IS a challenge for you—find out one interesting thing about everyone you meet (or at least five people a day). If you are really as intelligent as you say you are, then you should be able to accomplish this.

There Are Interesting People Out There

WHAT DOES interesting mean to you? Name five interesting people—real or fictional, dead or alive. Now describe what it is that makes them interesting. What qualities do these people posses that match your own? Where would these interesting people be found? Would they be found in the places you frequent or are you more likely to find them at a different venue? If so, then why not hang out there?

Would the people that you find interesting find you interesting? If not, then why not? What work do you need to do on yourself?

Check out the exercises for combating boredom in the Gemini chapter (pages 76, 77, 84 and 88). Your relationships may be further enhanced by trying out some of the exercises for developing empathy and communication skills found in this chapter (pages 12–14).

COMPATIBILITY

ARIES IS OFTEN attracted to its fellow fire signs, Sagittarius and Leo, but, unless aspects in the chart suggest otherwise, fire sign romances can be explosive. Aries will get along well romantically with air signs (Aries–Gemini and Aries–Libra are often a great match, Aries–Aquarius less so). Sometimes an earth sign can ground all that fiery Aries energy. In a chart comparison, a Venus or moon in Aries in the other person's chart would indicate compatibility.

WHAT ARIES NEEDS

ARIES PEOPLE DON'T generally need hearts and flowers to give them a warm and fuzzy glow. Aries is far more interested in finding a partner who is strong and self-possessed and who will challenge them and take them to greater heights, both mental and physical. The person who can draw them out, shake them out of the boredom, cynicism, and lethargy that sometimes afflict this sign in private, and make them better is a catch worth holding on to. It also helps if Aries's partner can handle the occasional fiery argument and master the art of making up. Sexual adventurers are also very attractive to the ram, whether it's acrobatics between the sheets or the sensual art of touching.

The Aries lover is passionate, adventurous, and energetic, loves romance and revels in the art of the chase. Those who can stand the heat will be rewarded with a loyal companion who will take them to greater heights. Get ready for the ride of a lifetime!

THE END OF THE AFFAIR

BOREDOM USUALLY KILLS Aries affairs stone dead. Aries loves the adrenaline rush of new love and gets bored once love has been won. For Aries most of the excitement comes from overcoming the obstacles to love, so if you want to keep your Aries lover on his or her toes, always maintain a little hidden part of you for Aries to uncover. You should also enthuse wildly about all of Aries's new ventures, introducing the voice of reason at a later date. Too early and you'll find yourself frozen out and accused of being unsupportive.

Aries will try to keep a relationship vibrant and fresh, but if this fails, will storm out the door in search of greener pastures. If you hurt Aries deeply you can expect to be completely cold-shouldered—your red-hot lover will turn glacial instantly.

RELATIONSHIPS
(Family and Friends)

ARIES PARENT

THE TYPICAL ARIES will give children plenty of affection, hugs, and praise without spoiling them. Aries is a devoted parent who will defend their child to the death while being realistic enough to accept that their child needs to be disciplined in order to become successful. An Aries can carry its competitive nature too far in terms of trying to decide its child's future career. An Aries wants his or her child to be first at everything.

As Aries is a very playful sign, an Aries parent is likely to create a magical, fun-filled, fantasy world for his or her offspring.

ARIES CHILD

THE ARIES CHILD loves to explore and possesses tremendous energy. If you want to be able to enjoy a peaceful evening, then after-school activities are a must for this child. I would suggest that intramural sports are an excellent choice for the Aries child. Sports will appeal to young Aries's competitive nature and with a little luck will burn off all that excess energy.

Aries children are always eager to try something new, particularly if there is an element of danger in it. The Aries child will probably fall from a few trees and maybe break a few teeth or windows but should come through it all relatively unscathed! If you're watching out for this youngster's welfare, don't let them know it, as this child has a strong need for independence.

Aries children are often extremely impulsive and can find themselves getting quite a culture shock at school. Imagine having to learn to wait for other children to catch up academically and, worse still, having to raise your hand before speaking or leaving a room.

The Aries child is incapable of slowing down, so watch this child's intake of junk food—the fewer stimulants the better.

BRINGING UP ARIES—COACH'S INSIGHT

ARIES CHILDREN, LIKE Aries adults, are direct and to the point when sharing their likes and dislikes. They are extremely determined to have their own way and saying no to any Aries child just doesn't work. Neither does coaxing, cajoling, or holding up other better-behaved children as examples, for that matter. The way to get the best out of your Aries child is to set him or her a challenge.

So, for example, if they're always coming in late, suggest that they are not very good at keeping track of time. This should result in the feisty young ram going out of its way to prove you wrong.

Your young ram needs an opportunity to shine and to try new things. Young Aries needs to feel loved and valued to bring out his or her potential. The young ram also wants to know that it is a winner. Aries needs lots of love and reassurance in spite of the brave face it puts on.

WHAT TO TEACH YOUNG ARIES

ARIES CHILDREN NEED to be taught how to handle dangerous situations as soon as they are old enough so that accidents can be avoided. In addition to challenging situations, the young ram likes to challenge authority, so you will need to "trick" them into obedience by making obedience a matter of pride. Aries needs to be guided gently, with sound logic and frequent praise, rather than being ordered about.

Aries needs to be taught how to handle finances from an early age to avoid trouble in later life. Your little ram also needs to learn that others have feelings and opinions too, so dominating them is just not effective.

ARIES AND FRIENDS

ARIES LIKES A friend who is at the top of their game, provided that he or she is not in direct competition. Aries also likes a friend who is striking in some way. Aries needs to be number one in the friend's eyes.

FRIENDS, BE AWARE

WHILE ARIENS MAKE great hosts, there is usually an ulterior motive for having friends around. Given the choice, Aries would prefer to entertain on neutral ground—a restaurant, for example.

Unsurprisingly, since Aries is a masculine sign, Ariens of both sexes get on better with male friends.

Aries friendships often fall by the wayside due to your competitive nature, Aries—the friend who beats you can expect to be ditched. This leaves you two options: You can either work on your self-esteem (list what is great about you, get others to do the same, and list your successes) or you can find a nonthreatening, unambitious friend who is nonetheless interesting in their own right.

HEALTH

ARIES is typically a robust and healthy soul who fights off any ailment with sheer willpower. When Ariens are laid low they can suffer a loss of self-esteem and require a great deal of comfort. In spite of their tough-guy image, Ariens are extremely vulnerable emotionally and can be laid low by rejection.

STRESS BUSTING FOR ARIES

MARS-RULED ARIES is a cardinal sign, which means that Aries places the emphasis on action. If you become a stressed Aries, rather than hanging around allowing the tension to build, get out there and do something physical to burn that excess energy off. Try some high-adrenaline competitive games like squash, basketball, or boxing—anything that totally absorbs your attention. Fencing may be a good choice, as your ruling planet, Mars, also rules iron. You could even take the car for a spin (avoid rush hour), or just tinker around under the hood. Doing this will allow your subconscious mind to process the problem at hand and enable you to get things into perspective.

Weigh up all your options for dealing with the crisis at hand. Write down the pros and cons of each action before committing yourself. Also write down the steps that you are going to take. This will force you to slow your thought processes down and prevent you from acting erroneously in the heat of the moment. By doing this you will also focus on the details (which is not an Arien strong point) and thus reduce the likelihood of taking the wrong course of action.

Aries rules the head, so try to avoid stimulants like coffee and alcohol, which can add to your stress levels.

As Aries is a sociable sign, why not go out with some upbeat friends—avoid whiners until you're over whatever has deflated you. Better still, why not burn off some of that energy between the sheets with a hot, passionate lover?

FITNESS

ARIES RULES THE head, eyes, ears, bones, and sinuses. The Aries metabolism is very high, and you have to work really hard at getting fat! You work hard, and play even harder. You do everything with gusto: eating, working out, and making love. You always live in the present and are optimistic about the future. As an Aries, you lack patience. You demand instant results from exercise and diet regimes, otherwise, you give up in disgust. However, the human body doesn't usually work at your frenetic speed, Aries, so you may have to get used to nature's slower pace.

In terms of keeping fit, Aries people need to take advantage of their strengths and do what they love. You excel at strenuous team sports and exercise regimens, because your ruling planet Mars—the warrior—imparts to you awesome strength, endurance, confidence, and drive. Highly competitive, Aries can also outlast any opponent in terms of sheer determination. Goal-oriented Aries wants to win and does.

Aries can overheat when exercising, so drink plenty of water. This tendency to be dehydrated is exacerbated by a love of fine wine and spicy foods—Aries is a sign that finds eating bland foods for health reasons practically impossible.

You may experience tension headaches, migraines, and head injuries; however, recovery is usually very quick. You can also suffer from jaw ache from grinding your teeth, so watch out for painful teeth and see your dentist on a regular basis.

TOOLS FOR MAKING A DIFFERENCE

ARIES IS A sign in search of an identity and usually establishes that identity through its interactions with others. Aries will also experience intense bursts of personal growth by throwing itself headlong into all that life has to offer. The ram is a sign that seeks extreme experiences and embraces them with gusto, adoring challenges, change, and risk.

One of Aries's tasks is to learn to allow for shades of gray. So, for example, if you find yourself adamantly saying "men are always," or, "women are always," then try the following exercise on for size. Through it you will begin to understand that the world is not always the way you see it. You could also try investigating the opinions of people who have a different take on life from you. Challenge yourself to find reasons why they might be right. Try doing the same next time you are entering a heated debate with a friend, instead of bearing down on them with adamant assertions and self-righteousness.

EXERCISE SIXTEEN

Losing Deep-seated Beliefs that Are Holding You Back

THIS EXERCISE can be used to change beliefs about colleagues, family members, friends, and people in general, as well as to potential partners.

Do you keep picking the wrong partners, thinking they are the right ones? If so, don't worry. You can pick the right partner, with a little work. Here are some steps to help you to do this.

1. Fill in the blank with a few items that readily come to mind:
   All men (or all women) are . . .
2. Think about the following:
   Is it true that all men or all women are . . . (terms from above)?
   Do you personally know any that are not . . . (terms from above)?

3. Get to know and build friendships with men and women who are not . . . (terms from above)

1. Fill in the blank with a few lines that readily come to mind: All relationships are . . .
2. Think about the following: Is it true that all relationships are . . . (terms from above)?
3. Do you personally know of any that are not . . . (terms from above)?
4. Get to know and build friendships with couples that are not . . . (terms from above)

1. Fill in the blank with a few items that readily come to mind (don't write what you think, but what you feel): I deserve many positive things in a partner, except . . . , which I don't feel I deserve.
2. Think about the following: Have you ever received . . . (terms from above) from people?
3. Did they provide you with . . . (terms from above) because you deserved it, or because they cared about you?
4. Get to know and build friendships with people who readily give you . . . (terms from above)

In this way you begin to change the deep-seated beliefs that are holding you back.

Another tool that Aries needs to develop in order to realize its true potential is persistence, the ability to hold onto a great idea and run with it rather than letting go and watching someone else capitalize on it.

Aries needs to learn to stop taking his or her frustrations out on others and to stop blaming others for his or her weaknesses. From its opposite sign, Libra, Aries needs to learn to develop more cooperative attitudes, patience, and respect for others, and to appreciate his or her environment. If you move too fast, Aries, you sometimes miss out on the lessons that life has to teach.

Aries must also learn that there are times when a pushy, me-first attitude does not serve you well in the long term; sometimes it is better to defer gratification. Practice this by getting a loved one to give you double the treats if you can wait a day or two longer.

SPIRITUALITY

ARIES is likely to sample everything before deciding which spiritual belief is best. From paganism to conventional religion, Aries will embrace any faith with passion until he or she gets bored.

Aries's spiritual goal is to learn the meaning of selfless love. Their spiritual quest comprises the slow process in which their desires become less selfish and expand to include the rest of creation. Only then will Aries attain the love and acceptance that it seeks. Once this sign becomes more self-aware and aware of the needs of others, then it can truly play out its role as the archetypal hero or heroine.

Aries's task is to initiate, challenge, and generally shake things up. Aries is the divine spark that initiates great changes; he or she represents the power of the individual, the "unreasonable man" who changes the status quo and reshapes the world.

CHAPTER 2

TAURUS

April 20–May 20

THE SECOND SIGN OF THE ZODIAC IS CONCERNED WITH:

- ◆ MATERIALISM, WEALTH, PROSPERITY
- ◆ APPRECIATION OF VALUES, TALENTS, ABILITIES
- ◆ NATURE, HARMONY, A LOVE OF LIVING THINGS
- ◆ CAUTION, CONTROL, HABIT, SECURITY, POSSESSION
- ◆ TRUSTWORTHINESS, DEPENDABILITY, CALMNESS
- ◆ BEAUTY, ROMANCE, SENSUALITY
- ◆ SENTIMENTALITY, KINDNESS
- ◆ SHYNESS

TAURUS is the fixed earth sign of the zodiac and lives in a world of concrete reality and sensory perception. For the sun in Taurus, whatever cannot be touched, heard, smelled, seen, or tasted is either denied or made as concrete and tangible as possible. The sun in earth is a consciousness sold on physical security—it lives in the here and now.

Of all the earth signs, Taurus has the greatest need for physical security. The bull has a reputation for being possessive and valuing material things because Taurus feels safer owning plenty of possessions.

Taurus energy—practical, solid, and reliable—dislikes change and may be slow to get moving. It's difficult if not impossible to change the mind of Taurus. The harder you try, the harder he or she digs in. Taurean characteristics are solidity, practicality, extreme determination, and superlative strength of will. No one will ever drive them, but they will willingly and loyally follow a leader they trust. They are stable, balanced, conservative, virtuous, law-abiding citizens and lovers of peace, possessing all the best qualities of the bourgeoisie. The typical Taurean has a deep respect for property and a horror of falling into debt, so he or she will do everything in their power to maintain the security of the status quo and be somewhat hostile to change. In short, don't expect Taurus to join any revolutions!

Mentally, they are sharp-witted but practical more often than intellectual—far from the plodders they are made out to be; however, they are apt to become fixed in their opinions due to their preference for following accepted and reliable patterns of experience. The Taurean character is generally dependable, steadfast, prudent, just, firm, and unshaken in the face of difficulties. As you can probably guess from the preceding paragraph, Taurus's main vice is obstinacy and occasionally rigid self-righteousness.

On rare occasions a Taurean may be an obstinate, irritatingly self-righteous, unoriginal, rigid, ultraconservative, argumentative, querulous bore, firmly stuck in a rut. They may also develop a brooding resentment by nursing a series of injuries received. Whether their characters are positive or negative, they need someone to stroke their egos with a frequent "Good job!"

Strengths to Focus On

- Dependable and loyal
- Thoroughness
- Artistic
- Calmness and patience
- Resourcefulness, realism
- Loving, kind-heartedness
- Admiration of the talents of others, supportiveness
- Caution and conservativeness in outlook, frugality
- Attentiveness
- Gentleness and placidness
- Excellent time-management skills
- Orderliness
- Superb cook

Building Positive Characteristics

MAKE a list of all the positive characteristics that Taurus has. Are there others besides the ones listed? If so, list them.

Do you have all of these characteristics? If not, how would you go about developing them? For example, if you wanted to enhance your time-management skills would you decide to buy a book, take a class, or hire a coach? How do you feel that you learn best?

As Taureans need to make everything as concrete as possible, I suggest that you try for some quick wins to gain a feeling of progress. So, for example, find yourself a time-management exercise that seems logical and that you can implement quickly.

WEAKNESSES THAT CAN TRIP YOU UP

▶ **Self-indulgence**
▶ **Slow moving, laziness**
▶ **Tendency to believe your way is the only way of doing things**
▶ **Materialistic**
▶ **Taciturnity**
▶ **Procrastinates due to over-lengthy deliberation**
▶ **Insensitivity**
▶ **Easily embarrassed**

For a way to change these so-called negative character traits into powerful tools for personal growth, see the Love Your Weaknesses exercise in Aries (page 6). (But you might prefer to sing out your affirmations rather than shouting them out while excited.)

Let's look at one negative Taurean trait, which can block your road to success pretty quickly: stubbornness. Obstinacy in any part of your life gives you a payoff. It could be control, or it could be an affirmation of what you hold to be true about yourself.

Let's say you have a deep-seated belief that there are no interesting people out there, but that you want to make friends or meet a partner. Assuming you feel that this belief is holding you back and that you are having trouble letting go of it, you might like to try the following exercise.

EXERCISE TWO

Letting Go of Unhelpful Beliefs

ASK yourself the following questions:

1. How do you know that there are no such people? Please focus on tangible evidence, rather than on assumptions or intuitions.
2. In what ways are you similar to the kind of person whom you want to meet?
3. You are focusing on something that you want at the same time that you are saying that this goal is unachievable. The goal needs to change, the belief needs to change, or you need to accept living in this tension. What would you prefer? (Actually, you have far more choices than those three, but it may be useful to stick to three options for now!)
4. What does your belief say about you?
5. Would you rather be right or be happy?

If you decide that you'd rather be happy than right, try some of the exercises for meeting interesting people in Aries (page 32). If you cannot decide whether you want to be right or happy, or suffer from procrastination go for the Decision Making for Libra Bosses exercise (page 198).

What about jealousy? How do you deal with your tendency to be jealous? Well, you could try this exercise on for size.

EXERCISE THREE

Letting Go of Jealousy

GET an empty chair, sit across from it, and imagine that the person you are feeling most envious or jealous of is sitting there. Tell the person why you feel the way you do. What does this tell you about what you want for yourself?

Take one step to acquire for yourself the quality you are jealous or envious of in this person.

TAURUS MAN

Unless there are influences in his birth chart that are stronger than his Taurus sun sign, the typical Taurus male will have some or all of the following characteristics:

- ▶ **Rarely changes his opinions**
- ▶ **Can evaluate a situation very quickly in financial terms**
- ▶ **Works hard to build security, abhors debt**
- ▶ **Is wary of others taking advantage of him**
- ▶ **Uses influential connections for advancement**
- ▶ **Quiet**
- ▶ **Unpretentiousness**
- ▶ **Is extremely well mannered and can be charming**
- ▶ **Dresses conservatively**

Taurus often has a stocky body, which can be plump or muscular, depending on whether the bull works out or overindulges. He usually has a clear complexion, a rounded face, large eyes, and a steady gaze. He is likely to have plenty of hair and often sports a beard. He usually has a swift sure walk. If disabled or injured, he will bear himself with dignity and stoicism.

TAURUS WOMAN

In addition to the personality and behavior traits exhibited by the Taurean male, Taurus woman:

▶ Accepts people for who they are
▶ Has tremendous courage—both moral and emotional
▶ Can be shy and self-conscious
▶ Prefers the real to the artificial—no cubic zirconium for this lady, buy her diamonds, or, better still, emeralds
▶ Is extremely sensual and romantic
▶ Is totally loyal to those whom she likes
▶ Is pragmatic and realistic
▶ Has plenty of practical, common sense

Physically, Taurus woman tends to have a rounded body and air of mystery about her. If she is uncomfortable with her Venusian, rounded curves, she may find herself on a permanent diet, which is a tragedy for a sign that adores the sensual taste, feel, and smell of a delicious meal. Too much dieting can also cause her to lose her beautiful complexion and dull her lustrous hair—the birthright of every Taurus lady.

THE HIDDEN (OR NOT-SO-HIDDEN) TAURUS

A PERSON WITH strong Taurean tendencies is a person who worries about security—physical, social, and emotional. I find that my Taurean clients really "buy into" the coaching concept of building a reserve of resources. I always advise my clients to pay themselves first, save a minimum of 10 percent of their earnings, even if they have to cut back on their spending to do so, and build up a minimum of three years' living expenses. This removes the need to make bad decisions out of financial necessity and allows you to take the odd calculated risk. Taurus also loves the concept of compound interest and long-term investments.

Taurus is a sign that takes the long-term view and proceeds slowly but surely—because Taureans believe that only the best will do and that the best things in life are worth waiting for. The bull positively embraces the material side of life—minimalism and poverty are not for Taurus. His or her two main fears are poverty and disturbances of any nature.

TAURUS LIKES

▶ **Soft, sensual textures**
▶ **Sensual pleasures**
▶ **Savings and a healthy bank balance**
▶ **Repetition and reliability**
▶ **Dinner dates or just dinner**
▶ **Gifts of value, lovingly wrapped**

TAURUS DISLIKES

▶ **Being disturbed**
▶ **Changing**
▶ **Being made to hurry up**
▶ **Sleeping in strange places**

POSSIBLE PROBLEM AREAS FOR TAURUS, AND SOLUTIONS

EACH SUN SIGN has particular personality traits, the suppression of which leads to problems. However, with a winning combination of astrology and coaching we can examine the problem and assess the proper solution based on sun sign characteristics. If, as a Taurus, you see things below that really strike home, try the solution. You may be amazed at the results.

PROBLEM: People taking advantage of you and your good nature, feeling used and manipulated.

SOLUTION: Understand that magnetic people like you will attract givers and takers. Establish strong boundaries and make sure that you choose your friends rather than letting them choose you.

PROBLEM: Feeling disappointed with life. People and things no longer hold any pleasure for you. You feel that life is meaningless and that you are developing an addictive personality.

SOLUTION: Revisit and realize the value of the spiritual things in life. (Spirituality is not the same as religion.) Take control of your life and your attitude to it by accepting that it is not material things in themselves that matter but your enjoyment and appreciation of them.

PROBLEM: Inexplicable anxiety and paranoia.

SOLUTION: Remember that you have the ability to attract loyal friends and partners. It is a law of metaphysics that "like attracts like," and you are one of the most steadfast and loyal signs of the zodiac.

PROBLEM: Material things lose their appeal and you sometimes feel out of touch with the world you have created.

SOLUTION: Don't worry; it's just your spirituality kicking in. Relax and enjoy the ride, making sure that you don't overindulge in spiritual pursuits at the expense of providing for your family.

EXERCISE FOUR

The Magnificent Seven Steps to Setting Boundaries

Are you getting what you want and need from your life and relationships, or are you simply getting a surfeit of what you don't want?

If your experience with other people makes you uncomfortable, think about setting your boundaries. Think about how you can sell these boundaries to them as being in their best interests and to their benefit. If you can successfully express your interests in terms of their interests, there's no limit to what you can achieve.

Boundaries make you feel successful in your environment and minimize the risk of being hurt. Personal boundaries let people know what you want and they will respect that. Your behavior becomes more consistent and you are more likely to persuade others to act in your interests, as opposed to antagonizing them and encouraging them to undermine you.

So what are your boundaries? Try asking yourself the following questions:

1. There are things I won't tolerate in my life and in my relationships—list them.
2. Certain behaviors irritate the hell out of me—list them.
3. I want people to behave around me so I can enjoy myself—list how you want them to behave.

Look at your answers. Make your boundaries big enough so you feel safe—and encompass the needs of others, *in a way that works for you.* Start to educate people about them. Be careful not to make people feel wrong about past behavior—otherwise they'll feel defensive. Calmly inform them that you'd now like to be treated in a *particular* way. Describe to the *specifically* what they can and cannot do around you. Also give them a benefit—work out what's in it for them—otherwise whey'll continue to behave exactly as before.

The following exercise should help you to educate people to behave the way you want them to. Make your voice as level as possible while doing this, as you are more likely to be heard that way.

The credit for this process goes to Thomas Leonard, founder of Coach University.

Seven steps to do when someone exhibits unacceptable behavior toward you:

Inform	"Are you aware that you're swearing?"
Request	"Please don't swear at me."
Instruct	"I want you to stop swearing."

Warn	"Do not swear at me."
Take a stand	"Stop swearing, now."
Time Out	"I'm going off to do something else until you stop swearing."
Extended Time Out	"I'm going to minimize my involvement with you until you . . ."

Setting boundaries allows you to feel in control. It's a way to exhibit self-respect and to gain respect.

Remember to work out what you will do if they are not prepared to change their behavior toward you—you may need to cut them out of your life altogether.

CAREER/BUSINESS

IN their work, Taureans are industrious and good craftspeople who are not afraid of getting their hands dirty. They are reliable, easy to get along with, and a good team player. They are also methodical and ambitious, within a framework of obedience to superiors, as befits an earth sign. Taureans can be a little slow to get to get going, so if you want Taurus to do something, you may have to ask them a couple of times before they get around to it. Taureans are notoriously strong-willed, so it's a good idea for a brave colleague to lay down the law first in order to prevent the bull single-mindedly heading in the wrong direction.

Taureans are at their best in routine positions of trust and responsibility, where there is little urgency, even less risk of change, and a pension at the end. Yet they are creative and good founders of enterprises where the rewards of their productiveness come from their own work and not that of others. They can flourish in many different trades and professions (see below). While the bull can do well in business, and is likely to become a respected pillar of the community, an artistic streak is also present, sculpture and singing being two talents strongly associated with the bull.

The Taurus office is likely to be a comfy, cozy den, a place where guests will feel welcome and the bull can hold court. Driving around between appointments is likely to be done in a comfortable, well-built vehicle, with ski racks on top, as a sign of practicality and success. If it's a lunch date you crave, the bull can just as easily take you for a burger or Chateaubriand—it all depends on your value to this discerning member of the zodiac.

Taureans excel in any profession that requires patience and determination. The bull must be careful not to undo all its good work climbing steadily up the corporate ladder by excessive stubbornness or an outburst of Taurean temper. So long as you can keep your focus on the steady accumulation of material goods and frequent doses of sensual, earthy pleasures, life will be perfect.

TAURUS CAREER GUIDE

HERE ARE SOME occupations that a Taurus might consider:

Accountant	Confectioner	Gardener
Antiques dealer	Cosmetician	Investment banker
Architect	Dancer	Makeup artist
Assessor	Decorator	Musician
Auctioneer	Economist	Patron of the arts
Bank teller	Evaluator	Perfumer
Banker	Farmer	Real estate agent
Biologist	Financial advisor	Singer
Business person	Florist	Venture capitalist
Cashier	Fund-raiser	Woodworker
Clothing designer	Furniture maker	

TAURUS BOSS

THE TAUREAN NEED for order and structure makes the bull ideally suited to corporate life. Your logic in building from the bottom up inspires you to make sure that everything is present in the right amounts at the right time for success to follow. You rarely act without considering the ramifications of each action. Action will not occur without a firm basis to support it. Such a mind-set is perfect for corporations, where individual initiative without taking the organization as a whole into account can have a negative impact on business performance.

Once you reach a senior level in business you will find yourself having to make decisions based on less-than-perfect knowledge. This can be a problem for a sign that is uncomfortable with ambiguity. For although you are great at processing information, you can have a problem changing direction when new facts come to light. You will also vigorously resist any threat to the organizational structures that you have put in place.

Ultimately, Taurus, you must learn to do the best with the information that you have and take a leap of faith to make the most of those golden opportunities. Look at the Decision making: Cultivating Your Inner Voice exercise in the Aries chapter (page 10).

Taurus's main strength lies in laying out the business blueprint for your colleagues to follow. You have the strength to command, as your calm way of communicating reassures others and gets them on your side. You are dependable, steady, and project an air of stability and calmness. Like my mother, a typical Taurus, you will probably be called upon by colleagues to resolve their disputes. Colleagues brought my mother their grievances, suggestions, and problems, knowing that she would put in place a means to deal with these issues promptly and effectively. She, like other Taureans, was trusted to be discreet and to provide a solution that had the organization's interests at heart.

Taurus is the one of the most hard-working signs of the zodiac. A workaholic, you are almost 100 percent certain to bring your work home with you. I can remember my mother bringing home a great deal of work so that she could walk into her office the next day knowing that, as far as possible, everything was in place for the day to run smoothly. While she was, and still is, fantastic at crisis management, it's not her favorite occupation.

Most Taureans are steadfastly loyal to the organizations they work for, and hate the upheaval of changing jobs, so it is essential that you find the right company and role for you.

EXERCISE SIX

Career-U-Like

THIS is a fact-gathering and analysis exercise for Taureans. Imagine your ideal job. Write it down in as much detail as possible, i.e., what exactly does the work entail, what will you be doing, what are your working hours, what's the salary, what are the benefits being offered, for example, pension, company car, health insurance, etc.?

Now imagine that you are interviewing someone for that job. Draw up a questionnaire and application form for the role. What skills and experience would the candidate require? What sort of person are you looking for?

Fill in your questionnaire and application form. Include your resumé.

Did you give yourself the job? If not, why not? How could you ensure that you get it the next time?

What further experience, skills, training, and qualifications do you require?

This exercise was inspired by watching my mother, who, having returned to teaching, decided that she wanted to leap from a low-ish-paying teaching role to a deputy headship—a jump of some six grades. Being a Taurus, she sat down and looked at what experience and skills she would need to land a deputy headship and then threw herself into acquiring them. She put in extra hours, including volunteer work, to pick up the management skills required and took plenty of courses. A typical Taurus, she naturally got the support of the family, and we took turns doing domestic chores and role-play interviews with her. All this focused activity paid off: She made her leap and attained the job of her dreams.

EMPLOYEE

AS A SUBORDINATE you follow superiors' orders thoroughly and willingly because you expect people to do the same when you're the boss. Taurus tends to lead by example and is a sign of great integrity. Whatever your current role in an organization, you will be pulling more than your weight, steadfastly working away until your efforts are rewarded.

A highly goal-oriented person, you are able to focus intently on whatever you do, making you efficient and effective. However, you are at risk of getting too close to what you are doing, focusing too intently on one portion of the project, which can put you at risk of missing an important detail or misjudging circumstances. You could find out later that the premise that formed the foundation of your plan is faulty, causing everything to collapse. Remind yourself to stop and question your assumptions now and then.

You are a deferential and, on the whole, even-tempered employee, who works at their own pace and hates to be rushed. You are a self-motivated and self-directed individual. This is partly due to your perfectionist streak and partly due to your strong belief that some day you will lead the company. Interestingly, with your desire to do well, you often outgrow a role before moving upwards—you can be too valuable in your current position for your own good, Taurus. If you feel that your progress is too slow, you may start quietly implementing plans to run the business—your business as you see it—more efficiently while you wait expectantly for someone to hand you the reins. Should this fail to happen, you, like some of my Taurus clients, will simply take your talents elsewhere.

COACH'S TIP

Sit down and talk with your boss about one thing you are uncomfortable with in your job. Stick to one thing only and position the change you are looking for as being to your boss's advantage. Changing one thing will reinforce your belief in your ability to achieve total comfort in your work.

Is there anything a coach can teach Taurus about goal setting? Well, you could go to the Aries Personality section and try the S.M.A.R.T.est Goals For Aries exercise for size (page 3) or even the Ego to Go exercise in Leo on page 156.

FINANCES AND WEALTH

THE slow and steady bull is one of the zodiac's great providers. Those born under this sign are terrific with money, probably because they value it so much. They also love the good life, and that usually costs significant sums. Fortunately, Taurus is prepared to work for the good things in life and is well aware of the value of material comfort and security. The bull also loves the kind of beauty that money can't buy—a beautiful sunset or melodic birdsong, for example.

As an earth sign, Taureans also enjoy owning a piece of the earth, so real estate makes for a particularly attractive investment for these folks. It's also a great way to take care of the ones they love.

Taureans have a wonderful ability to keep their eyes on the prize and apply the effort required to attain it, which means that they will slowly and steadily get the things they want. The bull loves everything about money—Taurus is a sign that feels comfortable with money—and also feels entitled to it! You recognize where money should be placed relative to people and possessions in terms of value—after people and before possessions. Money, after all, is what enables you to acquire your possessions. This comfort level around money helps to make you extremely good with it.

Liking security in general (a partner, their own home), Taureans aren't likely to make rash financial decisions that will cause them to lose their treasure trove. A favorite coaching exercise for my Taurean clients is called Building Up A Rainy-Day Fund and is found in the Finances section of Aries (page 27).

Tangible assets are best where Taureans are concerned—things they can see, feel, and touch. Consequently, antiques and real estate are far more appealing than stocks and bonds. Bulls are often long-term investors as well, since they like both making and keeping money.

The bull is a master at making deliberate decisions where money is concerned, which means that bills will be paid on time and accounts are always in order. Before making any investment, you look for practical, logical reasons to participate, and you put a great deal of emphasis on careful, painstaking research. You carefully factor in all the possible future ups and downs of a particular stock before you buy it. Do Taureans ever sell their stock? Sure, but only after they have lost faith in the management of the company they've invested in.

Taureans are patient and disciplined financial planners and, unlike my fire sign clients, usually keep close tabs on their finances. There are no unopened bills or bank statements hiding in the bull's closet. Taurus also tends to avoid lending or borrowing money, except for mortgages.

Does this sensible sign have any financial failings? Not really, just a couple of areas that might need watching. First, a tendency to overspend—not in terms of buying something overpriced, but in terms of buying a major investment that reduces your cash flow to a trickle short-term. Second, a tendency not to make your money work hard enough for you—you can be too conservative and have too much of your money tied up in low-interest bonds. You can forget the maxim that to make money you need to spend money, and end up holding onto your money so tightly that you barely keep up with inflation. To combat this tendency you might like to try this exercise—which I particularly recommend to Taureans with Libran or Aries partners.

EXERCISE SEVEN

White-Knuckle Finances for Taurus

TAKE a small portion of your money and call it "white knuckle money" (this is money that you can afford to lose). Give it to an Aries or Libra to invest. Now comes the hard part, Taurus—do not get involved in the trading he or she does for you, unless you are suffering substantial losses. If your Arien or Libran partner is true to their sign, the greater than average return on investment you experience should encourage you to add more to your "white knuckle money," and teach you about diversification as a tool for financial risk management.

LOVE, ROMANCE, AND SEX LIFE

THE bull, as you would expect from an earth sign, is a grounded and devoted kind, but that should never be construed as boring. Taurus can settle into a steady relationship with breathtaking speed. The bull generally wants a harmonious and beautiful relationship, and is easily hurt by a partner who just wants a quick flirtation. To avoid this hurt, Taurus, try the following exercise to determine how much commitment you need from a partner.

EXERCISE EIGHT

Choosing an Available Partner

WHEN I ask clients to tell me about why their past relationships have not worked out, I usually get the same response. They tell me their past partner(s) have been unavailable. When asked for a description of an unavailable partner, they have given the following examples:

- ◆ Uncommunicative
- ◆ Keeps secrets
- ◆ Doesn't talk about feelings
- ◆ Doesn't talk about his/her life
- ◆ Doesn't have time available
- ◆ Wants a relationship on weekends only
- ◆ Geographically distant and doesn't want to change the situation
- ◆ Doesn't want a commitment
- ◆ Doesn't want to move to the next step in the relationship

The list above can be reduced to three areas where there is a gap between what the two partners want:

1.   A gap in communication
2.   A gap in time spent together
3.   A gap in the level of commitment

The existence of these gaps makes one partner feel the other is unavailable. But what if there is no such thing as an unavailable partner? Instead there is the individual's definition of an "available enough" partner.

- What kind of a partner is "available enough" for you?
- Under what circumstances do you function best in a relationship?
- How much do you need of:
  - Communication?
  - Depth in communication?
  - In-person communication?
  - Together time?
  - Personal space?
  - Depth of connection?
- What is your definition of a committed relationship?
- Do you want a commitment?
- How long are you willing to wait for a commitment?

One way to answer the above questions is to look at what you want now and for the future. To gain even more insight, look at your past relationships as well. Was there a gap in what you wanted and what your partners were willing to give? Did you get enough closeness, distance, communication, and commitment?

If, in a relationship, you have asked for more and not received it, don't force your partner to close the gap. Instead, look to see if your partner is "available enough" for you. You cannot force anyone to do what they don't want to do. Only when both partners perceive a gap and seek to bridge it will the relationship work.

How do you recognize a partner who is "available enough" for you? It's not a good idea to talk about your deep needs on the first date. It is a good idea to listen to your date and watch their behavior. They will communicate to you clearly who they are and what they are looking for. If your date says he is not interested in a committed relationship, and you know you are, then he is not "available enough." If she says she loves working eighty-hour weeks, while you want someone with you every night, she is not "available enough."

Now that you are working on attracting a partner who wants

similar things, and has a similar value system, recognizing people who are not right becomes easy. You can weed out people who are not "available enough." Now you are free to attract a partner who is "available enough."

Whether it's a sweet serenade or silky sheets, Taurus loves anything luxurious and anyone who can bring that aspect into their lives. Taureans are very attracted to physical beauty and are extremely sensitive to perfume, color, light, and sound. Does this make the bull all style and no substance? Certainly not: In addition to being an earthy and physical lover, Taureans are sentimental, romantic, and possessed of a dogged determination, which virtually assures that they will get what they want. You can scare lovers off with the intensity of your ardor, Taurus, so learn to give less intense partners some space. Remember that love can only be freely given and lovers are not possessions.

COMPATIBILITY

TAURUS TENDS TO be compatible with fellow earth signs and water signs—remember that water nourishes the earth and you won't go far wrong! The earth–water mix that requires a great deal of effort to make flourish is that of polar opposites Taurus and Scorpio due to the fixed nature of both signs.

WHAT TAURUS NEEDS

THE BULL CRAVES someone who is strong and practical, qualities they value in their own life. They are traditionalists who like men to be men and women to be women when it comes to partnership. One who comes bearing gifts is also guaranteed to win, since Taurus is responsive to both material goods and sincere, heartfelt compliments. Making Taurus feel safe is a very smart strategy for a lover, for this approach will bring out the bull's most sensual self.

The Taurus lover is dependable and considerate, someone who

wants to be in a beautiful world and have that special someone to share it with. Anyone lucky enough to enter that world will find a sensual soul waiting to be nurtured and explored.

THE END OF THE AFFAIR

IT TAKES A long time for Taurus to give up on a relationship and cut their losses. However, once Taurus decides to leave a relationship, there is no turning back. While Taureans find it hard to admit that they have been wrong about a person, they are not the best judges of character. As the bull tends to be an honest and straightforward individual, he or she will tend to assume that all is well even if a partner is deceitful. When Taureans do discover that a lover has been less than honest, they may still cling to some hope.

The lover who abandons Taurus will leave behind a bewildered and disbelieving person, who may suffer physically and psychologically as hurt and rage bubble up from the subconscious.

COACH'S TIP

Taurus needs to learn to take risks in the course of developing or improving relationships. Here is something for you to try:

Tell your lover the sexual fantasy you've held back from telling him or her. Be really brave and say it out loud when you're making love.

RELATIONSHIPS
(Family and Friends)

TAURUS PARENT

THE TYPICAL TAURUS parent is affectionate and patient, with a tendency toward dominance and possessiveness. Taurus will support, protect, and nurture children, and will expect high standards. Taurus will encourage his or her children and teach them self-respect.

The Taurus parent provides the very best for their children and will save for the future. Taureans will have complete confidence in their parenting abilities.

TAURUS CHILD

THE TAURUS CHILD is remarkably placid. He or she will enjoy thinking about things and will generally appear consistent in their approach. A practical mind is a large part of the makeup here, so explaining things to a Taurus child by saying "This is how it is" is useless. Taurus needs to understand the "why" behind the rules, or they will take no notice of them.

The Taurus child has an insatiable need for affection. You can never hug the Taurus youngster enough and they can never get enough of your company. Your Taurus youngster could turn into a real "mother's little helper," particularly in the kitchen. "Home is where the heart is" should be this kid's motto. They're stubborn as well, making it pretty hard to sway them once they get an idea in their head. The positive side to this characteristic, however, is patience and persistence, something that renders the Taurus child a good student and an eager reader.

BRINGING UP TAURUS—COACH'S INSIGHT

THERE IS ABSOLUTELY no point whatsoever in trying to force young Taurus to do anything; you will be met with firm resistance. This child will hold his or her ground longer than anyone else except, possibly, a Taurus parent. Young Taurus does not respond well to harsh commands; however, a loving hug will break down the bull's resistance, providing that is backed up with an explanation as to why young Toro should behave in the required manner.

Generous doses of physical affection are essential to the healthy growth of the Taurus child. No smothering, though. Young Taurus also needs harmonious surroundings. Colors and sounds will have a deep effect on this youngster. Harmonious music and calming shades of blue and rose will have a soothing effect.

WHAT TO TEACH YOUNG TAURUS

MOST CHILDREN WHO are typical Taureans will have soft harmonious voices accompanied by a good ear for music. This is a sign that loves music—many of my Taurean clients love to sing along to the radio or enjoy singing in a choir. This love of music frequently surfaces in childhood, so introduce them to singing or other forms of music at an early age. Young Toro will probably express a heartfelt preference for classical music over pop. Taurus will also love other artistic activities where he or she can use their hands and eyes—painting, making collages or pottery, for example. This love of making things continues through to adulthood. Whereas other signs visualize what they want by cutting out photos or holding an image in their head, Taurus is likely to paint, make a collage or, in the case of one Taurus client, make plasticine models representing the desired outcome.

In general, Taureans will take a methodical and practical approach to schoolwork, learning steadily as they go along. Taurus has an excellent memory, so every lesson learned will be consolidated and built upon. Young bulls should be encouraged to communicate through words, pictures, and music, as they tend to mask their true feelings behind an inscrutable facade.

TAURUS AND FRIENDS

TAURUS HAS A tendency to prefer friends who are reliable, consistent, and not given to sudden mood swings or springing surprises.

Taureans are warm and very affectionate toward their friends. They are likely to choose people who have similar tastes to them, and with whom they can enjoy a quiet conversation, an excellent meal, or trip to a concert.

Taureans will be drawn to those people whose strength of character and endurance matches their own. Taurus will always be gentle, considerate, loyal, and completely trustworthy toward these friends.

WAYS TO HELP WITH FRIENDSHIP

TO HELP IMPROVE your relationships with your friends, try being a little less possessive. Give a gift to your friend for no special reason and without hoping for something in return. Maximize the impact by making sure that it's something your friend cherishes.

Apologize to a friend (or other) who you self-righteously argued with when you knew you were wrong.

Take a risk, open up, and tell a friend something that has been bothering you about the relationship for a long time.

Get out and meet new people, and talk with each one for at least fifteen minutes.

FRIENDS, BE AWARE

TAURUS, LIKE ITS neighbor Aries, can be extremely possessive and jealous of any attention a friend bestows on another.

Taurus cannot bear any sign of weakness—physical or emotional—and can be quite blunt about it. Cowards need not apply to be in Toro's gang. Taurus is prepared to give its best to a sick, heartbroken, or disabled friend, provided that the condition is bravely endured and not used as an excuse for underperformance.

The bull prizes friends who have some power, which the bull can share and enjoy. People who are all show and no substance are unlikely to attract the friendship of a typical Taurean.

HEALTH

IT takes a lot to get a Taurus ruffled, but once done, the magnitude of the bull's temper can appear in full force and just about anyone in your way could bear the brunt of it. You need to have time out when you are feeling enraged, Taurus, and wait for your temper to dissipate. This usually happens quite quickly, provided that there is no one around you to set you off again.

EXERCISE NINE

Roar, Toro, Roar

THINK of a situation to which you feel you habitually react or have reacted "irrationally"—that is, where your reaction is either inappropriate or out of all proportion to the response required to deal with what is happening to or around you. For example, every time someone criticizes me, I feel like bursting into tears, and then I get really, really angry.

In a safe space, recall those feelings. Really let go and throw a huge tantrum. Stamp your feet, throw things, thump a pillow or a punching bag, and roar at the top of your voice, if you feel like it. Don't attempt to analyze or evaluate what you're saying—just scream it out.

Once you've let go of your aggression, return to the real world. Tense and relax your body, take a deep breath, and relocate yourself in your physical surroundings.

This exercise is a great way of breaking a pattern of ingrained behavior—it is not intended to replace medical or psychiatric treatment.

STRESS BUSTING FOR TAURUS

WHEN CONCERNED ABOUT something that stresses you, like, "How on earth am I going to pay these bills?" Taurus needs to be left alone to meditate. Decision making is a lengthy process. An earth sign, Taurus needs to carefully consider all the options and weigh each for practicality. Yours is a fixed sign, so change comes slowly and deliberately.

To give you better perspective and time to unwind, you need creature comforts. Taurus is one of the few signs that would benefit from watching a little TV. You might also opt to have a brandy or a small chocolate bar—whatever makes you feel relaxed and mellow. In summer, if weather permits (yours is a sign that tends to feel the cold) open the window and feel the refreshing breeze. In winter you might opt for a nice warm bath or log fire. Your sign also enjoys music, but Taurus likes it best with the proper speakers and stereo unit. If you've set up such a system, now is the time to sit back and let music soothe your savage breast.

You have other options, too, Taurus. Your Venus-ruled nature always feels soothed by greenery, so get closer to nature by doing some gardening or landscaping. Planting tulips, fuchsias, and roses in the fresh air will give you quiet time to think and make you feel better. The rich, fertile, moist soil in your hands will soothe you, too. Even if you live in a city apartment you can still get in touch with nature. Plant some seeds or a hyacinth bulb for your windowsill, get a lush green tree for your living room, fresh flowers for your desk, or just go and immerse yourself in the sights, smells, and sounds of your local park. Even better, why not drive to the country to see homes with elegant manicured gardens. Spend a Saturday morning or afternoon strolling around, stop to sit down and watch the world go by—no beeper, no cell phone allowed.

If you prefer, treat yourself to a little pampering and human contact. Have the very best massage you can afford. Taurus is highly sensual, and responds very well to soothing touch. If you can't afford a professional—complete with aromatic herbs to relax you— ask your partner to give you the deluxe treatment complete with candlelight and special oils. You could follow this up with some tender, relaxing lovemaking. Lose yourself in your partner, Taurus, and feel your cares disappear. If you only have time for a massage, then remember the following tip. Taurus rules the neck, the first place your tension strikes, so be sure your lover works on that part of you. Afterwards, cuddle up together.

FITNESS

TAURUS RULES THE tongue, tonsils, neck, veins, kidneys, genital organs, throat, thyroid, and vocal chords. Your metabolism is low.

As a Taurus, you are aware that you use all of your senses to explore the world. How something feels, sounds, smells, or tastes matters to you—a lot. You adore sex, fabulous food (you're a gourmet rather than a gourmand), the touch and feel of certain fabrics against your skin (not to mention skin against skin), and are very responsive to beautiful music. An innate fondness for chocolate, French cuisine, and sedentary pursuits, combined with a slow metabolism can pack the pounds on you, bull.

Play to your strengths, Taurus, and work with your sensual nature to keep a program of regular physical exercise a fun part of your life. Instead of your beloved old sweats, spend a little on comfortable and flattering clothing to wear at the gym and enjoy the feel of your emerging, svelte physique. Bring along your portable tape player and earphones so you can listen to your favorite music, and treat yourself to an after-workout sauna and massage, if you can afford it. Women Taureans seem to be especially responsive to aromatherapy massage. When your muscles are aching as you pull into that last abdominal crunch, just grit your teeth and remind yourself that exercise always makes your sex life more active and pleasurable.

If you can find a sport that you enjoy, make the most of it. Leave sports that require lightning-fast reflexes to fire and air signs, as you'll hate them. Your true forte is sports that require concentration and good hand–eye coordination, such as archery, marksmanship, or golf.

Combine whatever sport you do with other activities that you love, for example, being outside enjoying the scenery. Try working in your garden to give you the dual benefits of gorgeous, healthy fruit and vegetables and a firm abdomen. The more you can enjoy an exercise regime the more likely you are to persevere.

Beware of radical dieting, Taurus. If you allow yourself to feel deprived, sooner or later you will rebel, binge, and pile on those pounds! You'll also be short-tempered and a nightmare to live with. The trick is to gradually make healthy changes in your diet so that you keep your enthusiasm—and your metabolism—high. Do try to exercise, as this will speed up your sluggish metabolism—dieting alone will just lower it even more, so that once you start eating normally, the pounds will pile on with a vengeance. Make sure that you don't give up if you reach a plateau. You are ruled by Venus, a fairly hedonistic, pleasure-seeking planet, and you will have the most success if you get regular rewards. So write down all the milestones that get you to your final goal and list a reward for yourself (a healthy one!) next to each milestone. Fortunately, you have a will of iron and plenty of persistence working in your favor once you commit to getting fit.

TOOLS FOR MAKING A DIFFERENCE

Change is rarely easy for you, Taurus, since the threat of losing something can be taken quite personally. Your resistance and stubbornness are the stuff of legend, and if you feel threatened you can be downright uncooperative. How many change management programs have been thwarted by Taureans, I wonder! Change becomes easier for you if you realize that you are far, far more than your possessions. You can then learn to let go of situations and possessions that no longer serve you—in fact, why not clear out all the clutter that you no longer need from your home. Be ruthless and get a friend to help if necessary. Why should you do this? Well, since you like explanations, I'll tell you. You do this with the intention of freeing space to allow room for the goodies that will inevitably flow in to fill this vacuum that you have created.

EXERCISE TEN

Clutter Buster

STEP ONE: *make a list of the "clutter" in your life.*
Divide your clutter into three categories:

1. Things you don't use, for example, old clothes. Include anything that you haven't used for a year!
2. Things you no longer gain any pleasure from, for example, unwanted gifts and bad purchases.
3. Things that use you, i.e., anything that takes more time being maintained than being used. Examples might be the second house where you were going to spend every weekend but which

you never go near, or the pleasure boat that's always breaking down.

STEP TWO: *start eliminating clutter.*

This can be a painful process initially for some people, but once you experience the incredible energy that is released with every item of clutter, you'll become a clutter-clearing dynamo! If you do find yourself resisting getting started, here's a tactic that works well for me: Start with the smallest items, and if that doesn't work, dispose of the thing that irritates you the most, like the size ten you bought at a sale that doesn't fit, now that you've finally lost weight!

As you eliminate the would-be "luxuries" that clutter up your life, your sense of how much is enough will become clearer and clearer. This will enable you to see that if you lost nearly all your possessions, you would still survive.

Learn how to say good-bye to relationships that no longer serve you, for this will strengthen your power, Taurus. Learn also to connect with your inner voice, which will reassure and center you during times of disquiet and change.

COACH'S TIP

Let go of a project or relationship that you've been working on for a long time, which you feel will probably never be beneficial to you.

CHANGE MANAGEMENT TACTICS FOR TAUREANS

WE KNOW THAT navigating successfully in a world that is changing as fast as ours can be tricky at times. In fact, if we allow it to overwhelm us, change can feel extremely stressful and frustrating. If we're smart, however, we've learned that although we can't alter the fact of constant change, we can learn to manage our response to it. Here's a sample of how I coach my clients to manage change in their lives:

1. Accept change as a fact of life.

2. Commit yourself to lifelong learning. If change is constant, then learning must also be continual. Learning helps us feel as though we're moving with the ever-changing world, which in turn helps relieve our anxiety at feeling left behind.

3. Get healthy, then stay healthy. Change, even positive change, is stressful, so stay physically healthy with proper nutrition, enough rest, and regular exercise.

4. Look at change as an opportunity. Changing our attitude about change is one of our best management tools. Look for opportunities in every change in your life. Rather than digging in your heels and resisting change, allow yourself to flow with it and see where it takes you.

5. Develop and maintain a strong network and support team. Many changes in our lives require us to lean on others for emotional support and advice. Have your team in place, ready to see you through the inevitable significant changes in your life.

6. Develop your spirituality.

7. Engage in rituals. Performing a task or celebration in the same way, week after week or year after year, gives us a sense of stability, a feeling of being grounded, a sense of security.

8. As much as possible, eliminate the irritations in your life. Major or minor, these drain your energy—energy you need to manage change. An irritation can be something as simple as a missing button or as significant as a "toxic" person.

9. Keep a daily journal. When change is viewed over a period of time, there is more sense to it. Seeing this historical perspective of past change in our lives can give us more objectivity in meeting the current changes that are facing us.

10. Engage in meditation. Being centered within yourself grounds you for the changes you're required to face every day.

EXERCISE ELEVEN

Avoiding Self-sabotage

TAURUS, with its resistance to change, needs to learn how to combat self-sabotage. I have lost count of the number of people who, just when everything seems to be going perfectly, manage to snatch defeat from the jaws of victory.

Self-sabotage is caused by our perception, often at the subconscious level, that what we say we want is in conflict with what we really want. (For example, we may feel that there is a conflict between wanting to be rich and wanting to be a good person, or between wanting to move up the corporate ladder and wanting more time for ourselves.)

The solution to this problem is awareness, and the simplest way to increase our awareness is by paying attention. The following ten questions are frequently used in the coaching process and are designed to focus your awareness on the most common areas of hidden conflicts in goal setting.

Choose a goal to work with, and ask yourself the following ten questions. To heighten your awareness, take five minutes per goal. You can write down your answers or just answer the questions in your head.

1. What do I want?
2. Why do I want it?
3. Why don't I want it?
4. How much energy will it take to achieve it?
5. What skills will I have to use or develop in order to achieve it?
6. Who else does it involve? Who else does it affect?
7. What's the time frame? Is it imposed externally, internally, or both?
8. Financially, how much will it cost? How much will it make? How important (on a scale of 1–10) is the money factor to me?
9. How likely (on a scale of 1–10) do I think it is that I will get what I want?
10. If I could have it right now, would I take it?

To avoid self-sabotage, Taurus needs to connect with his or her deepest and highest values. For more on values, see the Define Your Values exercise in Aries (page 20).

SPIRITUALITY

ULTIMATELY, the Taurean needs to discover their truest, deepest, and highest values. When they know what is truly valuable, they are no longer chained to people and to things that have to do with lesser values. The greatest indication of value to a spiritually mature Taurean is beauty, which cannot be owned, only appreciated.

No other sign in the zodiac is closer to earth then Taurus. No other sign has the same sensual intelligence. The bull will often seek and find spiritual answers in nature.

The main objective in leading a Taurean life is to maintain stability and look after physical concerns. Taurus is here to teach us to collaborate wisely with the natural world—it is the zodiac's environmentalist. Your inner spiritual sense longs for earthly harmony and wholesomeness. When you fully understand this and work toward this end, you will no longer need to blindly reassure yourself with external possessions and comforts. When Venusian Taurus is truly at peace with the natural world there is no divide between the physical and spiritual realm. Taurus, by appreciating the beauty of the physical world, immediately connects with the spirit running through all things.

Taureans flourish both physically and spiritually by accepting, and reveling in, the fact that their true tasks are tending, caring, nurturing, and mating.

CHAPTER 3

GEMINI

May 21–June 20

THE THIRD SIGN OF THE ZODIAC IS CONCERNED WITH:

- ◆ COMMUNICATION, ARTICULATION, SPEECH, WIT
- ◆ INTUITION, INSTINCT
- ◆ CHANGE, VARIETY, ADAPTABILITY
- ◆ DEXTERITY, NIMBLENESS, LIGHT-FOOTEDNESS, MOVEMENT
- ◆ FREEDOM, YOUTH
- ◆ ATTENTION TO DETAIL, COLLECTING FACTS
- ◆ EDUCATION, LEARNING, INTELLECT
- ◆ EXPLORATION, SHORT JOURNEYS

RULED by Mercury, the Roman messenger god, Gemini is associated with communication. Mercury is the ace communicator, the magician, and the jester. Gemini's quick-witted changeable energy may at times appear to others as scattered, disorganized, and chaotic, but there's usually a keen sense of logic behind Gemini's frenetic activity. (Although, truthfully, Gemini's constantly active right hand doesn't know always know what his or her constantly moving left hand is up to.) And with the sun in Gemini, you may also have a tendency to "bend" the truth at times. You are more than capable of deluding everyone, including yourself.

Gemini energy tends to be constantly questioning and skeptical of "eternal truths." Gemini is an extremely curious sign and will always be searching out different points of view. The Internet was made for Gemini—so many different perspectives to try on for size!

Gemini sun belongs to the element of air. Air signs are stimulated mentally and tend to have a detached perspective. Air is motivated and recharged by intellectual concepts, social interchanges, and the communication of ideas and ideals. The element of air tends to produce a fairly active mind. The world is approached with reason and everything (everyone) is open to analysis. This tendency is exacerbated by the fact that Gemini is a mutable, or changeable, sign.

Gemini is communicative, versatile, extremely talkative, and very curious. It has to know how things work, including other people. Gemini thrives on knowing what makes other people tick.

When curiosity really gets the better of a Gemini, he or she may say scandalous, shocking things or perform outrageous acts for no other reason than that they wanted to see what would happen.

Gemini enjoys knowing a little about everything, and can be the ultimate "jack-of-all-trades, master of none." Geminis are, however, so good at communicating that it takes a real expert to see through their posturing.

Mythology teaches us a key thing that we need to know about Gemini. Hermes (Mercury), by some accounts, was the god who originally owned and wore the "Helmet of Invisibility." Mercury, like Pluto (or Hades—ruler of Scorpio), revels in working silently and invisibly behind the scenes. So, like Scorpios, Geminis specializes in being secretive and keeping things under their hat.

Gemini, the sign of the twins, is dual-natured, elusive, complex, and contradictory. Wow, what a mixture! On the one hand, sun in Gemini gives rise to the virtue of versatility, and on the other the vices of two-facedness and flightiness. Mercury is the planet of childhood and youth, and its subjects tend to have the graces and faults of the young. Like children, they take up new activities enthusiastically but lack application, constantly needing new interests, flitting from project to project, as boredom overwhelms them. To Gemini life is a game, which must always be full of fresh moves and continuous entertainment, free of hard work and routine. Vacillating between courses of action is another quirk in the Gemini personality, which makes making and sticking to a decision particularly hard for them. This is why I find it imperative to get my Gemini clients to understand what values they stand for. Once Gemini has done this, decision making becomes far easier. For an exercise on values, see Define Your Values in the Aries chapter (page 20). For more on decision making, you might also want to read Chapter 7, on Libra.

As Geminis lack the quality of conscientiousness, not to mention conscience, on occasion they are apt to fight a losing battle in any attempts they make to be moral (in the widest sense of the word). Their good qualities are attractive and come easily to them. They are affectionate, courteous, kind, generous, and thoughtful toward the poor and suffering—provided none of the activities resulting from expressing these traits interferes too greatly with their own lives and comforts. This is fair enough; at least Gemini can give without resentment. They quickly learn to use their outward attractiveness to gain their own ends, and when striving for these they will use any weapon in their armory—unscrupulous lying, cunning evasiveness, and escaping blame by contriving to put it on other people, all wrapped up in all the charm they can turn on. Company politics was made for Gemini. Gemini may strive to be honest and straightforward, but self-interest is almost always the victor.

Gemini is not a sign that needs to connect with its inner child—quite the reverse, in fact. Like children, Geminis demand attention, admiration, and the spending on them of time, energy, and money, throwing tantrums if they don't get what they want. If the conditions of life become really adverse, their strength of will may desert them entirely. They can become uncertain of themselves, either withdrawn or nervously excitable worriers, increasingly focused on themselves. On the other hand, their versatility can make them very adaptable. They can adjust themselves to control the world around them by using their inherent ingenuity and cleverness.

Most Geminis have a keen, intuitive, sometimes brilliant intelligence, and they love cerebral challenges. However, their concentration, though intense for a while, does not last. Their mental agility and energy give them a voracious appetite for knowledge from youth onwards, though they dislike the labor of learning. Gemini is quite likely to try playing tapes while sleeping, driving, or engaged in some other activity in the hope that the tape will program their subconscious and save them the effort of learning. They easily grasp most things requiring intelligence and mental dexterity, and are often able to marry manual skills to their qualities of mind. Their intellect is strongly analytical, which can lead them to overanalyze situations and vacillate between too many options. Wise Geminis will use their intelligence to unify the duality of their natures into a most efficient unit.

If faced with difficulties, Gemini can rarely summon up the motivation to worry about a problem until they find a solution—they will pick the brains of others. In their intellectual pursuits, as in other departments of their lives, they risk becoming dilettantes, losing themselves in too many projects, which they follow until they become difficult.

Gemini people are often successful in many walks of life even though their general characteristics tend to make them unreliable. This is in part due to the Gemini skills in perception management. They are often able manipulators of language, in speech and writing, and are able to convince people to take them at face value. Geminis can become even more adept communicators if they develop their listening skills. A great set of exercises for doing this can be found in the Aries Personality section of this book (see pages 1–3).

STRENGTHS TO FOCUS ON

▶ **Curiosity and cleverness**
▶ **Quick**
▶ **Entertaining and charming**
▶ **Expressiveness**
▶ **Broadmindedness**
▶ **Inventiveness**
▶ **Exuberance**
▶ **Stimulating**
▶ **Versatility**
▶ **Youthfulness and agility**
▶ **Open-mindedness**

To acquire desirable characteristics before you get bored, you may want to try the 911 Affirmations exercise in the Aries chapter (page 7).

WEAKNESSES THAT CAN TRIP YOU UP

- ▶ Restlessness
- ▶ Easily bored
- ▶ Capriciousness and fickleness
- ▶ Gossipy
- ▶ Nervousness
- ▶ Manipulativeness
- ▶ Impatience and irritability
- ▶ Noncommittal
- ▶ Dual personality

So how do you turn these so-called negative traits into powerful tools for personal growth? First visit the Love Your Weaknesses exercise in Aries (page 6). Now let's look at how some of the ideas introduced there might be applied to your own sign. First of all, how boredom can be used to develop greater self-awareness.

EXERCISE ONE

Share the Task

ASK A friend to help you complete a task that you find boring—it'll only take half the time and, therefore, half the boredom. This will enable you to develop the discipline to see boring tasks through to the end, allow you to connect more deeply with your friend and enable you to reach out and ask for help to complete tasks that you find tedious.

EXERCISE TWO

Define Your Boredom

LOOK in a mirror when you are feeling bored and answer the following questions:

1. When did I become bored?
2. Why?
3. Where and how did this boredom originate?
4. What is this boredom? (Is it fear, frustration, resentment, anger?)
5. Who and what am I bored with? (Me or other people?)

EXERCISE THREE

Developing Gratitude and Acceptance

LOOK in a mirror and accept that the boredom you feel is the price you pay for being energetic, mercurial, and creative. Be grateful and thankful for your boredom—it's a small price to pay for all your better features!

If you are a Gemini who tends to lie, you might like to look at whether you should be creating a better life for yourself—one that gives truth to the lie. It is likely that creating a fantasy life where you're successful, devastatingly attractive, or whatever you lie about is telling you what is currently lacking in your real life. So get out there and grab the success, wealth, or whatever it is that you crave.

One of my Gemini clients, Neil, was always letting clients and colleagues down by not phoning them when he'd agreed to. By recognizing that the reason he did this was that he resented having his time encroached on by others and the restrictions that this caused, he was able to come up with a way of working via E-mail at times when he felt like it. When "selling" to clients he manages to turn the fact that he works almost solely via E-mail into a major selling point.

GEMINI MAN

Unless there are influences in his birth chart that are stronger than his Gemini sun sign, the typical Gemini male will have some or all of the following characteristics:

▶ **Gets impatient with routine**
▶ **Likes to influence**
▶ **Hates being misunderstood**
▶ **Is eager and always on the move, with a great deal of nervous energy**
▶ **Needs new challenges and intellectual stimulation**
▶ **Is a natural salesman**
▶ **Can talk himself out of difficulties**
▶ **Is intelligent and witty**
▶ **Likes people**
▶ **Is adroit, socially skilled, and diplomatic**
▶ **May change occupations frequently**

GEMINI WOMAN

In addition to the personality and behavior traits exhibited by the the Gemini male, Gemini woman:

▶ **Needs people around her**
▶ **Is a lively conversationalist, who has many interests and loves to gossip**
▶ **Is career-oriented**
▶ **Can be charming and very persuasive**
▶ **Notices every detail**
▶ **Can be loyal and sincere with the right partner**
▶ **Is optimistic**

- **Is very intuitive**
- **Will never turn down a cry for help**
- **Is a composite of many different personalities**
- **Makes a great friend and is stimulating company**
- **Takes an interest in any new subject**

So how do you turn these so-called negative traits into powerful tools for personal growth? First visit the Love Your Weaknesses exercise in Aries (page 6). Now let's look at how some of the ideas introduced there might be applied to your own sign. First of all, how boredom can be used to develop greater self-awareness.

THE HIDDEN (OR NOT-SO-HIDDEN) GEMINI

A PERSON WITH strong Gemini influences is likely to be searching to find their true soulmate, that mysterious other half who will make them feel complete. More mature and self-aware Geminis will realize that their missing twin lives within them waiting to be embraced.

Gemini can be a lonely and lost sign, seeking a deep connection yet keeping it at bay by giving up too quickly. Communication is this sign's lifeblood—contact through ideas, philosophy, or just plain gossip keeps Gemini devoted and happy.

GEMINI LIKES

- **Knowledge and information**
- **Company**
- **Pseudonyms and role-playing**
- **Variety, change, novelty**
- **Doing several things at once**
- **Gossip, chatting**
- **Playing devil's advocate**
- **Travel**
- **Gadgets**
- **Freedom**
- **Acting quickly**
- **Getting to the bottom of things**

GEMINI DISLIKES

▶ **Listening to complaints**
▶ **Fixed points of view**
▶ **Losing**
▶ **Having to make irrevocable commitments**
▶ **Wasting time**
▶ **Delay**
▶ **Uncertainty**
▶ **Focusing on one thing for extended periods**

POSSIBLE PROBLEM AREAS FOR GEMINI, AND SOLUTIONS

All sun signs have unique personality traits. When these traits are suppressed, problems will arise. However, with a winning combination of astrology and coaching we can examine the problem and assess the proper solution based on the sun sign characteristics. If, as a Gemini, you see things below that really strike home, try the solution. You may be amazed at the results.

PROBLEM: Superficiality could be a big problem for you in your relationships with others. Superficiality can also hold you back in jobs where you must learn something thoroughly in order to advance.

SOLUTION: Make a deliberate and conscious effort to control this trait. If you make a commitment to something or someone, you should compel yourself to keep that commitment where possible, assuming of course that you aren't in a situation that is not right for you. This will be hard to do but can be, and has been, accomplished by many born under this sign.

PROBLEM: Not one who cares for peace and quiet, you create your own problems with loved ones by picking arguments or causing trouble. You have a tendency then to stand back and enjoy the show.

SOLUTION: While this may relieve your boredom, you should not let it happen, as it can easily go out of control and cost you the love and companionship that you desire. When you feel like picking an argument, take a long walk and let the feelings pass. If you really can't help yourself, then provoke a few people in Internet chat rooms. That way you can enjoy the fireworks and keep your friends.

PROBLEM: Boredom is one of your biggest problems.

SOLUTION: You have a great many creative talents, and if you put these to work for you in some sort of hobby or project, you will find you do not have time to be bored. Alternatively, try some form of physical activity.

PROBLEM: You may have health problems brought on by overindulgence in food, drink, or nightlife. These seem to get worse as you age.

SOLUTION: Moderate your urges. Save the party times for weekends only, and then try not to overdo it.

PROBLEM: You may not be able to keep a spouse or a lover due to your pursuit of the opposite sex.

SOLUTION: Cultivate the habit of not flirting with every attractive person you see and make up your mind to be a true and loving spouse. Don't commit until you are really ready to do this. Alternatively, find a secure partner who will tolerate your flirtations.

CAREER/BUSINESS

IN Gemini you have those power twins the Great Communicator and the Great Facilitator combined in one human dynamo. This means that Geminis can talk twice as fast, twice as much, and come up with enough new (and good) ideas to be considered the ideas person at any firm. Possessed of a restless and quick mind, the twins are constantly moving from one project to the next; however, it is a good idea to have an earth sign colleague along to complete those half-finished projects!

Geminis work well as an intermediary or go-between as they love to talk. If someone needs contacts, a Gemini is bound to be able to help, as they are usually excellent networkers. Networking is usually conducted in a fast-paced, social whirl where they are being continuously challenged and stimulated. If things get dull, Gemini will simply insinuate themselves into a more stimulating and dynamic group. The twins are curious to a fault, something that can get them into trouble every now and again, as can their brutal honesty.

When wanderlust creeps into Gemini's life, it can generally be relieved with a quick business trip or a few days of play. Back at the office, the twins would be well served by a diligent and detail-oriented assistant to keep tabs on their work flow and to be sure they're getting things done.

The Gemini office is likely to be filled with multiple phones, a computer or two, fax machines, a TV—anything that will aid communication. A packed bag is in the corner, just in case. Their preferred car is likely to be a speedy convertible with a cell phone or two, the perfect way to plan a lunch date at the most happening spot in town.

GEMINI CAREER GUIDE

HERE ARE SOME occupations that a Gemini might consider:

Ad copy writer	Driver	News commentator
Announcer	Franchiser	Novelist
Auctioneer	Illustrator	Orator
Author	Impersonator	Playwright
Auto dealer	Information analyst	Printer
Bookseller	Information clerk	Reporter
Broker	Interviewer	Salesperson
Bus driver	Journalist	Speech pathologist
Cartoonist	Librarian	Spokesperson
Commentator	Linguist	Taxi driver
Concierge	Mail carrier	Teacher
Correspondent	Manicurist	Transcriber
Courier	Media person	Truck driver
Debater	Mime artist	Weather forecaster
Dispatcher	Mimic	
Distributor	Narrator	

GEMINI BOSS

HANDS-ON MANAGEMENT is not the twins' forte. Gemini prefers a state of continuous chaos in the workplace, and just when a routine is settling in, you come along and shake things up. You thrive on the energy of disarray; it gives you an opportunity to watch human interaction. You have multiple talents warring for expression, and spontaneous troubleshooting is more in keeping with those talents than maintaining orderly business. You are far too changeable to stick to a consistent management plan—any situation with definite structures and boundaries stifles you.

You are far too interested in intellectual pursuits and mental stimulation to master personnel management. Bossing others around is of no interest to you. You can get excited about masterminding business growth and success strategies, however.

You are superb in times of crisis, for you can keep your head in a chaotic environment. You maintain a detached, almost amused air as you assess and analyze unseen influences. Just as disaster appears to be about to strike, you will come up with a brilliant solution that saves the day.

GEMINI EMPLOYEE

GEMINI IS A bundle of creative energy that thrives in and enhances any free-thinking environment. Your ability to conceptualize, and your crisis management skills, sales ability, diplomacy, and charm make you a fabulous asset for the right organization. You need an organization where you are free to unleash your imagination and act quickly. You also need an organization that values a generalist with a dynamic personality, possibly a high-growth enterprise where crises are the norm and nobody is too obsessed with who does what.

You rarely possess the ambition or stamina to remain focused on a particular goal for long, so I recommend following an approach to goal setting that stimulates your creativity and fights off boredom. Set goals that really challenge you. A great exercise to help with this is S.M.A.R.Test Goals For Aries (see page 3).

You are not backward coming forward and will always voice any complaints or concerns that you have, including feelings of boredom and confinement. In fact you are likely to place a higher value on mental stimulation than on status.

TIPS FOR DEALING WITH BOREDOM AT WORK

WHEN YOU SEE a boring project looming on the horizon, try to ensure that it is preceded and followed by something more stimulating. And if a project bores you to tears, finish it!

Negotiate with your boss to see if you can exchange one of the more boring aspects of your job for something more stimulating in order to maintain a higher level of interest and productivity. If you need any help with negotiating skills, look at the Preparing for Negotiation exercise in Aries and The 100 Point Guide to Negotiating exercise in Virgo (see pages 25 and 171).

Any attempt to confine you at work is likely to send you straight off to an employment agency. In fact, you may just walk out, explaining your reasons for departure as you go—Gemini just has to have the last word. If you're feeling very playful (or just downright manipulative) and want to exercise your debating skills, you may attempt to win some concessions before departure. If you're thinking of doing this, try the Mining "Hidden Gold" Opportunities exercise for Capricorns (see page 276) before departing.

FINANCES AND WEALTH

THE GEMINI FINANCIAL plan is not to have a plan. Playing to your twin strengths of adaptability and flexibility often works well for you. You have no trouble finding freelance work, so somehow everything works out. You might also be considered the dealmaker of the zodiac, albeit a guileless one. A crowded cocktail party with its potential for new contacts and endless possibilities is a place where the fun-seeking twins can maximize their strengths and make a few useful contacts, which is fortunate, as holding down a long-term job is not Gemini's forte. You are unlikely to be picking up a gold watch for long and faithful service.

Jobs are what the twins crave, and lots of them, since keeping busy is great fun. The twins enjoy juggling many tasks, so developing several streams of income comes naturally to a Gemini. A Gemini client of mine combines book writing, journalism, coaching, and running workshops with other activities, and she thrives on it.

Changeable, unpredictable Geminis love spending their money and rarely worries where the next check will come from. Why should they when they have a deep-seated belief that their charisma will surely lead to something? The twins really can't be bothered with the details of balancing accounts, since there are so many more interesting things to do. Gemini usually sees money as a means to an end and takes an approach to finances that involves making money as and when they need it. It's the moneymaking journey that is all-important to Gemini, and it had better be an interesting one.

It may sound as if Gemini has a near-perfect approach to finances. Don't plan and just see what happens appears to be this sign's philosophy. Is this the right way to approach your Gemini finances? Unfortunately, as a coach I would have to say no. It's important to have some kind of a plan to fall back on when you hit a rough patch. I would also advise you to discipline yourself to do the Building Up a Rainy-Day Fund exercise in the Aries section of this book (see page 28). You can also try the following exercise.

EXERCISE FOUR

The Nice and Easy Does It Way to $1000

1. Go out and buy a container suitable for holding a large number of coins.
2. Put $2.75 (a sum that you might spend on coffee, magazines, or any other treat) into that container, every single day for a year.
3. In one year you will have accumulated $1000. Now what are you going to do with it?

Of course you could have your treat in six months if you saved $5.50 a day. How about going for $11.00?

COACH'S TIP

If you have the sign of Cancer on the cusp of the second house—the house of income—in your natal chart, you could have an emotional approach to spending and saving. Think about what money really means to you. Does money represent success? Energy? Power? Options? Freedom? Shame? Anger and resentment? Or is it just a means to an end? Do you keep changing your mind on this very subject? Write down five things that money means to you to help clarify your feelings toward it, as negative feelings can push money away.

At times, you are susceptible to impulse purchases, or can undergo swings in spending modes, such as saving like a miser for months and then entering a shopping frenzy. Do try to be sensible. If you have a strong emotional involvement with money, then saving can be a little like being on a diet: If you deprive yourself too stringently, you'll wind up rebelling and undoing all your hard work. Treat yourself to little things now and then so that you won't be tempted to splurge. Don't assume that because you've spent too much one day you might as well give up and spend the lot. Treat yourself with compassion and congratulate yourself on what you have achieved. A solid goal, like saving up to buy a house, could help motivate you to save. Make sure that this solid goal is powerful enough to keep you motivated.

Beware of taking on more work than you can handle. You are very versatile, so you can find yourself taking on projects just because you can do them. Learn to focus your attention on your most lucrative prospects. If you tend to take on too much, vow to do a little experiment: Finish whatever you start in the next six months. You may find that you become more discriminating about what you choose to put your time into once you've made this commitment.

Money does not motivate you—ideas do. The maxim "Do what you love and the money will follow" was meant for you to heed. You will accumulate wealth by doing what you love doing, provided there is a market for it. If your occupation bores you, you won't give it your all. Many Geminis are able to accumulate great wealth by heeding this sage advice.

LOVE, ROMANCE, AND SEX LIFE

IN LOVE, GEMINIS tend to be fickle, not intentionally so, but because of the basic inconsistency of their emotional nature, which has an amoral aspect to it. There is a side to Gemini that can become deeply involved emotionally, but warring with another side, hostile to sentimentality, which stands back from a romantic situation, dissecting it and analyzing it intellectually. Gemini subjects take nothing seriously, including love. In love, in spite of their temporary depth of feeling, they are often superficial and completely oblivious to the pain they may give others. They like intrigue and the excitement of the chase, but once they have caught the prey, they lose interest and look around for the next creature to pursue. Imagine a cat playing with a mouse and you see Gemini in love. In less serious situations, like those where the investment of emotional capital is not involved, they make witty, entertaining companions. Their lack of emotional involvement means that they make good acquaintances rather than friends. Even at their worst they are never dull—there is usually playfulness below the surface, and they can be brilliant conversationalists—but they can also be quarrelsome, idle chatterers, boasters, liars, and cheats.

COMPATIBILITY

GEMINI CAN GET along fine with anyone on a superficial basis. They tend to get along best with polar opposite Sagittarius and fellow air sign Aquarius. However, for compatibility purposes, you should really compare individual charts.

WHAT GEMINI NEEDS

GEMINIS NEED someone who can be attentive to them and who will naturally enjoy their sparkle and wit. It also helps if the partner is thick-skinned, because Gemini's razor-sharp wit can really wound. They also prefer a strong partner who is not necessarily as smart as they are but who can pick them up emotionally when necessary. If the twins can make a deep mental connection, life will be just perfect.

The Gemini lover is easygoing and caring, yet daring and a ball of fire at the right moments. Mental fireworks—their own and a partner's—are high on their agenda. Only those with plenty of fire of their own need apply for this celestial light show!

THE END OF THE AFFAIR

GEMINI ENDS THE affair when he or she gets bored or when a partner makes too many emotional demands. While the affair may appear to end suddenly, Gemini has no doubt been secretly unhappy for a long time. Once a decision to end the affair has been made, it will be irrevocable, and Gemini will freeze the lover out or vanish.

If a partner ends the relationship, Gemini will be deeply insecure and at a loss. Gemini will mask these feelings from the outside world with a display of dazzling confidence, while continuing to search for that elusive soul mate.

TIPS FOR COMBATING BOREDOM IN YOUR RELATIONSHIP

- ◆ Make a list of five things that you find boring in your current relationship. Make it a priority to sort them out.
- ◆ The next time that you are bored having sex with your partner, share a fantasy with them. Ask them to co-star.
- ◆ Call attention to the boring spots in your relationship with your lover. See if (s)he's bored at the same places and times. Work out how you as a couple can address this.

RELATIONSHIPS
(Family and Friends)

GEMINI PARENT

THE TYPICAL GEMINI parent can get on a child's wavelength very easily. He or she will love playing, communicating, and teaching offspring. Gemini will tend to use rational argument when disciplining or teaching a child. The Gemini parent may find it hard to show their real emotions, but will feel deeply nonetheless.

GEMINI CHILD

THE GEMINI CHILD is extremely sharp mentally. He or she will revel in doing several things at once and is likely to do them all pretty well. It goes without saying that the Gemini child is a clever sort who will always be full of surprises. This child is also a real trickster, like the god Mercury.

Geminis hate boredom, so be sure this youngster's schedule is jam-packed (sports, book clubs, you name it). In keeping with all this activity, the Gemini child will collect plenty of friends. This kid will enjoy being the class clown, making faces, and telling goofy jokes for a laugh—a clever ruse that enables Gemini to shine academically while avoiding being seen as the school brain. Gemini's rapid-fire mind craves stimulation, so be sure that this child always has plenty of good reading material.

BRINGING UP GEMINI—COACH'S INSIGHT

THE GEMINI CHILD needs the freedom to explore, investigate, and learn. The young Gemini needs plenty of opportunities to change direction and explore multiple interests simultaneously. Confinement and boredom strike horror into the heart of a young Gemini.

Gemini needs to be understood and paid attention to. The Gemini child flourishes when a parent accepts them for who they are and joins in their dreams with them.

What to Teach Young Gemini

Young Gemini needs to learn how to distinguish between illusion and reality, which can be hard for a sign that inhabits the world of thought so wholeheartedly. Encouraging Gemini to tell the truth will encourage this to happen. The twins are not maliciously dishonest; they will only avoid telling the truth so as not to be misunderstood or rejected.

Gemini children love to read and communicate—learning a foreign language is a great source of stimulation and pleasure to them.

Teach young Gemini to slow down a little and not to be too hasty in abandoning old ideas and pursuits.

Gemini and Friends

Gemini enjoys friends who are spontaneous. A Gemini friend is always ready to embark upon a new adventure.

He or she will always help a friend in need.

Gemini is bound to keep friends amused with interesting and amusing anecdotes, pieces of information, and plenty of gossip.

Friends, Be Aware

Gemini can be a little dishonest, embellishing the truth to make it more exciting. They also make poor timekeepers, arriving early or late to avoid missing anything good.

Gemini will drop a friend who no longer interests or stimulates them.

EXERCISE FIVE

An Awareness Exercise for Gemini

Talk to the next person who bores you—go on, I dare you! Ask if (s)he ever becomes bored with people and what (s)he does to combat this.

EXERCISE SIX

Interesting People

FIND out one interesting thing about anyone you meet (or at least five people a day).

Alternatively, pretend, just pretend, that actually everyone you meet is exactly the kind of person you seek to meet. Get to know them with this in mind and uncover all the ways in which they are interesting and fabulous.

Also, try some of the exercises for meeting interesting people in the Aries chapter (see page 32).

HEALTH

WHEN crisis hits, the first thing a Gemini does is pick up the phone and a call a trusted friend. This is the perfect reaction, for reaching out and listening to get an objective observer's opinion will offer air sign Gemini another perspective, fresh insights, and new information they may not have considered. Highly cerebral and analytical, Geminis like to see all sides of their situation, to feel that they have thought of all the possible options. Simply by relating what is wrong, Gemini often finds a solution to a problem. At the very least, articulating your dilemma enables you to get some clarity.

Keep in mind, though, that with all this input from others, you could get confused or overwhelmed with all the varying responses you get. Eventually you will have to draw the line and come to a decision. Sometimes Gemini procrastinates, so ask yourself why you're holding out and if there is something troubling you about the situation. Dig deep to uncover whatever is preventing you from proceeding with your usual vigor and enthusiasm. Remember, your mutable quality makes you highly flexible and adaptable, a real asset in times of change.

STRESS BUSTING FOR GEMINI

IF POSSIBLE, GET a change of scene by going away for a few days—any problem can be solved more quickly when a Gemini is away from home and not distracted by everyday duties. The trip need not be to a distant place as long as it provides enough stimulus to keep high-IQ Gemini busy and entertained. Nothing rejuvenates a Gemini from stress like a trip, even a weekend getaway. You could enhance the effects of a relaxing break by inviting a few entertaining friends over to dinner.

Gemini is the sign that rules sisters, brothers, and cousins, and often Gemini is close to one of these relatives. If you have a sibling or cousin who always gave you good advice while you were growing up, seeing them again now could be comforting. The break in routine will refresh you, and getting an opinion from a relative who knows you well and who loves you could do much to steady your nerves.

If you can't find the time (or the money) to go away, taking a long walk or drive in the country would be the next best idea. Make sure this is an area you're unfamiliar with, so that you focus on the experience rather than traveling on automatic pilot.

Gemini rules the written word, so keeping a journal or pouring your energy into creative writing is an excellent idea. (One of my Gemini clients writes fantastic poetry when her emotions are raw.) Being surrounded by new books is ecstasy for the twins, so get to a bookstore! Try tackling the self-help section to spark some creative ideas on dealing with whatever is disturbing you. Look at the magazine section and review what's there—how about tackling a magazine in a foreign language that you learned at school? Try downloading an exciting e-book or article from the Internet—there are some true visionaries out there. The point is to vary your routine and break molds.

Gemini rules the lungs, which are often this sign's weakest link, so be sure you don't resort to smoking. Many Geminis begin to smoke because their friends do, and then find they can't stop. A doctor may be able to help if this is the case for you. Another part of Gemini's sensitive body to stress is the fingers, for Mercury rules the hands. Mercury's influence gives Geminis great dexterity in their fingers, but they tend to overuse them, so remember to pamper your hands, Gemini. A gentle hand massage can work wonders.

Lastly, Gemini is known to have lots of hobbies and interests. So why not pick up an old pastime that you haven't done in a while? Or, think of a new hobby. The point is to try something that will absorb your conscious mind while your subconscious gets to work and comes up with a solution when you least expect it. You ought to be an expert at this, Gemini—you practically invented doing two things at once.

FITNESS

GEMINI RULES THE hair, nervous system, speech, lungs, hands, shoulders, arms, and fingers. Your metabolism is high.

Gemini is always doing two things at once. When you eat, rather than read or talk, concentrate on the flavors. Otherwise you might not remember having eaten at all. Luckily, you are usually slim due to your abundance of nervous energy and the fact that you are always on the move.

However, being slim does not always translate into being healthy. Resolve to eat more fresh foods and to exercise more. If you do ever find yourself with a weight problem, it is because of nervous tension. You tend to eat quickly and obsessively to calm yourself down. At these times, you find yourself consuming crunchy foods (sweets and chips) to ride out your aggression. Try eating a crisp, fresh apple instead. Try to stay off the junk food, Gemini, even though you have a tendency to find healthy cooking a drag and prefer to grab whatever you want when the urge takes you.

The lungs and upper part of your body need strengthening, so start doing some aerobics or jogging. Gemini likes quick, active sports that stress agility. Anything slow and meditation-like (such as yoga) can make you fidgety. Since you are prone to bronchial problems, you need to take extra care of your lungs and avoid anything that could lessen their ability to perform.

All Geminis are prone to illnesses that stem from nervous tension. Therefore it is more important for you than for most signs to find ways to unwind and keep life in its proper perspective.

TOOLS FOR MAKING A DIFFERENCE

FROM THEIR OPPOSITE sign, Sagittarius, Geminis can learn to take a broader view of things and to structure the masses of information that they collect. By doing this you will penetrate beneath the surface to attain the wisdom you crave. You will also have something meaningful to communicate.

Be aware, Gemini, that talking about something is not the same as doing it—actions usually do speak louder than words. Part of your growth lies in sticking with things—projects, relationships, jobs—through the hard, dull parts. To help with spiritual growth, make sure that you do at least two of the exercises in this chapter for combating boredom.

Your adaptability comes to your aid when you're facing unusual circumstances or stubborn attitudes, and you are likely to be called upon to act as negotiator because you are the one who can identify common ground. Making connections comes naturally to you and attracts both the people and experiences you need to grow.

Through your ability to connect with people from all walks of life you are likely to develop a multifaceted personality. You blend intuitive awareness with logical perception and are aware that some things cannot be explained by rational thought alone. Your creativity and ingenuity stem from this marriage of left- and right-brain thinking. Your thirst for knowledge and experiences eventually leads you to surrender your mind to the universal mind, where you discover your true nature and purpose in life. Know that you can indeed alter your future by altering the quality of your thoughts.

SPIRITUALITY

GEMINI is so restless mentally that you generally don't do well in organized religion, unless you've chosen that path for yourself. You are likely to sample spiritual belief systems in the way that the rest of us try new foods. However, once you find a spiritual path that makes sense to you, you usually stick to it.

Your sense of power will emerge when you connect to the source of divine intelligence, and from that lofty plane you can lift humanity to heights that empower us as a whole.

Gemini is like the nerve synapses of a culture, continually receiving and transmitting information, causing change wherever they go. Like nerves in the human body, Gemini does not implement these changes or see them through—that is left to the muscles (or other signs).

The task for Gemini is to take themselves seriously so that others will too, and to understand the power of language. To talk is to create or invoke, whether we are uttering affirmation, negative self-talk, or song. Whenever Gemini is in our charts, we are assigned the task of understanding the power and creativity of words.

CHAPTER 4

CANCER

June 21–July 22

THE FOURTH SIGN OF THE ZODIAC IS CONCERNED WITH:

- ◆ HOME, PROTECTION, FAMILY
- ◆ FOOD, NURTURE, RESPONSE TO PUBLIC NEED
- ◆ DREAMS, RECEPTIVITY, PSYCHIC PHENOMENA
- ◆ SECURITY, DOMESTICITY
- ◆ MONEY, BUSINESS
- ◆ HISTORY, MEMORY, PATRIOTISM
- ◆ NOSTALGIA, SENTIMENT, SENSITIVITY, ROOTS

CANCER is the most difficult sign of the zodiac to describe, possibly because it is a cardinal water sign. Of the four astrological elements (fire, earth, air, and water), water is the most ancient, primitive, and instinctual. The most primal element, water is the element furthest away from rational, describable, consciousness, and thought. This means that water energy tends to defy our attempts at coming up with rational explanations and descriptions. All three water signs (Cancer, Scorpio, and Pisces) are extremely difficult to describe in left-brain language.

Cancer combines the tough, self-assertion of the cardinal signs (interested in promoting change and influencing the environment) with the powerful emotions and sensitivity of the water signs. A very potent mix! The crab, Cancer's zodiacal symbol, represents the contrast between cardinal and water energy, with its hard, protective shell covering a soft, fleshy body.

Nurturing, protective Cancer represents the archetypal bond between mother and son (as well as the archetypal bond between father and daughter). Ruled by the moon, Cancer reflects the mysterious continual cycles of nature and the ebb and flow of the tides—and therefore also the ebb and flow of emotions.

There is no typical Cancer. Cancerians can range from the timid, dull, and emotionally closed to the brilliant and outgoing. However, many Cancerians possess fundamentally conservative and home-loving natures, appreciating the nurturing quality of a secure base to which the male can retire when he needs a respite from the stresses of life, and in which the Cancerian woman can exercise her strong maternal instincts. Cancer's home is likely to remind one of a hermit crab's shell—a dark and mysterious but comfortable house which belongs to the family rather than existing as a showcase to impress visitors. As long as Cancerians have a firm base to which they can return to recuperate, they are able to venture out into the world and make their cardinal presence felt.

People with the sun in Cancer generally develop best through having an emotional relationship with their surroundings. Cancer evaluates everyone and everything in terms of feelings and values. Hard, cold logic is not a part of Cancerian energy.

Cancerian emotions fluctuate, puzzling loved ones, associates, and Cancerians themselves. However, they are tenacious, even ruthless, when it comes to defending family and friends. Cancer is a sign of compassion that embodies all that is best in the caring maternal instincts, but it often hides its emotions behind a mask that denies this inner feeling. Cancerians are vulnerable and easily hurt; the confident mask they wear in public serves as a defense against a hostile world. When upset, Cancerians may withdraw further into their shells, and they may snap at people, imitating the crab's sharp pincers.

Due to your emotional sensitivity, Cancer, you are seldom comfortable in a wider and more impersonal social setting, so you may tend to create a small, enclosed environment and only allow a few select people into your sphere of influence. Once you do allow someone or something into your sphere, you often experience great difficulty letting go (even when you know you ought to). See some of the Taurean exercises for letting go of possessions and people (see page 44) to help with this one, Cancer.

STRENGTHS TO FOCUS ON

▶ **Shrewdness and intuition**
▶ **Tenacity and ambition**
▶ **Compassion and kindness**
▶ **Sensitivity to need and adaptability**
▶ **Protectiveness**
▶ **Caring**
▶ **Helpfulness**
▶ **Domesticated**
▶ **Excellent memory**
▶ **Faithful**
▶ **Affectionate**

EXERCISE ONE

Act Out Your Positive Traits

As an intuitive and sensitive Cancerian, you might like to maximize your strengths by doing the following:

Imagine how someone with the characteristics you desire would act. Try to see them in your mind's eye. How would they behave? You have nothing to lose by trying this, so really immerse yourself in becoming this person. Feel yourself taking on their characteristics, Cancer. Put on an Oscar-winning performance.

Now act as if you already had those personality traits. Take your cue from your audience and refine your act until those characteristics become a part of you.

You might also like to look at the exercise for enhancing your positive traits in the Taurus chapter (see page 43).

WEAKNESSES THAT CAN TRIP YOU UP

- Selfishness
- Manipulativeness
- Holds on to insults
- Matriarchal/Patriarchal
- Irritability and unpredictability
- Too easily hurt
- Introspection
- Overpowering
- Possessiveness
- Moodiness
- Prone to despair

So how do you turn these so-called flaws into powerful tools for personal growth? Begin by doing the exercises in the corresponding section of Aries (see page 6).

CANCER MAN

Unless there are influences in his birth chart that are stronger than his Cancer sun sign, the typical Cancer male will have some or all of the following characteristics:

- Is patient and persistent
- Adaptable
- Is conventional and needs approval
- Has a strong and retentive memory
- Wears clothes with a conservative cut
- Is very sensitive
- Hates being conspicuous and avoids the limelight
- But enjoys being in the spotlight once it falls upon him

- Loves security, money, food, and children
- Has an uncanny business sense
- Gives people the runaround to get what he wants
- Dislikes discussing his personal life
- Is usually very attached to his mother
- Has some favorite, old casual clothes that he always wears

CANCER WOMAN

In addition to the personality and behavior traits exhibited by the Cancerian male, Cancerian woman:

- Is usually very good at business
- Needs a close partnership
- Has a strong maternal instinct
- Can be dramatic
- Is imaginative and sensitive
- Is adaptable
- Puts on weight in middle age, can overeat when unhappy or frustrated
- Puts family first, but domesticity can hold her back
- Is introspective and emotional
- Uses intuition rather than logic
- Wants material security and comfort
- Never does anything impulsively
- Is shy but very sexual, and can associate sex with vulnerability and surrender
- Will use all her maternal instincts to look after her friends and family
- Easily takes offense at minor insults
- Is patient, subtle, and often unconsciously manipulative

THE THREE FACES OF CANCER

Face 1: Large head, high cheekbones, and prominent brows.
The eyes are small and far apart.

Face 2: Rather moonlike and babyfaced, round with soft skin,
a wide mouth, and charming grin. Eyes are usually
round.

Face 3: A combination of the two above, but with distinctive,
especially strong cheekbones.

THE HIDDEN (OR NOT-SO-HIDDEN) CANCER

A PERSON WITH strong Cancerian tendencies is someone who
was very shy when young and still tends to use harshness and brit-
tleness as a defense against perceived slights from others.

The most vulnerable part of the Cancerian personality is a fear
of unnamed dangers that often reduce a wonderful dream to a pes-
simistic worry. This indefinable fear is often what drives a Cancerian to invest so much time and effort in activities, which will
enhance a feeling of security and self-preservation. Try the Building Up a Rainy-Day Fund exercise from Aries (page 28) and look
at the Taurus chapter for material on change management and risk-
taking to help with this, Cancer.

EXERCISE TWO

Fear Zapper

HOW OFTEN have you talked yourself out of going for an opportunity, rejecting yourself long before life has had a chance either to
reject you (sometimes we don't get what we want) or to give you
what you really wanted?

This is certainly what I used to do when I was younger, until I
realized how much it was costing me. Lost opportunities, lessons,

thrills, and fun. So now when I ask myself those questions that used to stop me in my tracks:

- ◆ Can it be done?
- ◆ Can I do it?
- ◆ Will they laugh if I fail?
- ◆ Will he tell me I'm too ugly, fat, whatever, to go out with him?

I always answer, "Well, it's time to find out!"

1. Think of a goal—something you want to do, be, or have.
2. What stops you from achieving it?
3. Is this a feeling or external circumstances?
4. If it's circumstances, then see what you can do to change them. If it's inside your head, you can try using the fear-zapping questions and answers above to get you unstuck and moving forward.

COACH'S TIP

When faced with fear, we often talk ourselves out of taking action. Yet most of the time, we have nothing to lose and everything to gain. Try the following strategies:

1. Breathe! When we are excited, we feel body sensations that can prevent us going forward. So stop, take some deep breaths, and then proceed.
2. Remember, it isn't personal. When you get rejected, it is usually because the other person doesn't need what you are offering.
3. Picture the worst. Can you live through that? Ask yourself, What is the worst that can happen? Most of the time, you can handle it.
4. Know your subject. If we feel confident in our knowledge, the fear about sharing it with others decreases. Even if they don't agree with us, we feel OK, because

we have developed an expertise that gives us confidence in ourselves.

5. Put something at stake or give yourself a reward. A reward or penalty that is big enough will motivate sometimes.

6. Get a partner. Taking on something fearful with another person often will get you through it and keep you from having those dialogues in your head that try to talk you out of it—provided that you don't pull each other down.

7. Read something inspirational or listen to tapes. Play your favorite motivational tape or read something inspirational right before you take action to help your mind focus on what is possible instead of what could derail you. Think about how you will feel when you have taken action. Write down the top ten feelings you'll have when you have done this thing.

8. Just do it!

CANCER LIKES

▶ **Anyone who loves his or her mother**
▶ **Gourmet food and fine wines**
▶ **Sentimental keepsakes**
▶ **History, especially genealogy**
▶ **Companionship and wry humor**
▶ **Birthday and anniversary cards on the right date**
▶ **Affection and demonstrations of affection**
▶ **Shopping**
▶ **A calm working atmosphere**

CANCER DISLIKES

▶ **Harsh, abrasive people**
▶ **Criticism of the Cancerian home**
▶ **Anyone who refuses their cooking**
▶ **Memory lapses in others**
▶ **Pressure to contribute to a conversation, as (s)he prefers to observe**

POSSIBLE PROBLEM AREAS FOR CANCER, AND SOLUTIONS

ALL SUN SIGNS have unique personality traits. When these traits are suppressed, problems will arise. However, with a winning combination of astrology and coaching we can examine the problem and assess the proper solution based on the sun sign characteristics. If, as a Cancerian, you see things below that really strike home, try the solution. You may be amazed at the results.

PROBLEM: You can be oversensitive, somewhat insecure, and clingy, which may cause you to harbor imaginary hurts and slights. This can make for a highly unsettling relationship with your spouse.

SOLUTION: Be sure that the love you are expressing is not simply your need to hang onto someone for moral support. If necessary, you should seek professional help in order to overcome this negative, clinging aspect of your personality.

PROBLEM: One of your biggest personality flaws is the habit of being so self-absorbed that you sometimes fail to notice what others are doing and accomplishing in their lives. You feel shut out and jealous if a family member has more success than you do.

SOLUTION: Make a special effort to change this in yourself by forcing yourself to rejoice over their good fortune. You will find that this eventually becomes a habit, and you, as well as they, will be happier for the change. Jealousy is also a call to action—if you are jealous of a family member's success, do what it takes to acquire some success of your own.

PROBLEM: Inability to take orders without getting angry or upset may be another one of your problems. This one could be very serious, as it affects your chances of earning a good living for yourself and/or your family, since you are apt to walk away from any job where you feel "picked on."

SOLUTION: Try keeping an ear out and find out how colleagues who have been on the job for any length of time get along with the boss and coworkers. If you follow their lead or simply decide that you will simply keep quiet and follow orders, you will soon see how well you can be really liked by all concerned.

PROBLEM: You tend to put things off until the last minute, which upsets your family and friends. Procrastination also has a tendency to make an unpleasant matter even more unpleasant

SOLUTION: Make taking care of the business at hand your prime objective from now on, for when you do not have all those worries in the back of your mind, you will find it more pleasant to be around people and that life goes smoothly for you. Releasing the energy tied up in thinking about things you "should" do will make for more effective living.

SWEET SIXTEEN—TIPS FOR PROCRASTINATION BUSTING

1. Design clear goals and set priorities. What do you want (outcome)? What do you need to do to achieve this (action)? How long will it take (time)? When is the deadline (realistic end date)?

2. Get organized! Get clutter out of your life; clutter is just one more distraction. List your tasks in order of importance and put the distractions where they belong—out of your life. Make a realistic deadline date for each item. Make sure you have all the materials or information that you need before starting a task.

3. Do the most difficult task first. If you put off the difficult tasks until the end of the day or the end of the week, they will "grow" in size and seem even more challenging.

4. Reward yourself. Pat yourself on the back when you finish a task, especially a task that you saw as difficult or challenging.

Choose a personal reward like a massage, a long walk, or a bubble bath.

5. Understand that you're worth it—you are worth having a procrastination-free life. You no longer want to be a victim to this behavior. When you believe this in your soul, you'll learn to say no and will take care of what is important to your personal and professional wellness. You'll stop aggravating yourself with procrastination.

6. Become extremely selfish—ask for what you need in order to create space in your life. This gives you the time to eliminate those things about which you are procrastinating. Think of the image of the oxygen mask extending down in an airplane. Put it on yourself first, and then minister to others.

7. Be accountable. Commit to complete each task by its deadline. Tell your partner, friend, or coach when this will be. Ask them to hold you accountable for your actions.

8. Use the one-touch system—whenever possible, take care of the task before it gets onto your procrastination list. For instance, pay your bills when they come in the mail; open your mail, sort it, file it, act on it, or throw it away immediately. Do this standing up!

9. Lighten up—procrastinating is often the little girl in you saying, "I won't do it" because she hasn't been taken care of. She's mad that you never take her out to play, so she's trying to create space for herself by keeping you from doing "one more thing." Sometimes this works. However, wouldn't it be better for the "adult" to choose when to "go out for playtime," thereby allowing the child within to leave "the working woman" alone?

10. Get some rest—sometimes we procrastinate because we're just too tired to do another thing. Go to bed really early at least once a week. Get eight hours of sleep whenever you can. Maintain boundaries in your day so that you can take breaks and end your work at a reasonable time. Take time for yourself!

11. Divide and conquer. Divide large tasks into smaller, manageable chunks. Limit yourself to one task at a time to reduce frustration. Delegate if you can. You don't have to struggle with this all by yourself.

12. Start somewhere! What is the most important task on your list? Look for something unpleasant but manageable. Divide it up into mini tasks. Take action!
13. Schedule time. Allocate a specific amount of time to your tasks and stop when that time is up. Start with just five minutes, and then consider another five minutes at the end of the first.
14. Use reminders. Keep your tasks visible in front of you. Write lists or notes to prompt you into action.
15. Identify your best time. When are you most productive during the day? When do you have the most energy and feel really alert? Use this time for your most important tasks and use other times during the day for more routine tasks. If you feel an impulse to work on a task, follow it up right now. When you have had enough, stop.
16. Cultivate self-motivation. Try telling yourself some of the following: "There's no time like the present," "The sooner I complete this, the sooner I can play," "I don't have to do this all by myself—I can ask for help." Reward yourself each time you complete a task.

Of course, procrastination is not always bad and sometimes it is better to work with a tendency to procrastinate rather than trying to overcome it. For example, one of my former clients, Graeme, is a very talented freelance writer. He came to me because he was having trouble meeting deadlines. He was in a terrible state—stressed out, no social life, and no time to take care of himself. Initially I advised him to look for and implement ways to reduce his stress and also to build up his levels of fitness so that he could deal with the stress that was unavoidable.

Accompanying Graeme's deadline problem was a tendency to procrastinate, something he saw as a major flaw. He would procrastinate before settling down to work. Once he began to write, he would write intensively, working through the night to produce work of a superb standard. His initial request of me was to help eliminate this serious flaw.

I asked Graeme to see his perceived flaw as a great strength and to create a schedule that allowed for this "wasted" time. Once

Graeme stopped putting himself down for procrastinating, he began to see that the longer he procrastinated, the longer he ultimately worked and the more he got done. A period of procrastinating also resulted in far better-quality work. He was now able to use the time that he had wasted trying to force himself to work—and feeling bad about not being able to—on creative projects of his own. By being able to devote time to projects that inspired him, he no longer felt resentful about the time his assignments were taking. Previously, he'd been so obsessed with meeting his deadlines that there had been little time for anything else, which caused a massive buildup of resentment. Some of Graeme's inability to meet his deadlines was a side effect of this resentment.

There were, of course, other steps that needed to be taken, but once Graeme saw his natural creative style as a strength rather than as procrastination, all resentment and deadline problems vanished.

How about following Graeme's example and feeling great about your worst weakness? Just imagine the peace you would feel inside and the increased amount of energy that you'd have for focusing on positive directions. Doesn't it make your heart sing just to think of it?

CAREER/BUSINESS

THEIR ABILITIES FIT Cancerians for a wide range of occupations. As they are interested in what people are thinking and able to judge what they can safely be told, they can be good journalists, writers, or politicians, though in this last capacity they are more likely to remain in the background rather than attain prominent positions of power. As the zodiac's idealists and romantics they may change their party affiliations. They will go where they feel that they can do the most good. Cancerians can serve in other departments of public affairs, especially those that involve looking after others. They are good in services from welfare to catering, and their own love of comfort and good living makes them an excellent chef or housekeeper.

Cancerians have a penchant for trade or business and are often successful as a captain of industry. This is because they are excellent organizers with a good sense of value and economy, which they may combine with a flair for inventiveness and originality. The romantic side of their natures make them enjoy exploring places where exciting discoveries may be made (old artifacts lurking in attics, etc.), and if they can do this professionally, as a secondhand dealer or specialist in antiques, they will be happy. Other occupations that suit some subjects of Cancer are estate agent, gardener, and sailor. Cancerians are well suited to any career where they can feel truly useful.

The Cancer office feels like home, with a couch for snoozing, a teapot for fixing something warm and comforting, and favorite mementos all around. The office is the crab's favorite place for a business lunch, although a homey neighborhood spot is a close second.

CANCERIAN CAREER GUIDE

HERE ARE SOME occupations that a Cancerian might consider:

Agricultural worker	Farmer	Nutritionist
Archaeologist	Fisherperson	Nonprofit organi-
Baker	Gardener	zation founder or
Banker	Genealogist	manager
Builder	Historian	Oceanographer
Caterer	Homemaker	Plumber
Chef	Hotel worker	Producer
Coal miner	Landowner	Programmer
Collector	Lifeguard	Real Estate Agent
Cook	Manufacturer	Sailor
Crop grower	Merchandiser	Shipping clerk
Dairy farmer	Merchant	Teacher
Deep-sea diver	Midwife	Veterinarian
Dietician	Nurse	Writer

CANCER BOSS

CRABS LIKE TO lead, and so long as they are comfortable with their proscribed duties and their colleagues in the quest, they will probably succeed. The crab expects colleagues to be neatly dressed and hardworking. Forget frivolity with a Cancerian boss. The crab has one aim—to make money—and takes work extremely seriously. They are perceived as being stern yet fair.

As long as their emotions can be kept in check, Cancerians can create a space of harmony and happiness for all. They are usually benevolent leaders, with a compassion for others that breeds loyalty and team spirit. Those born under this sign may not look like they're out to conquer the world, but in their own way, they're getting a lot of good done. Cancerians are very creative and love family, qualities that can lead to bliss in the workplace if properly expressed. They show genuine interest in people and their nonthreatening manner nicely neutralizes overly competitive types. They are very sensitive toward the feelings of others and can diffuse highly-charged situations.

Cancer will actively pursue management positions, as developing a team of loyal, devoted employees strengthens the crab's grip on power and financial rewards.

You see personnel issues as being vital to business profits. You grow your business from the bottom up, building on solid foundations, and no management task is too mundane for you, Cancer. You plan your moves carefully, so that your employees can rely on you to come through for them when needed.

I have mentioned that you treat colleagues as family; your true family comes first, however, and the company that cannot respect these values loses out on a first-rate manager.

CANCERIAN EMPLOYEE

DON'T MISTAKE A Cancerian for an underachiever—they're working it as much and as well as the next person, albeit in a subtle, low-key manner. The crab's sensitive nature is readily apparent in business dealings, in which a nonconfrontational approach that protects them as well as those around them is preferred. Caution is the Cancerians' motto, lest they be forced to retreat into that hard, protective shell of theirs.

The Cancer employee works for the security of money earned, and little else. You constantly worry about future financial stability and these fears drive you hard. Crabs are reliable and determined and pursue monetary success above all else—you expect to be paid for your efforts, and any company that undervalues your efforts can expect to lose you. (See the Determine Your Value exercise in Capricorn [page 274]—you'll love it).

There is a very popular theory that suggests you can never get rich working for someone else, which would suggest that Cancerians might be at a disadvantage when it comes to getting rich. However, as many corporate Cancerians will testify, nothing could be further from the truth. You can get rich working for someone else, but how likely it is depends on three unshakable rules:

1. You must work in an industry that rewards its top performers with financial riches.
2. You must work in a field within that industry whose top performers are rewarded with financial riches.
3. You must work for a company within that industry that rewards its top performers with financial riches.

The fourth, generally unwritten rule is equally inviolable: You must do whatever it takes to become a top performer within your company, field, and industry.

EXERCISE THREE

Get Rich Working for Someone Else

YOU CAN benefit from doing this exercise whether you work for somebody else or for yourself. Answer the following questions as accurately as you can:

1. How much do you want to earn over the next five years?
2. What are you currently earning?
3. If you work for a company, what are the top performers in your company earning? The good performers? The average performers?
4. What are the top performers in your field and industry earning?

The good performers? The average performers?

5. Would you currently class yourself as an average, good, or top performer in your company? In your field? In your industry?

By taking a few moments to review your answers, it should quickly become obvious which of the three strategies for earned wealth will work best for you:

1. Study and train to increase your performance capability
2. Switch to a new company
3. Retrain in a new field

You are also highly sensitive and require appreciation and encouragement along with a regular paycheck. Although you are a steady, responsible worker, you can experience periods of extreme self-doubt—you can give up on your dreams far too early due to imagined feelings of inadequacy. Without authority figures' acknowledgement, you can talk yourself out of your dreams and ambitions.

While you dutifully and expertly perform those tasks requested of you, you are a leader rather than a follower and keep a close watch on the top of the corporate ladder, as this is what you are aiming for. So take the time to play with the Create a Political Map of Your Organization exercise in Aries (page 17) and the Culture Vulture exercise in Libra (page 202) to facilitate your rise to the top.

COACH'S TIP

When negotiating, be careful not to feel sorry for your opponent and give too much away, leaving both of you dissatisfied or sticking to your guns because of some emotional trigger. Use your skills for uncovering people's hidden motivations and likely responses, and, if possible, leave the negotiating itself to a less emotionally-driven air sign, which is better suited to on-the-spot decision making and confrontation.

When you are well prepared for debate, however, you can use your intuitive powers to come up with a good solution

that appeals to both sides. Somehow your sense of fair play
is transmitted to your opponent.

Intuition Workout

THIS EXERCISE is one that I and the more intuitive of my clients
use whenever we face a difficult decision that doesn't succumb to
facts and logic. It seems to work every bit as well with "serious" business decisions as it does with personal and relationship-based decisions.

Think of a decision you want to make, and make a list of the different options you are exploring. For your first go at this exercise, you
might want to consider a decision with no more than three different
options. For example, I have been offered two jobs, and I need to
decide whether to take one of them or stay in the job I currently hold.

Now close your eyes and imagine that each option you are trying to decide between is written on a door. Now stand in front of
the door and imagine walking through it. What is there on the
other side? Notice everything you experience. Write down all the
thoughts, feelings, and emotions that you pick up on. It may help
either to write down your experience or to speak it aloud—either to
yourself, to a friend, or even into a tape recorder.

Now do the same for all the remaining doorways.

You may find this exercise a little unnerving at first, however, this
is just fear (False Evidence Appearing Real) kicking in. This exercise is telling you what you fear from making a particular decision.
To help combat this, get as much information about what will happen if you commit to a particular course of action. This will stop
your imagination running wild and filling in the gaps in your
knowledge with negative images. If you write down your fears on
paper, they will look less threatening, and solutions will become
more apparent. Ask yourself empowering and solution-generating
questions like, "How can I turn this situation around?" "How can I
make this work for me?"

The more times you go through a particular doorway, especially if you keep arming yourself with more information, the less threatening it will become. You will be able to make a decision from a position of calmness rather than procrastinating or making a big mistake through fear.

Remember to balance your intuitive impressions with whatever factual information you have gathered. Our best decisions inevitably come when we balance our heart and our head.

FINANCES AND WEALTH

THE sun rules your second solar house, the house of income, which is always extremely helpful when you are thinking of new ways to make money! As a water sign, your instincts and intuition are always operating, which means you can sense important trends in the economy before the rest of us do. You do not, however, get yourself into a situation where there is a high degree of risk involved. You are in for the long haul, considering each financial move carefully. You are always able to make tough, calculated business or financial decisions when necessary. Saving to provide for your children's education or your family's security is your biggest goal, and winds up bringing you wealth. By taking care of others, you help yourself.

Many Cancers do well by investing in property—owning their own home is usually important to the crab. Overall, you are very financially prudent and, like Capricorn, you know all the best places to shop for the best deals. You love to buy household supplies in bulk and take advantage of sales. Not only do you steadily accumulate wealth, but you hold onto it—two great traits of the successful investor. Just be careful that you don't buy anything you don't need just because it's a bargain. Don't hoard either. When it comes to clothes, you like to get years of wear out of the outfits you buy. Some call you a little stingy, but you want a nest egg for retirement and a financial reserve to cover emergencies. Cancers like to keep their money in the bank rather than wearing it on their backs.

They know the current rates of interest and probably know how to multiply their savings better than their banker does (unless the banker is a Taurus, Scorpio, or Capricorn).

Sometimes, like Taurus, you stay in situations longer than you should. Your steadfast devotion leads you to pour energy into situations that have long outlived their usefulness. Learn to move on sooner rather than later.

COACH'S TIP

> When times are hard you tend to cut down on spending rather than coming up with ways to make more money. Spend more time figuring out how you can raise your income and less on scrimping.

LOVE, ROMANCE, AND SEX LIFE

IN your personal relationships you are a mixture of toughness and softness. You are often emotional and romantic to the point of sentimentality in your fantasies, but in real life—and especially in marriage—your loving is less sentimental than tenaciously loyal. Even if you have affairs (and you may do so, for the Cancerian male in particular is open to sensual stimulation), your first loyalty remains to spouse and family, of whom you regard yourself as the protector. Both the Cancerian man and the Cancerian woman love wholeheartedly and unreservedly, giving much and asking very little in return—in fact, one of the most important lessons they have to learn is how to receive gracefully. Cancerians are easily influenced by those they love and admire, and sometimes a loved one may exert too much of an influence. Cancerians make very loyal friends, the negative side of their faithfulness being a tendency to form cliques and close ranks in suspicion and coldness toward outsiders. This can deprive Cancerians of opportunities to learn about different points of view and to broaden their horizons.

Cancerians have a retentive memory, particularly for emotionally-laden events, which they can recall in detail for years afterwards.

They are strongly governed by childhood memories, and since they live intensely in the past in memory and the future in imagination, a chance meeting with someone for whom they had an unrequited love, even if they thought they had conquered the feeling, will easily arouse the emotion all over again.

The crab usually knows what it needs from a partner to make for a happy, loving relationship. If you lack this sixth sense, try the following exercises.

EXERCISE FIVE

Getting Your Needs Met

THIS IS a coaching exercise I have used with several clients who have been looking for love. It is based on three sound pragmatic and spiritual principles:

1. We look for a lover to fill missing gaps in ourselves, meaning we look for someone who has qualities that we lack.
2. Like attracts like, so we attract people who have the same gaps as we have.
3. Once we have a clear picture of what we want and believe that this is going to come to us, it always does.

For the first part of this exercise I want you to write down everything you need from a partner to feel loved. Here are a few ideas to start you off: fidelity, commitment, affection, and availability.

How many of these needs or wants can you get from someone other than a partner? Put in place a system that meets these needs for you. So, for example, if you need unquestioning devotion, lavish some love on a pet. The more needs you get met, the stronger a position you will be in to attract the right partner. You won't need a partner; you'll choose to have one.

To this end, address all the other areas of your life so that they are full and satisfying. By doing this, you will appear less needy and therefore more attractive.

Is there anything that you expect from a partner that you are lacking yourself? For example, are you looking for an honest partner when you are dishonest? If you are looking for someone who has different values and standards from you, you are likely to be unsuccessful long-term, so aim either to acquire and live by the values that you expect from a partner, or to settle for a partner with the standards and values that you currently have.

Once you have transformed yourself into the type of person you want to attract, go out and look for your ideal partner. Devote a certain amount of time to your search but do not neglect other areas of your life. Work out where you are most likely to meet a suitable partner—is it through clubs, mutual friends, family, or agencies, perhaps? Decide on your most likely options for success and put yourself out there.

COACH'S TIP

The success of a relationship depends on its ability to satisfy our needs. If we want a long-term relationship, we must look for a partner who will fulfil our long-term needs, for example, raising children. Conversely, a short-term relationship satisfies short-term needs. The reason many relationships fail is that we select someone who satisfies the needs we had years ago but who cannot meet our current needs.

EXERCISE SIX

Choosing the Right Partner

BEGIN by identifying your values—you are far more likely to have a long-term, successful relationship if you pick a partner who has the same values as you. See the Define Your Values exercise in Aries (page 20) for help with this.

Next, get your needs met. We all have needs. These can be physical, emotional, material, or spiritual, and are what we need to be truly, authentically us. Having our needs satisfied gives us the freedom to live happily and be comfortable in our skin.

The quality of your relationship, or the kind of people you attract, is intimately connected to whether you recognize and take care of your needs. If you are unaware of your needs, your partner will feel unable to give you satisfaction and may become resentful. If you don't know what you need, how can you tell a partner how to keep you happy? What kind of lover are you if you're continually wanting? You will put off emotionally mature mates and attract only those who need what you can give them.

At the same time, a haze of unmet and unrecognized needs clouds your judgment of whom you choose to date. When a potential partner fully meets one of your main needs, you may discount other qualities that will ultimately make the relationship impossible. This is one way that people end up in relationships where there is more resentment than love.

Here are some specific examples of needs you may have (this list is by no means exhaustive):

- ◆ To be liked
- ◆ To be wanted
- ◆ To be respected
- ◆ To be loved
- ◆ Independence
- ◆ Friendship
- ◆ Material things
- ◆ Spiritual meaning
- ◆ Trust in something greater than yourself

Did you find some of your needs on this list? What other needs can you list for yourself?

Find out what your needs are and then be creative and resourceful in how you take care of them. Once your needs are meet, you will be able to create the great life and relationships you desire. By getting your own needs met, you will avoid attracting needy and demanding partners.

COMPATIBILITY

YOU MIGHT EXPECT me to say that fellow water signs Scorpio and Pisces would be perfect for you crabs. However, Scorpio is probably just too intense and Pisces's vacillating moods will drive you crazy. Try earth signs, particularly Taurus and Virgo, for lasting relationships.

WHAT CANCER NEEDS

WHAT CANCER WANTS most is a partner who can take things slow and easy, secure in the knowledge that the ultimate victory will be sweet for both. A partner who can cope with the Cancerian mood swings and insecurities is also a must. An exchange of emotions is ideal for the crab, whether it's through sex, sports, or some passionately penned correspondence. Gifts that show you care are also a must.

Cancerians are great one-on-one and love that type of interaction, but they are also good at parties and enjoy dazzling a crowd. Consequently, an understanding lover is key. Accept that Cancer has a strong need for friends and do not become possessive. Cancerians must guard against devouring or becoming overly possessive of their partner and stifling them. Guard against hanging on to relationships that no longer serve you.

A partner as intuitive as the crab will also help to draw lovers out of their shell and keep them out. The crab needs a partner who can accept their intuitive and psychic abilities and encourage them to use their abilities in a positive vein. Ultimately, a strong partner who can set the table and be there for the crab is heaven-sent, and if they know how to retreat when necessary, even better.

The home is the most natural place for the affectionate crab to be, and if they can share that space with someone special—well, that's just perfect. The emotional nature of this winning sign helps to make Cancerians empathetic and caring lovers, the sort of people who glow like the moon and flow like the sea.

Cancerians do need to be aware of the necessity for setting

boundaries. See The Magnificent Seven Steps to Setting Bound-aries exercise in Taurus (page 48) for an exercise for this.

I also sometimes advise water signs to imagine themselves sur-rounded by a circle of protective white light to avoid picking up on others' emotions too much.

Cancer's biggest lesson in sex and relationships is to learn to let go. Timing and action are two valuable tools, and the Cancerian woman needs to learn to use them to her advantage. The Cance-rian woman needs to know exactly what she wants; only then she can have it. Most problems in her sex life, indeed, her life as a whole, arise from erroneous decisions.

THE END OF THE AFFAIR

THE CONFUSION BETWEEN emotional neediness and love can lead to problems in Cancerian relationships. Cancerians often feel that they are not loved enough, and so become clingy and demand-ing if a partner appears disinterested. The Cancerian will cling more and more tightly as the relationship deteriorates, making separation very difficult.

If the partner has been unfaithful, the Cancerian will react with jealousy and, occasionally, aggression because the hurt has been so great. See the exercise for Letting Go of Jealousy in Taurus (page 45) for help with this tendency, Cancer.

A Cancerian who feels unloved may stray in search of loving attention. The crab is unlikely to divorce, however, no matter how unpleasant the marriage becomes.

RELATIONSHIPS
(Family and Friends)

CANCER PARENT

THE TYPICAL CANCERIAN parent may worry too much about their offspring. They are also characterized by a tendency to be overly possessive.

As a parent, Cancer will protect and support the children and will do anything to encourage and foster their creative development. Cancerian parents love looking after and playing with their offspring and will remember every birthday and anniversary.

CANCERIAN CHILD

THE CANCER CHILD is the stay-at-home of the zodiac, a shy and sensitive type who would rather play in their room than play rough-and-tumble with the neighborhood kids. Emotional as well, this child will cry easily if things aren't going their way or if there is some upset going on in the family. As they can occasionally be moody, it's best to give the Cancer child room when they're feeling blue. They might at times feel sorry for themselves and even become lazy, but this won't last for long. It's much more fun, after all, to be involved!

Staying close to home, the Cancer child can be expected to cling to their mom. This child loves to be helpful. Maternal in nature, the Cancer child is a good choice to look after the younger kids in the family. These children are natural baby-sitters and can keep the neighborhood kids happy for hours with games and other domestic pursuits.

As this child possesses an excellent memory, studying and test-taking will come easily.

Most of all, the Cancer child appreciates family, so expect this youngster to revel in family reunions and any and all family adventures.

BRINGING UP CANCER—COACH'S INSIGHT

MOST CANCERIANS ARE fascinating and delightful youngsters whose faces convey every changing mood. They love to use their imagination and are easy to discipline, provided that any disciplinary act is backed up by warmth, love, and reassurance. The Cancerian child also has a great need for attention and approval.

Parents should relate to the Cancerian child wholeheartedly and reassure him or her when fear strikes, which is likely to be often. Cancerian children are very sensitive to emotional hurts and rejections and must have parental support at these times. If Cancerians grow up feeling unloved and rejected they are likely to become withdrawn and reclusive.

The Cancerian child needs to be free to express his or her emotions through creative activity, be this drama, painting, writing, or some other pursuit. All you as a parent need to do is to give your Cancerian child the tools, some basic training, and the space to express themselves adequately.

When Cancerian children use their vivid imaginations to embellish the truth, they should be taught the difference between reality and imagination. I really cannot overemphasize the need for Cancerians to be able to find an outlet for their rich and vivid imagination.

CANCER AND FRIENDS

CANCERIANS REGARD THEIR friends as treasured family possessions, which means that friends are treated with loving care, consideration, sensitivity, nurturing, protective hospitality, and great tenderness.

Although friends may come and go, those from early days are regarded as the most precious.

FRIENDS, BE AWARE

CANCERIANS CAN BE a little insecure, so friends can expect to have their loyalty tested severely over the course of time.

The crab is likely to remain angry for a long time with any friend who hurts them, and they may abandon their friend, permanently. If the friendship is a deep and long-standing one, a reconciliation may occur.

Cancerians are quite competitive and do tend to set their standards by the progress that a friend is making. This can be circumvented if Cancer learns to define its own criteria of success and concentrates its efforts on meeting them. With Cancer's strong links to family, the crab can be at risk of accepting other family members' definitions of success rather than having the confidence to define its own.

HEALTH

WHEN a Cancer is stressed out, he or she will become withdrawn and refuse to discuss things with anyone. This is Cancer's self-protective device, and friends and family will probably have become very used to this by now. Water signs need regular time alone, especially in turbulent periods, so don't discount this need if you yearn for space. At the same time, Cancer needs tender loving care in tough times. If you love and trust a partner, get the affection you need, even if you can't get the words out.

Cancers have the capacity to remember events and details well, which can occasionally get in your way when you allow your past to overly influence your future. If you keep remembering the bad relationships you've had, for example, you'll convince yourself that you can never have a good one, as opposed to learning the skills required to make a relationship work. History doesn't have to repeat itself. Whether you make the wrong recommendations at work or handle a relationship less diplomatically than you should have, as a Cancer you will tend to beat yourself up with reruns and recriminations. Just let go, and don't torture yourself that way.

Some new experiences are just that—new—and you won't have any past references to prepare or guide you. All you can do is plan, prepare, and enjoy the experience.

Realize too, that emotionally, you are a delayed reactor. Cancers tend to stay in situations long after they have outlived their use-fulness, mainly out of habit, misplaced loyalty, or fear of making the wrong decision. Forget about failure, learn from each less than ideal experience and move on. Life is a creative process, and it will occasionally involve some wasted effort. That shouldn't stop you from pressing forward.

STRESS BUSTING FOR CANCER

YOUR SECRET ASSET is your profound intuition, so use it to find solutions. Listen to your inner voice; it is waiting to help you. If you are pulled in two directions, follow instinct over logic, whatever your intellect might tell you. (Yours is a sign that can "hear" the messages of the subconscious above the clamoring chatter of the conscious.) The logical reasons usually do appear later, and should give you confidence to continue to follow your hunches. Your cardinal nature will boost your ability to deal with change and help you to investigate a number of opportunities. If you find yourself getting really uncomfortable with change, try the Fear Zapper exercise (page 124).

COACH'S TIP

Instead of using the word "problem" to describe your situation, use the word "challenge." For example, instead of "financial problems," you have "financial challenges." This will begin to put you in the frame of mind to come up with ways to rise to your financial challenges. As soon as this starts to happen, you can see that your problems are really opportunities in disguise.

Now here's the magical part. Imagine that you have successfully exploited your biggest opportunities. What happened to your problems?

Cancerians are in tune with the sea and may unwind by walking barefoot by the sea, collecting shells, or sailing. If you do feel like a little company, make it someone equally as sensitive as you, perhaps a Pisces, or a practical Capricorn—someone who will not criticize or undermine you. You could even go to the park and have a tasty, lovingly prepared picnic. Talking of food, stress tends to play havoc with your appetite, so treat yourself to some comfort foods (rice pudding is my favorite) until your stress subsides. Later, when you feel better, you can add other items to your diet.

Cooking is a favorite activity of Cancerians, so you might want to do some therapeutic cooking even if you don't feel much like eating yourself (certainly you won't find your family complaining). The creativity will engross you and give you pleasure. Cancers enjoy all parts of the process: carefully selecting a delicious recipe from a favorite cookbook, shopping for the ingredients, the creative work in the kitchen, and, finally, the feeling of closeness and appreciative feedback from your guests.

Your moon-ruled sign would enjoy playing with a child as a way to let go of tension. Mind a relative or close friend's baby for an hour or two, and soon you will have forgotten your problems while nurturing the infant and giving your friend a much needed rest. Older children are also a real joy for Cancers, since they can communicate with them easily. Some people find peace with pets— Cancerians find it with children.

Since you are very sensitive to your home surroundings, when you feel blue, try rearranging your furniture, redecorating or buying some new things to revamp your home. If you're feeling really adventurous and want to immerse yourself in creative activity, why not draw up dream plans to renovate your home completely? The process of fantasizing about what you would like to happen next and, more importantly, how you will make it happen will be highly productive for you. You could exercise your powers of visualization, creativity, and planning by creating a bright, new, compelling future. Yours is a creative sign, and fantasizing is one of your best methods of effecting change. To help you with this, try the Career-U-Like exercise in the Taurus chapter (page 53) and extend the exercise to other areas of your life that you want to re-create.

FITNESS

CANCER RULES THE sternum, ribs, diaphragm, stomach, womb, esophagus, breasts, gallbladder, and upper lobes of the liver. The Cancerian metabolism is low.

Cancers worry, and when they do, their sensitive tummies feel it first. Watch what you eat when you are in an emotional turmoil, as you could end up binge-eating and piling on the pounds. Not all stressed-out crabs overeat, however; some Cancers avoid food altogether when emotionally upset. Find a course for yourself that is moderate, neither too little nor too much eating when you're not feeling your best.

Make sure that you are getting enough of the right vitamins and minerals too.

Cancer is sensitive to the phases of the moon, which can cause them to feel moody. Give yourself—and others—a little slack near full-moon periods. You may need a little more privacy during that time.

Cancers have a very sensual nature—moreso than most of the other signs. If a sport or exercise program "feels" good in a physical sense, it is likely to stay a part of your routine. You may love water sports, since Cancer is a water sign and finds being near water akin to going back to the womb. Don't disregard the power of water for you—it works magic on your nerves. Swim, run on the beach, sail, windsurf, or try whitewater rafting—anything water-related.

Be sure to avoid fitness programs that are overly regimented, as you will tend to rebel against prescriptive regimes. Allow your intuition to guide you to the perfect exercise regime. You are naturally drawn to exercise that has a steady, rhythmic flow. Aqua-cize—callisthenics that are done in a pool using the weight of the water as resistance—could be soothing and strengthening at the same time.

Cancer may be the most nurturing sign of the zodiac, but creating and tasting those delicious meals you cook up for your loved ones may be hard on your waistline. Don't stop cooking—you enjoy it and you're great at it—just switch to lighter fare or go for smaller portions. Investigate recipes that combine great flavor with interesting texture (Cancer's standard of excellence) and have fun experimenting.

Finally, Cancer men and women of all nationalities have radiant, beautiful, and translucent skin, which usually makes them look younger than they are. However, since a Cancer's delicate skin can be damaged by sun, be sure to keep using that sunscreen.

TOOLS FOR MAKING A DIFFERENCE

VISUALIZATION IS A powerful tool for manifesting your goals, Cancer. By creating goals that reflect your deepest hopes, and by doing the inner and outer work necessary to achieve them, you'll surpass even your own expectations.

Visualization for Beginners

VISUALIZE the kind of life you really want to have—let go of your doubts and don't hold back. Let your imagination run riot and get in touch with your feelings about the images that appear. With experience you'll learn to distinguish between illusion and those images that arise from a higher source. When you find that the images leave you feeling excited and hopeful, you're seeing what you can create for yourself if you dare. Write down affirmations that help you keep focused on these goals, place them where you can see them every day and say them out loud. For extra backup, commit them to tape and play your tapes when you go to bed at night.

If you run into your own resistance to change, have a look at the exercise for Avoiding Self-sabotage in Taurus (page 70).

Buy some aromatherapy oils to help with clarity and concentration if necessary. If you find yourself getting stressed, do something to relax—meditate, make a cup of chamomile tea, or listen to a recording of ocean sounds.

SPIRITUALITY

INTROSPECTION is the key with you, Cancer. When you find the rightness of a set of spiritual beliefs, you'll persist with it, explore it, and use your intuition to understand it fully.

Cancer's spiritual goal is to learn how to take a balanced view of things. If you can reconcile the personal conflict of your urge to be outgoing with the reserve that causes you to withdraw into yourself, then at best you can inspire a generation, especially the youthful part of it, by your idealism.

From your opposite sign, Capricorn, you can learn how to distinguish reality from imagination, thus getting things into a proper perspective and consequently making better judgments. Your life-long challenge is to bring your own ceaseless changeability, akin to the ebb and flow of the tides, into balance with your equally deep-seated resistance to change. You must learn to live without needing to control life, to accept that life is an ungovernable force, and to transcend your mother-protector role to become a fully-fledged human being with much to teach us about looking after the living world, which will in turn look after us.

CHAPTER 5

LEO

July 23–August 22

THE FIFTH SIGN OF THE ZODIAC IS CONCERNED WITH:

- PLEASURE, FUN, PLAYFULNESS
- CHILDLIKE ACTIVITIES, CHILDREN, CHILDISHNESS
- SEX, ROMANCE, LOVE AFFAIRS
- CREATIVITY
- RECOGNITION, LIMELIGHT, APPLAUSE, SELF-PROMOTION
- RISK TAKING
- SPORTS
- PERFORMANCE, DRAMA

LEO, the fifth sign of the zodiac, is a fixed fire sign. The key to the Leo personality is held in the words "fixed fire."

Ruled by the sun, creative Leo is characterized by flamboyance, a strong sense of drama and expansiveness. Leo sees a future full of endless possibilities for success and is a true visionary. Leo is a sign that sees the "big picture"—a great, big, bright picture with Leo center stage, feted by one and all.

Fire, as an element, transforms and all Leos love transforming things with their energy. Think of the sun in all its splendor, think of the fire that transforms formless glass into a work of art. As a Leo life coach I adore working with clients to transform their lives so that they express and honor what is great about the person living them.

Leonine energy is motivated by inspiration and aspiration. The lion brims with fire energy, which can be warm, vital, welcoming, cheerful, and loyal to whatever attracts it. Leo must be careful to ensure that its loyalties are not misplaced. As a fixed sign, Leo is at risk of holding onto situations that are no longer appropriate. The lion can become obsessed with the goal of the moment, blinding itself to other, more appropriate opportunities.

Leo needs to guard against excessive spending and a tendency to keep up appearances. I've had more than one Leo client who, not taking the step of informing partners or friends that their financial circumstances had changed, spent themselves deep into debt. Being a sunny, optimistic sign, Leo can be slow when it comes to heeding wake-up calls. When talking to Leo clients, initially I tend to assume that business or financial problems are worse than they let on.

Take John, for example, one of the most charismatic clients I have ever worked with. A born showman, John had homes in some of the most exciting cities the world has to offer—London, Paris, New York, and Rome. He owned a Porsche, an Aston Martin, a Ferrari, and a mountain of debt. Business had been less than good over the past few years. He had not paid his staff for three months—those who hadn't walked out were getting pretty fed up. However, this state of affairs wasn't going to bother John—after all, he had this hot new idea that was going to get venture capital funding. No way was John going to sell his possessions and give up his playboy lifestyle—he had an image to project.

John was less than enthusiastic when I suggested that he start looking at reducing his debt—venture capitalists do not as a rule sponsor those who can't budget. He worked extremely hard to convince me that a miracle was on its way that would clear his debts, allow him to escape paying outstanding tax, and give him plenty of money to enjoy.

I was less convinced, a judgment backed up by the fact that his second check to me bounced! When I called him to discuss this, he had already woken up to the fact that if he didn't take action now, he would lose everything. Far from grand designs, we were looking at damage limitation.

The first task I gave John was to clarify exactly what state he was in financially and to draw up a plan for financial recovery. I also instructed him to get support in implementing his plan from loved ones and outside agencies as well as a coach. One of the hardest steps for any Leo to take is to ask for help, but John took this step with fortitude.

Two years into coaching, John has sold two of his homes and is renting out a third. All of the cars are gone, replaced by a classic E-Type Jag. He has now paid most of his outstanding tax bill and is aiming to have his credit-card bills and outstanding loans paid off within the next three months.

The venture capital funding hasn't happened, but by focusing on his core business (executive search) John has more than tripled his profits. He is now feeling confident enough to be considering launching a couple of more ventures, once he has two years' living expenses in the bank.

Although John's story may read like a cautionary tale, Leo's tendency to role-play is far from all bad. The Leo aspirant lives by the maxim "Fake it, till you make it." Typical Leo employees will dress for the role to which they aspire and act as if they have already got it. Getting that job then becomes a natural progression. Leo builds self-confidence by putting on demonstrations and shows of bravado. By acting self-confident, Leo becomes self-confident in truth as well as deed.

Interestingly, Leo's fixed nature is balanced by fire energy that craves freedom, opportunity and, of course, a steady stream of new experiences. The fire energy of royal Leo can be assertive, competitive, ambitious, and full of confidence for the future. Fire energy learns best when actively engaging in and grabbing hold of life. Fire loves adventure and hates routine. Once Leo decides to tackle problems head-on, a laserlike beam of commitment, creativity, and enthusiasm is focused on uncovering a solution. Give Leo a motivating challenge and it will be tackled with great energy—but don't ask Leo to do something low-status and mundane, unless you are a smart operator who can make even the mundane low-grade job sound sexy.

But, Leo is much more self-reflective and inner-directed than the average person might ever suspect. Over the years, Leos learn that, first and foremost, they have to be able to live with and please themselves. As Leo matures, a strong, burning inner desire for self-authenticity comes to the fore. So "To thine own self be true" could be another really good Leo motto.

Playful, creative, warmhearted, and risk taking are all character-istics common to Leos who are living out the fullest potential of their birth sun placement.

Leos are uncomplicated, knowing exactly what they want and using all their energies, creativeness, and resolution to get it, as well as being certain that they will get whatever they are after.

STRENGTHS TO FOCUS ON

So how does this combination of fixed fire express itself outwardly? What is Leo like in terms of personality? This is a general guide; sun sign alone does not solely determine personality.

▶ **A sunny disposition**
▶ **Strong leadership skills**
▶ **House proud**
▶ **Generosity**
▶ **Hospitableness**
▶ **Courage**
▶ **Self-sacrifice for the right cause or person**
▶ **Responsible**
▶ **Vivacious**
▶ **Pride in appearance**
▶ **Pride in achievements**
▶ **Open, warmhearted friendliness**
▶ **Loving disposition**
▶ **A sense of dignity**
▶ **Tolerance and acceptance of people at face value**

For exercises to help you make the most of your strengths, you might like to look at S.M.A.R.T.est Goals for Aries (page 3) and Act Out Your Positive Traits in the Cancer chapter (page 98).

WEAKNESSES THAT CAN TRIP YOU UP

▶ **Stubbornness**
▶ **Wilfulness**

- Contempt bordering on arrogance
- Gullibility
- Petulance and sullennedss
- Erratic worker
- Coldheartedness and withdrawal when hurt
- A tendency to take undue credit or to take credit for other people's ideas
- Smugness
- Indifference or an uncaring attitude
- Tendency to cut others down to size

So how do you turn these so-called negatives into powerful tools for personal growth? Look at the Love Your Weaknesses exercise in Aries (page 6).

LEO MAN

Unless there are influences in his birth chart that overpower those of his sun sign, the Leo man:

- Has an impressive appearance
- Is a good host
- Can turn failure into success
- Is warmhearted
- Has great presence
- Can adjust to difficult conditions
- If disabled will fight to prove his physical prowess
- Can be over-generous
- Likes to show off
- Is trusting
- Likes everything he does to be exciting
- Gives and expects loyalty
- Appears to be in control of himself
- Needs to be adored and admired
- Is generous with his time and money
- Is popular
- Uses charm to get what he wants
- Likes an elegant environment

LEO WOMAN

The Leo woman is everything the male Leo is and more. Unless there are influences in her birth chart that overpower those of her sun sign, the Leo woman:

▶ **Has real presence**
▶ **Has sex appeal**
▶ **If disabled will use it to her advantage, making her attractive**
▶ **Is well-dressed**
▶ **Appears to have an inner sense of royalty**
▶ **Can be domineering**
▶ **Always looks fabulous even in adverse circumstances**
▶ **Is trusting and loyal and needs to love**
▶ **Loves to show off**
▶ **Likes everything she does to be exciting**
▶ **Frequently misplaces faith in people: broken engagements, separations and divorce likely**
▶ **Needs to be admired and adored**
▶ **Is a social leader**
▶ **Uses courtesy to get what she wants**
▶ **Is generous with affection and hospitality**
▶ **Likes to be in elegant surroundings**

THE HIDDEN (OR NOT-SO-HIDDEN) LEO

INSIDE ANY LEO beats the heart of a cat, which wants to be top dog. Leo is not interested in being an unsung hero or an unrecognized hero(ine); Leo wants to be undisputed ruler and often gets more satisfaction from being a one-man band than the leader of a team of thirty. A natural status junkie, Leo would prefer to rule the world!

Like the sun in the center of its universe, Leo expects everything in life to revolve around Leo. In astrology, the radiant, beaming sun is life giver and font of creativity. In common with the sun, the best Leos are a source of life-enhancing warmth for all.

In order to flourish, Leo needs to be loved, cherished, and adored. Leo needs to surround itself with supportive, loving, and appreciative colleagues, friends, lovers, and family in order to perform at its best. An unloved Leo, like a Sun eclipsed by clouds, fails to shine.

Leo, even when taking center stage, can have self-doubts. Leo consultants and coaches can doubt their worth and end up undercharging. Leo needs to touch base with an objective partner to understand his or her true value. A successful Leo can have moments when they feel like a fraud, who will be uncovered and cast out. (Look at the Determine Your Value exercise in the Capricorn chapter on page 274 for help with this, Leo.)

LEO LIKES

- Activity
- The promise of pleasure
- Being creative
- Receiving gifts, praise, or thanks
- Luxury and glamour
- Pets and children
- Being seen as the best at something

LEO DISLIKES

- Being ignored
- Being laughed at
- Being told something they don't know
- Being back stage, or second place
- Being sedentary
- Physical pain
- One-upmanship or being put down

EXERCISE ONE

Value Yourself

TO COUNTERACT the tendency to undervalue yourself, Leo, make a note of what's great about you and ask friends to do the same.

Repeat this step for your achievements.

This should enable you to see that you have got where you are due to your innate talents and value.

POSSIBLE PROBLEM AREAS FOR LEO, AND SOLUTIONS

ALL SUN SIGNS have unique personality traits. When these traits are suppressed, problems will arise. However, with the formidable combination of coaching and astrology we can identify the problem and come up with a likely solution based on sun sign characteristics. If the following problems strike a chord with you, Leo, come up with a plan of action and implement it.

PROBLEM: Getting upset and angry with others when things do not go the way you expected them to.

SOLUTION: Work out what outcomes are solely dependent on you, and therefore subject to your control. Where results are dependent on others, accept that you cannot control everything, but you can influence the odds of getting a favorable outcome—all you can control is your own reaction to events.

PROBLEM: You are sometimes your own worst enemy, especially so when you are striving for attention in such obvious ways that you turn off the very people you seek to impress.

SOLUTION: First of all, stop trying to gain attention; give people the chance to notice the real you. Decide what it is that impresses you and then you will know what to do to impress others.

PROBLEM: Egotism and arrogance.

SOLUTION: Look for things you can admire in others so that you begin to get a sense of perspective.

PROBLEM: Loss in income from unwisely speculating, which leads to financial ruin. Possible loss of family and friends, due to a lack of concern for their financial welfare.

SOLUTION: You should always investigate all investments well before they are made. Look at your objectives and psychology, and research potential investments thoroughly before committing yourself. Involve your spouse before committing joint funds.

CAREER/BUSINESS

LEO loves to be the center of attention at work. People born under this sign are giving, proud, energetic, and confident—the world can't help but look! Which is as it should be, says the lion. Leos can't help but be in the limelight, thanks to their larger-than-life personality and infectious positive attitude. Leos are focused in their work, provided that the work excites them, and they make excellent team leaders. A motivated Leo will work extremely hard.

Leo needs to be in charge of a high-profile project, department, or company to shine at work. Fortunately, colleagues are often quick to seek out the lion as a role model, since those signature qualities of leadership, truth, and justice are ones that many look for. The lion is also a risk taker, someone who wants the world and often gets it.

Leos need to guard against indolence and complacency, and must be careful not to use Leonine charm to manipulate people. Machiavellian tactics can backfire—people soon wise up to the fact that someone is pulling their strings, Leo.

Leo loves being in the spotlight but has to learn there really is plenty of room for a team to assemble there with the lion. Is there a game to be won? A deal to close? The lion's team will be victorious, but teammates will have to watch for the lion's tendency to take credit for everyone's success.

Here are some occupations that a Leo might consider:

Actor	Entertainer	Principal
Architect	Entrepreneur	Professor
Announcer	Exhibitor/Marketer	Publicist
Art dealer	Fashion designer	Resort manager
Artist	Inventor	Spokesperson
Athlete	Manager	Stockbroker
Cardiologist	Master of	TV anchor
CEO	Ceremonies	Talk-show host
Celebrity	Money	Teacher
Coach	manager/trader	Theatrical agent
Comedian	Moviemaker	Theater manager
Counselor	Park ranger	Tour guide
Director	Performer	Writer
Educator	Politician/president	

If you are a typical Leo, both money and an excellent quality of life will be of great importance to you. To help you find out which comes first, visit the Define Your Values exercise in Aries (page 20).

Leo Boss

LEO MANAGERS ARE exactly where they want to be—in control and in a position of power and respect. They have, or appear to have, huge self-confidence, which only slips when their authority is threatened.

Leos make strong leaders in an organization, as long as they curb their control-freak urges. Leos tend to have difficulties delegating work, unless they're of a more indolent disposition. They also have a tendency to interfere. No matter how good a job everyone else is doing, the Leo manager will be convinced that they could do it better. Leo managers have to keep their fingers on the pulse of everything and everyone at the organization. They find it difficult to cope with a sneaking suspicion that people are keeping secrets from them.

Leo's followers know where they stand. Leos think and act bigger than others would normally dare; the ambitiousness of their schemes and idealism sometimes daunts their followers, but their practical hardheadedness and ability to go straight to the heart of any problem reassures those who depend on them. If Leos meet with setbacks, they thrive on the adversity.

Managing to be such a control freak and yet still remaining popular with colleagues is one of Leo's special talents. Leos achieve this through their natural friendliness and warmth. They can charm people into working devotedly for them and get colleagues to buy into their great vision for the future. Leos believe in hard work and they'll make everyone around them work just as hard as Leo does. However, people are willing to work hard for a Leo boss because the boss is also seen to be pulling their weight. Leo loves showing people how to do things, so they take the trouble to explain to colleagues how to carry out the tasks delegated to them. The lion is also thoughtful toward employees and their families. One Leo client of mine thought nothing of paying for a subordinate's son to have laser surgery to save his sight.

ADVICE ON WORKING FOR A LEO BOSS

WORKING FOR A Leo manager, you will probably work harder than you ever have in your life—but also have more fun in the process. Leo believes in working and playing hard. If you work for a Leo manager, appear to take in all that advice they dish out with good grace and let them take center stage. Leo does not respond well to being upstaged. Never try to usurp their power but put your best image forward as well—Leo managers like good-looking people, as they see their employees as an extension of themselves.

LEO EMPLOYEE

THE AVERAGE LEO employee needs to have their worth and superiority acknowledged. They are loyal and hardworking and respond positively to genuine praise for their efforts. They are natural show people and motivators.

Leo delights in keeping colleagues and customers happy.

Whatever level Leo is at in an organization, his or her working space will be luxurious, convenient, and comfortable. Their office, or cubicle, will be personalized with pictures and status symbols. Leo will find some way of subtly making their office better, to their mind, than everybody else's, even if company culture ostensibly precludes this.

Leo is one of the most competitive signs in the zodiac and also performs superbly at interviews. This means that Leo could very easily find him or herself being offered an unsuitable job and being flattered into taking it. I know, because I, and quite a few of my sun sign clients, have done just this.

If you want to say good-bye to that sinking feeling you get when you know you've just landed yourself the job from hell, try the Career-U-Like exercise in the Taurus chapter (page 53). Culture Vulture in Libra (page 202) is also worth a look.

FINANCES AND WEALTH

LEO is a sign with truly champagne tastes—this is not a sign that settles for second best—but not always with the budget to match. From a coaching perspective, this is by no means bad, as those who expect to be poor end up poor. There are two things you have to guard against, Leo:

- ◆ Going over budget—so you are going to need to work out how much extra work you have to do to cover the odd excess expenditure—and do that work.
- ◆ Believing that because astrology books tell you that you may have financial problems, you will have financial problems. This then becomes a self-fulfilling prophecy.

Just see yourself as financially responsible, act as if you are and, soon, you will become so.

As one of the most generous signs of the zodiac, there is a danger that you could overspend on entertaining and lavish gifts, particularly where your children are concerned. My coaching advice to you is to be aware that you don't have to spoil your family and friends by spending large sums on them. They will love you just as much without those frequent presents and dinners out. Find creative, low cost ways of treating yourself and others.

As a coach, I encourage clients to build up two years' worth of living expenses as a reserve—with Leonine clients, this is quite a feat. For extravagant Leos, I begin with the following pragmatic approach.

First, get into the habit of only treating yourself when you can afford it. While Leo is not known for being the most realistic sign, it is one blessed with great vision and creativity, so put these gifts to good use by devising affordable treats and creative ways of funding yourself and staying within budget.

Second, build up a rainy-day fund. See the Building Up a Rainy-Day Fund exercise in Aries (page 28) for help with this.

EXERCISE TWO

Combating Impulse Spending

IF YOU are a Leo who borders on spendaholism, try this little exercise:

1. First, sit down, relax, and think about why you have a spendaholic personality. Do this in a friendly but slightly detached manner, as if seeing yourself through the eyes of a close friend. You are not looking to cast blame, just to work out why you do things in a certain way. Do you shop gratuitously when you are feeling down, or are you simply a spontaneous shopper who loves the thrill of hunting out bargains, without really wanting or needing the item you wrest from the grasp of others? Look at the circumstances in which you shop for no other reason than shopping. This will help you understand why you behave in this way, and, forewarned is forearmed. Ideally, you are looking to spend for a reason—pure pleasure—in a controlled and responsible way.

2. For the next seven days, before you go into any shop, decide what it is that you are going to buy. If you cannot clearly state, out loud, specifically what it is that you intend to buy and why, don't go in. For example, for the purposes of this exercise, I would suggest that "I want to buy a designer outfit" is specific enough (i.e., you

do not need to have decided on the designer); "I want to get some stuff to cheer me up" is not!

3. Once in the shop, if you see something you really want but that was not on your list, leave it (for now). Once out of the shop, you can make the decision whether or not to buy it, and go back in with intention.

COACH'S TIP

If you are "comparison shopping," or "just trying to get a feel for what kind of car/computer/TV/lipstick/mutual fund" you want, be honest with yourself. How many times have you actually left the store or Web site without having spent any money? The less you think this tip applies to you, the more money it will probably save you!

Frustration may also kick in and this is something you need to watch out for. You may feel that after several fruitless shopping expeditions, you must buy something. This is the time when you may be most likely to buy an expensive mistake. So relax, take a deep breath, have some coffee, and if you feel you must buy something, try to keep the purchase small.

EXERCISE THREE

Maximizing Your Return on Investment

1. The next time you decide to make a purchase of any size, note the amount you have decided to spend.
2. Now ask yourself the following question: "Given that I have now decided it is acceptable to spend this amount of money, is there anything I would rather be spending it on?"
3. Make note of your answer and take action accordingly.

The Debt Filter

Today, and over the weekend, make a note of the many different ways you are invited by television, advertising, stores, E-mail, the Internet, newspapers, and magazines to get into debt. Here's a list to get you started:

1. No money down
2. No payments
3. Operators are standing by
4. Here's your preapproved credit card
5. Bad credit—no problem!
6. Send no money now
7. Buy now, pay later

Now, here's the game—you can make up your own scoring system if you prefer. What you are looking to achieve are creative ways of getting what you want without incurring debt.

- ◆ You get one point each time you notice an invitation to debt.
- ◆ You get two points each time you notice an invitation to debt only after thinking about it (i.e., it sneaked past you at first glance).

Now let's make this exercise more realistic by extending it in the following way. Let's say you are tempted to buy something for $100 on your credit card or store charge card. The cost of borrowing (interest) actually means that this item will be costing you a lot more if you do not pay your card balance in full by the specified time. If your credit or store card has an APR of, say, 20 percent, the annual cost of this $100 is in fact $120 over the year. So think about how you can make choices using actual cash to reduce your debt and to build up your financial reserves. For example, if you choose not to spend that $100 ($120), this either reduces your debt by that amount, or increases your cash reserves.

You can in fact try to have your cake and eat it if you see this amount reducing your debt by $60 and increasing your cash by $60. Magnify this logic to your spontaneous spending, and work out how long it could take to significantly reduce and then eliminate your debt and build healthy cash reserves. It works well if you use significant figures—so each time you resist the urge to blow $100, you are conserving your cash, which can be used to reduce your debt or simply to build cash reserves.

Becoming mindful of and resisting invitations to live beyond your means will improve your financial health dramatically, Leo.

LOVE, ROMANCE, AND SEX LIFE

The creative and romantic lion rules the zodiac's house of pleasure, ensuring that any love affair with this cat will include sensory as well as sensual delights. For Leo, love is a high-octane dramatic affair. This cat loves wholeheartedly and takes pride in this. The regal lion becomes even nobler in the presence of his or her lover. Romance is a princely quality for the lion, and those who ensnare this passionate animal may well be rewarded with a wonderful and inventive lover, not to mention an attentive one.

Leo loves to be in love and glows more brightly in presence of a soulmate. The lion is a strong advocate of romantic love and is caring, supportive, and protective. It is not unusual for Leos to make great sacrifices for love, even to the point of fighting to the death for the loved one.

While Leos love to be admired and adored, they can also take the lead in romance, since they believe their strength and power will win the day. When the lion gets going, watch out, as passionate sparks will fly. These cats know how to turn on the charm, and the heat. The charismatic lion will take risks in love, as losing is not a word that Leo understands.

The lion may test a lover from time to time in their quest for answers about love. What is it really? How can I feel it the most? The one with the best answers to these questions will surely make this cat purr.

Both Leo man and Leo woman expect the partner to be dependent in some way, which is just as well, since charismatic, dominant people can find themselves attracting the needy. Leos who want to break away from attracting needy types need to learn to be comfortable with letting potential suitors shine once in a while.

In his or her relations with others, the Leo type is open, sincere, genuine, and trusting. Leos are more disillusioned than the average if let down by those they trust. They are not good judges of character and are inclined to favoritism and an exaggerated faith in their nearest and dearest, which too often ends in disappointment. All Leos believe their loved one is a prize worth having, and expect others to feel the same.

Leos have a strong sex drive and are so attracted to the opposite sex that they find it hard to be constant. On the whole, Leos are intensely sexual and, like fellow fire signs Aries and Sagittarius, must guard against becoming dissolute. They are sexual gourmets who may have numerous love affairs for the sake of pleasure, and a love of beauty and excitement is liable to drive them from one attractive partner to another. The lion needs to be aware that liking sex with a partner is not the same as being in love with them. This is a sign that loves to be in love and loves the adrenaline high that accompanies the chase. Since Leos don't like hurting people, or being seen in a bad light, they can be very much inclined to deceive.

Leo marriages may fail due to the lion's need for excitement and adulation, yet Leos are sincere and generous to their lovers while love lasts, and will remain attached to their home so long as it is run for their benefit.

A relationship with the daring yet devoted lion will rarely prove dull. Leo may demand to have attention lavished on him- or herself, but can ravish a lover with riches and a breathtaking tenderness in return.

COACH'S TIP

A fiery lion requires a lover who can keep up with them and certainly one who can match them in wits. Otherwise, the risk of boredom and flight is large, since a Leo has very high expectations.

Look for a partner who can understand and indulge your

need to be the center of attention. Your ideal soulmate will
understand the pleasure principle and will work hard to keep
you satisfied.

Try to add variety and spice to your relationship in order
to stave off boredom.

If you are looking for a partner, try the Getting Your Needs Met
exercise in the Cancer chapter (page 116).

COMPATIBILITY

LEO IS LIKELY to be happy with other fire signs, particularly Aries.
Air signs Gemini and Aquarius also make this stellar cat purr.

WHAT LEO NEEDS

WHAT THE KING/QUEEN of the Jungle wants more than anything
else is to be appreciated for being special, and adored. Only a psychologically immature Leo with self-esteem issues will demand to be
worshiped. The lion will more than match a partner's devotion, and
delights in making a partner feel special. A lover with all the right
vibes, who comes bearing gifts, exudes class, and remembers that it's
nothing but the best for this cat, is clever and wise.

Those who wish to share Leo's throne must enjoy being in the
spotlight. Leo will look for a partner who is good-looking and successful, a real trophy partner—though not as successful as the lime-
light-loving lion or lioness.

THE END OF THE AFFAIR

When Leo wants to end a relationship, the partner is often still
needed as a friend. This state of affairs can lead to divorce if the
partner is, understandably, unhappy with this situation. Keeping an
ex as a friend can also interfere with Leo's ability to form new relationships.

Leo is not the best sign at letting a partner know when it's over, partly due to its fixed sign quality and partly due to pride. Consequently, some Leos withdraw from their partner or treat them shamefully, in the hope that the partner will drift off and Leo can rewrite history, pretending the whole affair never happened.

If the lion is deserted by a partner, they will take months to recover from the blow and may never risk giving their heart completely again.

EXERCISE FIVE

Saying Good-bye

LEO IS not always very good at setting an ex-lover free. Here is an exercise to help with this.

Take all your old love letters from this person and burn them. Visualize yourself saying good-bye to them and loosening the bonds that keep you together.

Bid them farewell and wish them peace and a brighter future without you.

Make your imaginings as vivid as possible and burn incense, play music, or use any other props that will heighten the impact of this ritual. You are telling your subconscious that you are letting go of this person. Your conscious mind should then follow suit and the unwanted lover will "pick up" that they are free to go.

RELATIONSHIPS
(Family and Friends)

LEO PARENT

A TYPICAL LEO parent is very conscientious about bringing up children and makes every effort to educate their children. Few parents are better at creating a stimulating, playful environment for children than Leo. Leo certainly knows how to reach and play with children. This can lead to friction if the Leo parent is more generous and indulgent toward their children than the other parent. Take care to back your partner up on matters of discipline, unless you feel they are crossing the line, Leo. Agree on how to discipline your children and what constitutes overindulgence—make sure you stick to your side of the bargain.

Leo parents insist on honesty and openness from their children.

Leo parents must beware that their natural desire to be proud of their children does not border on the obsessive. Be careful not to attempt to live vicariously through your children, not to diminish their achievements, and not to put too much pressure on them to succeed. No child wants to be made to feel a failure.

Leo Child

THIS IS A creative youngster who loves to lead and be center stage. If you're looking for a lead in the school play, look no further than this stellar kitten. Born to lead any group, the Leo child has many friends—or are those followers? After all, there's no mistaking who's in charge here!

The Leo child is generous to a fault and hates people who are mean. Blessed with a sunny disposition and limitless quantities of charm and optimism, this child is bound to succeed. He or she refuses to be undermined by the criticism of others and is very sure of their own self-worth. Intent on being seen to be the best, this youngster will get good grades if only to show that they're number one.

Bringing Up Leo—Coach's Insight

YOUNG LEO NEEDS plenty of love, hugs, and honest compliments. Do not ruin this child's trusting nature by telling lies, even flattering ones—you'll only cause hurt. Leo needs a good balance of affection and discipline—praise for desired actions is far more effective than heavy-handed admonishments for transgressions.

Make it a habit every day to find something you can praise genuinely and sincerely in your Leo child. Watch your child blossom.

You will need to teach your Leo child early on that boasting is not the right thing. Try suggesting that boasting is undignified. This seems to work, as no proud lion likes to feel undignified.

Another early lesson for Leo is to beware of strangers. The sunny, trusting Leo child needs to be told in a straightforward, non-frightening manner that not everyone is as friendly as they are. Take advice on the best way to do this.

In order to avoid raising a small tyrant, get young Leo used to sharing in some of the household tasks. (Coach's tip—try giving jobs impressive titles). Leo also needs to be taught the importance of regular study and given an understanding of the rights of others.

Finally, teach Leo financial skills early on. This will give your Leo offspring a good start if they decide to try their hand at the stock market. This is a way of making money that draws many Leos and, fortunately, they are usually very successful at it. However, Leo still has to learn not to spend all that money before it's been made.

HEALTH

LEOS are usually fit, happy, energetic people as long as they are loved. If Leo is struck down with poor health, it is likely to be in the form of a fever, sudden illness, or accident. Leo can also delay recovery by going back to work too early and is not well suited to resting in a sickbed and letting an infection run its course.

Since your sign adores fun and games, head for the great outdoors for strenuous athletic fun, such as football, or organize a volleyball team. Try to vary your sporting activities throughout the week, as Leo doesn't like to be in a rut.

In terms of eating habits, Leo, you tend not to put much effort into creating a meal, unless you're putting on a lavish spread for company. Your preferred way of eating is to be waited on hand and foot at one of the swankiest, most fashionable restaurants, where you can be amongst, and be seen by, happening people. Try to frequent fashionable places that have healthy, low-fat meals. This will enable you to indulge your love of luxury and status while avoiding the corpulent frame that tends to result from too many rich meals.

Learn how to say no to too much food and alcohol and too many late nights, as overindulgence is a vice to which Leos are prone.

Two clients of mine, a hardworking, hard-living Leo couple, addressed the issue of eating more healthily by engaging a personal chef to cook and serve them well-balanced, nutritious meals. They combined their love of gourmet food and being served with a pragmatic and cost-effective way of getting healthy. Not for the less affluent among us, maybe, but their personal chef costs less than the take-away meals they were eating twice a day.

STRESS BUSTING FOR LEO

WHEN LEOS ARE feeling stressed or down, they are best when spending time with friends, as Leo is a supremely sociable sign. Leo is a people-loving, big-hearted sign and needs plenty of affection. This is a key to how you can best cope with stress. The more love and support you feel from your partner, family, and friends, the faster you will recover from whatever has knocked you off course. Input from others will also indicate whether you are overdramatizing your plight. No sign is more dramatic than a Leo. Take a moment to find out whether you are overresponding to your present concerns. If so, you could be unnecessarily increasing your panic level.

Because you are such a competitive sign, stay away from those people who make you feel deficient in any way, whether in looks, status, or achievement.

COACH'S TIP

Line up some treats, Leo, if you can afford them. How about a ticket to a play or a rock concert? How about dancing at a club—something energetic with a good, driving, rhythmic beat—or going to an opera and immersing yourself in the vibrant music and glorious spectacle? Alternatively, go out and treat yourself to the CDs you've been promising yourself. Then let go and lose yourself in music.

Treat yourself to a good meal at a restaurant (make it an elegant, well-reviewed place—shabby surroundings will depress you even more). I've yet to meet a Leo who isn't cheered up by eating out. If you're down or worried, wear something new—clothing that is well designed in a becoming color. The compliments you receive will surely give you a lift!

Be aware, Leo, that while your fire element loves action, your fixed nature tends to deter you from implementing the innovative steps you should take. As a Leo, you hate being told what to do, even when it's excellent and well-meaning advice. Guard against your tendency to reject ideas just because you didn't think of them yourself—this is what I call the "not-invented-here" mind-set.

Lions are very creative and need regular expression of feelings. As a Leo, I deal with feeling really blue by writing dramatic poetry. In fact, I can only ever write poetry when my emotions are in turmoil. Other cats paint away the blues or grab center stage in an amateur theater club. Any emotion you are feeling now can be poured into your role and released. Leos make great actors, but even if you turn out not to be the world's greatest thespian, at the very least you should meet some lively, flamboyant people.

Leo rules the fifth house, the house of children, so indulge your love of play and children by doing something for a charity like the Make a Wish Foundation or, if you have children of your own, immerse yourself in doing something special for them. Break out of your self-absorption (a potential Leo failing) by looking after or entertaining children—as every parent knows, you can't take your eyes off of them for a minute.

FITNESS

LEO RULES THE heart, back, spine, ankles, legs, hair, reproductive organs, throat, wrists, dorsal nerves, spleen, shoulders, and circulation. Your metabolism is medium to high.

Keep your heart healthy and fit with good nutrition and frequent aerobic exercise. As you are usually happiest in a social setting, don't work out alone. Join a health club or exercise class to get the best results. As a music-loving sign, you probably enjoy working out to lively music.

You will love having the attentions of your own personal trainer or coach—and be assured of great results. Anything tailored just to your needs and tastes will give you support, confidence, and a chance to achieve your personal best. Just remember that you need a regime with plenty of variety.

As Leo rules the back, you need exercise that strengthens your spine. Leos also need to maintain agility, suppleness, and stamina. Power walking, calisthenics, yoga, or Pilates could address these needs perfectly.

Tools for Making a Difference

Remember that confidence is the key to your personality, and if it is shaken, you won't be able to move forward as smoothly as you might wish. Because you are a fixed sign, change is hard for you to adjust to, at least initially. So to enable you to cope with it better, surround yourself with only your most supportive friends. Reminisce over your biggest victories. Find the common factors that underpin all your successes, no matter how small, to discover your personal formula for success. Keeping your self-belief high and feeling pride in your accomplishments is the single most important factor for you in turning around negative situations. Build in some treats to reward yourself for each step that you take toward getting your life back on track. Record in a journal each step you take successfully to remind yourself that you can cope well with change if you break it down into a series of small steps.

Dramatic change jolts Leos out of their comfort zones. See change for what it is: an opportunity for personal growth and a freeing up of space for something better to arrive. To help you with this, try the next exercise.

EXERCISE SIX

All Change

THINK OF a situation in your life that has been getting you down.

Now imagine yourself wearing a hot, heavy, restrictive suit of armor. Feel it begin to weigh your shoulders down, pressing down on your whole body, exhausting you, and draining the life out of you.

Now imagine throwing off the oppressive, constricting suit of armor and enjoy breathing a huge sigh of relief. Feel a huge weight being lifted off of you.

Feel the air rushing into your lungs as your chest expands. Feel its delicious coolness. Feel yourself starting to fizz with energy and come alive again.

Continue to breathe like this for the next minute.

Now turn your attention to what is concerning you. If you have carried out this exercise correctly, you will no longer feel so overwhelmed. You should find yourself refreshed and far better able to tackle the situation head-on.

If you continue to do this exercise regularly, you will find yourself freeing up enough of that wonderful, creative Leo energy to find a solution to your problem(s).

EXERCISE SEVEN

Winner DNA

THE PURPOSE of this exercise is to become an expert on what works and how to apply it to your own life. You will be modeling yourself on people who have successfully achieved what you want to achieve in your life. You will be identifying true winners, learning from them and possibly exceeding their success! You will use the techniques of learning how to be successful, designing a strategy, visualizing, and actually feeling your success, and actualizing your dreams. Now is the time to think big!

1. Make a list of the top five things you want to achieve and why. Be honest about this—don't just put down things that "would be nice to do" or "sound good." Focus on your burning desires, the things you are really prepared to work at to get. Think about the practical reasons and what success will mean in terms of material things, such as a bigger house, better life for your family, financial independence. Now think about the emotional reasons, such as how happy and successful you will feel, how people will respect and look up to you, and so on. You are looking to capture the emotional adrenaline that will help drive you in your quest.

2. Now make a list of people who have achieved these things. It could be one person who has achieved all five things. Or, more likely, five people who have achieved one of your desires really well. For example, if one of your objectives is to be a best-selling author of fiction, look at writers whose very name is sufficient to evoke breathtaking advances and make millions of TV viewers tune in to adaptations of their books.

3. Find out everything you can about these people. Use the Internet, autobiographies and biographies, magazine articles; write to them if they are still alive. How did they achieve their success; how long did it take them; what lucky breaks and synchronicities did they have; who helped them on their path? How can you learn from their successes, and how can you learn from their failures? How can you apply these lessons to your own situation? Write down the key things that determined their success. Are there factors common to each of them, such as commitment, determination, and persistence? What factors are unique to them, such as having a unique idea, finding the right contacts, and so on? Can you synthesize their experience to design a process for success that you can apply to your life?

4. Now think about how you can actually improve on what they have done. How could you do this better, how can you streamline and enhance their performance? How could you measure your increased success? You are looking to model yourself on these winners to a degree, but basically to use their success as your win-

ner DNA. How will you feel if you actually better the achievement of the top performers in your chosen field? Remember, you should be thinking big here, so engage the emotions and the imagination!

5. You now devise a strategy for success in each of these five areas. Think about how your five goals complement each other—for example, becoming a best-selling author may also satisfy a goal you have for financial independence. Look at some of the success strategy exercises in this book. Write down this strategy, keep it short and sexy, and make it sound bold and exciting. Learn it by heart. Also make sure you keep it flexible, to meet changing circumstances.

6. One highly effective technique that should be used now is to write a short future autobiography from the perspective of having achieved those goals. Simply imagine you have achieved all that you want, write down how you did it and who you learned from. You don't need to show this to anyone. You are trying to imagine how you feel when you have got to that stage of success, and how you actually achieved it. Once again, engage imagination and the emotions.

7. Now put the strategy into action!

TOOLS FOR MAKING A DIFFERENCE

SELF-AWARENESS IS one of the most powerful tools a Leo can ever develop. All Leos love the feeling of being in control; self-awareness will increase your sense of how effectively you are taking charge of your life. Remember, Leo, that many situations are beyond your control, while your responses are entirely up to you. Self-awareness is the art of being conscious of who you are and how you are responding to events around you.

EXERCISE EIGHT

Developing Awareness

A GOOD exercise for developing self-awareness is simply to attempt to watch yourself more carefully, as if a part of you were a detached, outside observer.

EXERCISE NINE

Ego to Go

GOAL setting is another tool that can have a major impact on your accomplishments, since by defining your goals, you are establishing your priorities and creating a plan of action which, if implemented, will enable you to create the life you desire.

This approach just had to be designed for Leos, but it works for other signs too.

Forget the pleasure or pain school of motivation and try "the Superiority Factor," which simply says that, like it or not, we are motivated toward any action or goal that we believe will cause us to feel superior to our fellow human beings. When we are successfully living our "shoulds," we feel superior—just slightly superior—to the mere mortals around us who haven't exercised, stuck to their diet, or renounced feeling superior to others.

The inverse of the Superiority Factor is equally true: We are motivated away from any action or goal that we believe will cause us to feel inferior to our fellow human beings.

Try this: Think of some of the things you "should" do that you actually do or have done recently—exercise, cleaning out your closets, buying a present before you need it, and so on.

Notice how it makes you feel when you think of successfully doing those things—don't you feel just a teensy bit superior? (If you don't feel superior right now, do you feel a bit superior about that?)

Actually, if you're like most of us, you feel conflicted about feeling superior. There are two main reasons for this:

◆ You hear imaginary people in your head saying, "Pah! Who does he think he is?"
◆ You think that if you allow yourself to feel proud of what you're doing, it will demotivate you from attempting to do any more.

The Superiority Factor says: The more you allow yourself to feel good about what you do, the more you will want to continue to do it. When you feel so superior or inferior that you are no longer motivated to act, you have gone beyond superior and entered the "stupid" zone. Stay superior and succeed!

Set up a "superiority scale" for yourself—you can call it your "scale of optimal superiority"—where ten is wonderfully self-satisfied and ready for more, and one is either totally down on yourself or ridiculously overinflated.

Finally, design your day for optimal superiority. What do you need to do or get done today to feel perfect Factor 10 superiority? Do it.

Try S.M.A.R.T.est Goals for Aries too (see page 3).

SPIRITUALITY

LEOS are likely to sample every type of spiritual practice under the sun and are unlikely to stay within the confines of conventional religion unless it suits them.

From an astrological and coaching perspective, the positions of the planets in our twelve astrological houses tells us what lessons we have been placed on earth to learn. In other words, our spiritual quest. Leo is ruled by the Sun. This tells Leos that their job is to produce, direct, showcase, and stage life's riches. The key to how Leo can do this is held by its opposite number, Aquarius.

Leo must learn to be more Aquarian. The spiritual lesson that a Leo sun sign teaches us is that far from Leonine creativity emanating from within, Leo is in fact a conduit for creative energy. Leo is the steward of creativity. It is Leo's job to ignite the divine spark in all of us. In short, to coach us to be the best that we can be.

Leo's fulfillment comes through enabling others to be the best that they can be. How can the valiant lionheart achieve this?

Leo can choose to build leonine self-esteem to the level where the lion can bestow its radiant gifts without the need to be appreciated and can allow others to take center stage. This is the lesson of Aquarius. Leo is here to bring out the best in all of us.

CHAPTER 6

VIRGO

August 23–September 22

THE SIXTH SIGN OF THE ZODIAC IS CONCERNED WITH:

◆ INCISIVE COMMUNICATION, SELF-PERFECTION
◆ CRITICAL FACULTIES, SHREWD, LOGICAL THOUGHTS
◆ SERVICE, ALTRUISM, RESPONSIBILITY
◆ HARD WORK, EFFICIENCY, DAILY ROUTINES, RELIABILITY
◆ STRENGTH OF CHARACTER
◆ MODESTY, PASSIVITY, VEILED SENSUALITY
◆ CLEANLINESS, HYGIENE, HEALTH, AND HEALING

DOES any of this sound even vaguely familiar, Virgo? I thought so ... But hang in there with me until the end and you might even hear a few new and surprising thoughts about the sign of Virgo.

Virgo is the only zodiacal sign represented by a female, who is sometimes thought of as a potentially creative girl, virginally lovely; and sometimes as a somewhat older woman, intelligent but rather pedantic and spinsterish. The latter is how many people think of Virgoans, and is sometimes confirmed by the Virgoan preciseness, refinement, fastidious love of cleanliness, conventionality, and aloofness. Those born under the sign of Virgo are usually observant, shrewd, critically inclined, judicious, patient, practical supporters of the status quo—qualities shared by the other earth signs, Capricorn and Taurus—and tend toward conservatism in all areas of life. On the surface they are emotionally cold, and sometimes this goes deeper, for their habit of suppressing their natural kindness may in the end cause it to wither and die, with the result that Virgoans may hold back from committing themselves to friendship, having only a few superficial relationships.

The outward lack of feeling manifested by some Virgoans may be a way of concealing deeply held feelings, to which they are afraid of surrendering because they do not trust others or because they lack confidence in themselves and their judgments. This is because they are conscious of certain shortcomings in themselves in terms of worldliness, practicality, sophistication, and outgoingness. Thus they become masters (and mistresses) at the art of self-concealment, hiding their apprehensiveness about themselves and their often considerable sympathy with other people under a mantle of matter-of-factness and undemonstrative, quiet reserve. Yet in their unassuming, outwardly cheerful, and agreeable fashion, they can exhibit a good understanding of other people's problems, which they can tackle with a practicality not always evident in their own personal relationships.

Mention that you are a Virgo to most people and, aside from jokes about virginity, you are most likely to hear the word . . .

PERFECTIONISM

VIRGO IS CONSTANTLY aiming toward the eternally elusive goal of being "perfect." At the same time, Virgo is painfully aware that it constantly comes up short of this goal. As a result of this need for perfection, Virgo has gained the reputation of being the zodiacal "neat freak." In addition to this, because Virgos often extend their unconscious need for perfection to the people around them, this mutable earth sign has also earned the reputation of being overcritical in interactions with loved ones. This reputation is not always deserved, however; while some Virgos are into organization, discrimination, and neatness in their physical environment, many others have an untidy, chaotic home and working environment—yet have the tidiest, most organized minds you'll come across in this (or any other) lifetime. So while some Virgos are primarily into physical manifestations of neatness, many others are primarily into mental organization, and some Virgos fall into the middle and are into a little of both.

For those of you who are too perfectionistic, let's look at a few strategies for overcoming this negative trait, which can block your road to success pretty quickly. Perfectionism in any part of your life gives you a payoff. It could be control, or it could be a way to affirm what you hold to be true about yourself. Perfectionism goes hand in hand with disliking ourselves, and seeing things in a negative light. Since we know there is no real state of being perfect, we ensure we will never be satisfied with who we are. Talk about being unforgiving to yourself, Virgo! Perfection only exists where fault does not, so if we are looking for perfection, we must be constantly in search of our faults. What an ego trip! Here are ways to get over perfectionism, in order to free up time and energy for getting on with what matters in life.

1. Start by looking for the good in yourself as opposed to what is not perfect.
2. Shift from judging yourself and the world, to understanding. Judgment holds criticism and hatred, and is loaded with blocks to success and prosperity. Understanding brings us acceptance of others and the ability to love our imperfect/perfect selves. From a position of understanding, we can begin to move forward.
3. Start asking yourself, "Did I do the best I could? Am I doing the best I can?" as opposed to "Am I the best?" Who defines that, anyway? Remember, we will never make everyone happy, and we don't have to.
4. Set attainable goals, reach them, and celebrate all the bumps along the way.
5. Letting go of perfectionism may require you to change your internal dialogue. Start talking to yourself differently. No more undermining, negative conversations with yourself. This may take practice!
6. Know what your personal payoff is for being a perfectionist. These can be endless. For some it could be having a great deal of control. For others, perfectionism offers predictability—if you aim for perfection, you know that you're inevitably going to fail. Perfectionism does not serve any purpose well. It promotes misery and dissatisfaction. It prevents you from learning from success. If you can see

that it harms you, you can let go of it. Perfectionism can justify our low self-worth and sense of disapproval. When we are unable to fulfill our perfect goals, we get to say, for example, "I knew I wasn't smart enough to get that job."

7. Define what true fulfillment means to you. Perfectionism appears to offer a beautiful vision of fulfillment—we imagine a perfect life once we have refined ourselves enough to be worthy of it. Why wait? You're worthy of a great life, so work out what you want from life and get out there and create it. There is no perfect way of creating a great life; you have to find what works for you by trial and error.

8. Forgive yourself because you love yourself. Another reason for choosing to be perfectionistic is that deep down we know we are bound to fail. It is impossible to be perfect, so we are not to blame for falling short. We don't have to take responsibility.

9. Don't let the search for the ideal life get blocked by perfectionism. Practice being okay with who you are and where you are in your life. Keep taking steps to create the life you love and enjoy the journey. Accept that the life you have now is perfect for teaching the lessons you need to get to the next stage.

PRACTICAL INTELLIGENCE

WITH THE SUN in Virgo, you are especially attuned to the element of earth. This element is concerned with concrete reality, sensory perception, and feeling most comfortable in the world of the five senses—forget the sixth sense unless you have a substantial dose of the element water in your chart. Whatever cannot be touched, heard, smelled, seen, or tasted is either denied or made as concrete and tangible as possible. The sun in earth is a consciousness sold on physical security—on the here and now. And the search for security can often tend to make one a little too conservative and practical.

Ruled by Mercury, Virgo is infused with intelligence. Like its flightier cousin, Gemini (also ruled by Mercury), Virgo is a mental sign. However, Virgo's Mercurial intelligence is directed toward practical matters and practical solutions. Sun in Virgo desperately wants to be of practical service by fixing things, situations, or people. Virgo also enjoys focusing on the very smallest of details.

Virgoans are intellectually inquiring, methodical, and logical. They combine mental ingenuity with the ability to produce a clear analysis of the most complicated problems. They have an excellent eye for detail, but they may be so meticulous that they neglect larger issues. They are practical with their hands, good technicians, and have genuine inventive talents. Thoroughness, hard work, and conscientiousness are their hallmarks, and they are studious and easy to teach.

Virgoans are such perfectionists that if things go wrong they are easily discouraged. Due to their innate ability to see every angle of a many-sided question, they are unhappy with abstract theorizing. Appreciating the many different points of view as they do, they find philosophical concepts difficult—they tend vacillate and have no confidence in any conclusions at which they arrive. If this applies to you, Virgo, look at the Decisions, Decisions exercise in Aries (page 19), and What Commitments Do You Have? and How Balanced Are You? in Libra (pages 187 and 188).

COACH'S TIP

You are a great one for helping others, Virgo, but you may find it hard to let others help you, and this leads to unbalanced relationships—do you really want to be surrounded by lazy, needy people?

Try to let others help you—most people gain satisfaction and worth from being able to lend a helping hand. Use the free time you gain creatively, Virgo.

For an exercise to help you make the best of these good points, see S.M.A.R.T.est Goals for Aries (page 3).

STRENGTHS TO FOCUS ON

◆ **Sympathy**
◆ **Gentle with the helpless**

▶ **Organized**

▶ **Humane and helpful**

▶ **Painstaking, methodical, and exact**

▶ **Physically sensual**

▶ **Dedicated and industrious**

▶ **Emotionally warm**

▶ **Witty and charming**

▶ **Discriminating**

WEAKNESSES THAT CAN TRIP YOU UP

▶ **Scathing criticism of self and others**

▶ **Dogmatic**

▶ **Untidy**

▶ **Prudish**

▶ **Eccentric**

▶ **Undemonstrative, fears dependency**

▶ **Nervous and worried**

▶ **Hypochondriac**

▶ **Overly demanding**

So how do you turn these so-called negative traits into powerful tools for personal growth? Look at the Love Your Weaknesses exercise in Aries (page 6) to take your life to the next level, Virgo.

A FEW TIPS FOR A HAPPIER LIFE

- ◆ Do not be a know-it-all. Give others an opportunity to shine and display their expertise.
- ◆ Do not let perfectionism get in the way of living a fulfilling life.
- ◆ Create space for yourself and do not let others cross your boundaries and invade it. See The Magnificent Seven Steps to Setting Boundaries exercise in Taurus (page 48).
- ◆ Do not abuse your talent for making intelligent criticism, Virgo. Remember to remark on others' good points as well. Do not criticize yourself beyond what is constructive and

healthy. Remember to congratulate yourself when you've done well. This will build healthy self-esteem.

THE HIDDEN (OR NOT-SO-HIDDEN) VIRGO

INSIDE ANYONE WITH strong Virgo tendencies lurks a perfectionist who works too hard to mask their imagined inadequacies and lack of confidence. Virgoans are also driven by the need to serve others and a love of detail

A well-kept Virgoan secret is the fact that this sign has a strong, volcanic sexuality that is lying dormant, waiting for the right partner to unleash it.

VIRGO MAN

Unless there are influences in his birth chart that are stronger than his Virgo sun sign, the typical Virgo male will have some or all of the following characteristics:

- Is generally not a leader
- Lives simply
- Has high standards, can be critical
- Is careful with finances
- Is good at crisis management
- Is practical and unsentimental
- Is likely to be devoted to serving those less fortunate than himself
- Is accurate and methodical
- Is subtle and rarely obvious about his intentions
- May relax by working a little less hard than usual
- Takes his responsibilities seriously
- Instinctively loves his work

VIRGO WOMAN

In addition to the personality and behavior traits exhibited by the Virgoan male, Virgo woman:

- Is not very fond of children
- Is ingenious
- Can recognize the potential of others
- Is discriminating
- Is highly intelligent
- Can analyze situations in detail
- Is devoted to her work, usually serving others in some way
- Has incredible strength of purpose
- Will pursue happiness
- Is pure-minded, but not naive
- Believes herself to be more orderly and efficient than other people
- Can be soothing one moment and critical the next
- Is basically rather shy

VIRGO LIKES

- Muted, subtle colors and textures
- Sensible, tailored clothes
- Being of service to others and being appreciated
- Attending to the smallest details
- Very small animals
- Punctuality
- Self-improvement courses
- Making lists
- Grooming and self-care
- Mimicking others
- A well-stocked medicine cabinet

VIRGO DISLIKES

- Being under an obligation
- Slang, vulgarity, dirt, and slovenliness
- Crowds, loud, brash people
- Lids left off boxes, containers, and toothpaste, or toilet seats left open!
- Sitting still
- Disrupted schedules

- **Bright, bold, primary colors**
- **Having their personal possessions moved**
- **Any admission of weakness or failure**
- **Hypocrisy or deceit**
- **Whiners and complainers**

POSSIBLE PROBLEM AREAS FOR VIRGO, AND SOLUTIONS

All sun signs have unique personality traits. When these traits are suppressed, problems will arise. However, with a winning combination of astrology and coaching, we can examine the problem and assess the proper solution based on sun sign characteristics. If, as a Virgo, you see things below that really strike home, try the solution. You may be amazed at the results.

PROBLEM: Being unable to keep friends for more than a few weeks.

SOLUTION: Try to be less argumentative and cut the constant criticism that Virgos give to their companions. These are really not endearing qualities.

PROBLEM: People getting "turned off" by you.

SOLUTION: You can appear to be too preoccupied with health and make it a continual topic of conversation. Try to keep your tips and suggestions about health and health products to yourself unless asked for them.

PROBLEM: Dissatisfaction with the way your life is turning out—no excitement or change to speak of.

SOLUTION: You may be restricting yourself by reducing your life to a set of theories. Try to express the positive by asking yourself who or what you are serving. Are you devoted or are you enslaved? Now start a new path that includes your true worth.

PROBLEM: You may feel that your life is a steep hill that you will never be able to scale.

SOLUTION: Try to curb the perfectionist trait that causes you to give up at the first hurdle.

CAREER/BUSINESS

THOSE born under Virgo love to analyze and mull ideas over, and they are bound to come up with some answers. Their minds are such that they need the stimulus of practical problems to be solved rather than the mere routine of working to set specifications that need no thought. The mental, smart Virgo is also a talker and a helper and likes to facilitate solutions as a service to others. That said, Virgos crave independence and a space of their own, so don't expect them to be completely open with you—for them, some things are best kept private.

Members of this sign are pragmatic and realistic and will set practical, achievable goals for themselves and on their team. Virgos are task-oriented and highly organized, very loyal colleagues and often the conscience of their group. They will get things done but are often reluctant to take the credit. The Virgo's perfectionism can often lead to nervousness and ill health, so achieving balance is a lesson that must be learned.

If there's one thing a Virgo can do (and they can usually do plenty, thanks to their strong work ethic), it's to create a winning team. Their discerning eye and evaluating style is hard to beat. Virgos find it easy and a pleasure to be the thinker, problem solver, organizer, and supporter of the team. When Virgos remember to criticize less and emphasize the positives more, they are superb as team players.

Virgoans tend to make better subordinates than leaders. Responsibility irritates them and they often lack the breadth of strategic vision that a leader needs. They are essentially tacticians, admirable in the attainment of limited objectives. Their self-distrust is something they have a tendency to project onto other people, which makes them exacting employers. Most Virgos do, however, temper with justice the demands they make on those under them.

Virgoans have potential abilities in the arts, sciences, and languages, so a wide range of careers is open to them. They are, however, better suited to working in an office environment than in a workshop.

Their faults, as is usual with all zodiacal types, are the extremes of their virtues. Balanced criticism becomes harping and nagging; and concern for detail becomes overspecialization. Virgoans are liable to indecision in wider issues, and this can become chronic, leading to paralysis of analysis. Their carefulness, if turned in on themselves, can produce worriers and hypochondriacs.

The Virgo office is highly organized, with a battery of computers and other electronic gadgetry for maximum efficiency. When a car is required, Virgo will go for a model that is both elegant and reliable. If it's time to talk business, take the Virgo out for a light salad in a squeaky-clean restaurant, and you're bound to get results.

Virgos are well suited to be chemists, doctors, nutritionists, managers and entrepreneurs, and veterinarians—they especially like working with small animals.

VIRGO CAREER GUIDE

Here are some occupations that a Virgo might consider:

Accountant	Dental hygienist	Porter
Aide	Dietician	Programmer
Airline attendant	Doctor	Proofreader
Auditor	Draftsman	Psychologist
Bookkeeper	Dressmaker	Record keeper
Busboy	Dry cleaner	Repairer
Butler	Engineer	Scientist
Caretaker	File clerk	Secretary
Carpenter	Food server	Statistician
Chiropractor	Healer	Surveyor
Civil servant	Housekeeper	Systems analyst
Cleaner	Information	Technician
Clerk	processor	Usher
Computer analyst	Inspector	Valet
Contractor	Mental health	Volunteer
Copy editor	worker	Waiter
Craftsperson	Nurse	Welder
Critic	Personal assistant	
Data operator	Pharmacist	

VIRGO BOSS

YOU TEND TO lead by example rather than by forceful assertion of your views. You aim to be perfect and expect the same of others, taking on superhuman amounts of work in the expectation that others will do the same. While you are prepared to let employees have a reasonable degree of autonomy, you fly into a panic at the first sign of carelessness and are likely to be worried and irritable until standards return to normal.

Beware of a tendency to be so obsessed with perfecting your own performance that you neglect to monitor that of others. In order to thrive and stay sane, you'll need to surround yourself with people who are neat, disciplined, and never sloppy about their work. Try not to be so critical that you either lose or demoralize valuable members of your staff. You also need to steer clear of focusing so intently on detail that you fail to free your mind enough to produce the imaginative objectives required to acquire future business.

Avoid large organizations and positions of responsibility, as you will overload on detail and try to make everything perfect—policing and politics are not for the virgin. You will detest being distracted from your productive day-to-day practices by all the troubleshooting, irregular meetings, and schmoozing required of senior corporate players. Stick to leading a small work group where you can drive your team to precision without stressing yourself out.

As your work is important to you, put plenty of effort into ensuring that your job is satisfying, not just okay. To help you with this, try a logical, methodical exercise for you to work with called Career-U-Like, which can be found in the Taurus chapter (page 53).

COACH'S TIP

No one is indispensable, not even you. Find out what you really value and take the time to pursue it. Avoid workaholism—if you find yourself immersed in your work, ask yourself what you are afraid of finding—or of finding you—during your leisure time. Do not fob yourself off with a trite or facile answer.

Let go of any need to criticize others—apply your sharp, analytical mind to working out what you want in the future and go for it.

VIRGO EMPLOYEE

YOU ARE A dream employee with your attention to detail and commitment to serving others. Employers are more than happy to leave you unsupervised, which is when you are at your most productive, due to your focus on your own duties, sense of responsibility, high standards, ethics, and loyalty. Everyone should recognize that your value to the company lies in your ability to keep the practical side of the business running smoothly. You know all the facts about the business and are a walking knowledge-management system, as you know where every key piece of information resides.

Negotiating is not your forte, as you detest any criticism of your own ideas and you tend be too reserved to relish imposing your ideas on others. During negotiation, you can do one of three things—give away your entire hand, antagonize others by the forcefulness of your criticism of opposing views, or withdraw completely from the fray. You do not tend to adjust well to sudden changes in agenda or thought, and creative compromises do not come easily to you. If you do need to negotiate, read the exercises Preparing for Negotiation in the Aries chapter (page 25). Here is a further exercise that will appeal to many of you.

EXERCISE ONE

The 100 Point Guide to Negotiating

MOST OF us fall into one of two categories when it comes to getting things done: those who focus on what needs to be accomplished and those who focus on relationships, or the people they're doing things with. This provides us with a simple way of looking at negotiating.

1. Think of a meeting or phone call that you have coming up soon.
2. Now take a piece of paper and draw a line down the middle of it to form two columns. At the top of one column, write "Task/Outcome," and at the top of the other write "Relationships."
3. Now, looking at all the various people and elements involved in the task, imagine that you have 100 points to distribute between the two columns. How are you going to distribute them? What are your priorities? For example, I might place less emphasis (points) on developing a relationship with someone with whom I already do business because I already have a good working relationship with them. If I'm dealing with a potential client or supplier for the first time (and am looking to work with them on a long-term basis) I will place a great deal more emphasis on building up a relationship with them than in the previous example.

The value of this exercise is not only in helping you to prepare for your meeting but also in realizing that there are certain circumstances in which placing your focus on the opposite side from where you usually place it (i.e., emphasizing relationship building where you might otherwise have pushed for a quick result, or vice versa) can be a powerful and effective tool.

You tend to do better in an established concern than going it alone (unless there is a lot of fire in your chart), as you will tend to find plenty of reasons for not taking appropriate action. You may also lack the vision and confidence needed to get a fledgling enterprise off the ground or you may get too bogged down in detail. If you are going to set up a business, Virgo, go into partnership with an ideas person with plenty of initiative or get an advisor or coach who has successfully done what you seek to achieve.

If unemployment strikes, turn looking for a job into a job itself—you will find work in the end. Accept that it may take a while and use the time constructively. Losing your job does not mean that there is anything wrong with you.

COACH'S TIP

> Your biggest impediment to getting ahead professionally is
> assuming that others are more qualified for a job than you are.
> That's your critical, perfectionist nature getting in the way
> again. Nine out of ten times you are better qualified than they
> are. You need to highlight your achievements, dear Virgo,
> because your competitors certainly won't. Occasionally send
> out a status report so that your boss can keep abreast of your
> progress. If you are self-employed, draw up a press release and
> get a story written about your company in a local newspaper.

FINANCES AND WEALTH

VIRGOS are usually very good with money. Those born under this sign are blessed with common sense and self-reliance and manage their money (and that of others) very well. The accounts will always be in order, and most Virgos can really stretch cash flow, knowing exactly which creditors can be held off for a while.

The virgin hates wasting money, so will think long and hard before making an investment. Having money in the bank is a bonus for Virgos, since it will eliminate one more worry. While money isn't the most important thing in life to the virgin, Virgos will definitely save for a rainy day and don't mind working hard to do so, especially since it keeps them from having to depend on others—a perennial Virgo concern.

The virgin is also a budgeting magician, someone who knows how to live on little and still have fun. A Virgo can tell you that "some of the best things in life are free" and really mean it. Virgos are rarely big spenders, hate to borrow, and hate to lend money even more. About the only person they'll lend to is a family member in need or, even more rarely, someone who they're sure will pay them back.

A regular paycheck is an absolute must for Virgo, and if it's paid weekly, even better. Freelancing and other forms of self-employment are really not for the wise virgin.

Virgo is prudent and wise where money is concerned. No risks for you, that's for sure. Ask a Virgo what she spent today, and she'll be able to tell you down to the last penny, like her fellow earth sign, Taurus. After all, detail is your middle name. When a product breaks down, Virgo has the receipt to prove the warranty is still in effect—which never fails to save you money. When it comes to shopping, Virgo carefully compares manufacturers and prices, and knows all the benefits and drawbacks of each product. If you're buying a big-ticket item, you probably like to check magazine articles for test results before you buy. Your ability to research and attend to detail are your greatest strengths when it comes to handling finances. Virgos pay their bills on time and aren't into heavy consumerism or a flashy lifestyle, so are most unlikely to become trapped by debt.

You demand value for your money, simply because you work extremely hard for your cash and do not intend to squander it. Your biggest expenditure is usually a health-club membership, vitamins (Virgoans like to stay healthy) or computer equipment (Virgoans like to write and also enjoy being organized). As an earth sign, you are realistic about money. You know what you can afford, what it is sensible to pay, and when to say no to a new purchase. You spend wisely and you usually have enough money when you need it. Virgo understands that money stress is draining and unnecessary. Virgoans place a high value on productivity and tend to banish anything that gets in the way of it.

You might also want to try the Determine Your Value exercise in the Capricorn chapter (page 274) and White Knuckle Finances for Taurus (page 56), if your money isn't working as hard as it could.

COACH'S TIP

You know that if you should find yourself in a financial jam, you can rely on your intelligence and analytical ability to find a resourceful solution.

The fear that makes you hang onto your cash could be repelling money from you. I know that as a mutable sign you are more sensitive than most to the ebb and flow of the value of your assets, but if you appear "closed" and untrusting, people will not trust you and you will be deprived of potential opportunities to make more money. Relax, be prepared to give, and in so doing create a space for yourself to receive.

LOVE, ROMANCE, AND SEX LIFE

DEEP inside this hardened pragmatist there is a romantic who is yearning for passionate romance. Your ruling planet, Mercury, symbolizes communication, and Virgos are possessed of an ability to reason clearly, resolve issues, and take a romance to new heights. The Virgoan can, at times, be shy and repressed, with a well-hidden, smoldering sexuality. Someone who can bring Virgo out of these depths will be rewarded with a vibrant lover.

Virgo's easygoing nature and earthy qualities make for a reliable and steady partner who relishes the opportunity to be helpful to their partner. The virgin's devotedness means that a great deal of energy will go into making the relationship work. Those born under this sign tend to strive for the perfect relationship. They may also refuse to admit defeat when a relationship has clearly run its course.

WHAT VIRGO NEEDS

THE STRIVING ACHIEVER that is Virgo yearns for someone who can play at their level. Virgoans will often indulge in sports with a partner, and may even use sport as a kind of foreplay, since the virgin adores the one who shares their love of good health and excellence. Those born under this sign want and need a strong and free lover who will draw them out and acquaint them with sexual pleasure. Virgo needs a partner who is secure, can take the initiative, and can easily communicate sexual and romantic feelings. If Virgo mates with someone who will have sex at the beach as readily as in the bedroom, it can be a match made in heaven.

With Virgo, it's all in the details and doing things right. The caring and romantic virgin knows that the small things in life and love do count. Couple that with an eagerness to serve, and Virgo's lucky lover is in for a wonderful time.

COMPATIBILITY

SCORPIOS AND CANCERS are best for you, with mystical Pisces a close second. You'll find Gemini too taxing and are likely to find fault with fellow earth signs Taurus and Capricorn. The impulsiveness of fire signs Aries, Leo, and Sagittarius will depress you.

THE END OF THE AFFAIR

VIRGOS ARE VERY loyal and will try to avoid ending a long-term affair or marriage wherever possible—they also hate giving up and admitting defeat. Some Virgoans may keep trying repeatedly to make an unsuitable affair work rather than being pragmatic and cutting their losses. Although Virgo is a mutable sign, you can have a tendency to remain stuck in a rut, unless circumstances force you to change, yet when you have change forced upon you, you adapt very well.

However, it is rare for a Virgo to linger when a marriage really has failed. If sensible discussion does not resolve the issues, or if Virgo's sense of fair play is affronted, then a clean and final break will be made. This sign does not usually go for reconciliation and is virtually impossible to manipulate into starting the relationship again. If there are children involved, however, Virgo will see to it that they are properly educated.

WHAT VIRGO NEEDS TO LEARN

THE SEXUAL SIDE of relationships is very important to you. Do not allow your need for control and knowledge to snuff out your sensual side. You also need love and adventure, so don't shut these out of your life when they come your way.

Allow yourself to become more spontaneous—take a few risks. The world won't come to an end if you let yourself go a little.

Let others help you—it's good for both of you.

Never allow misplaced feelings of guilt to keep you stuck. Accept responsibility for whatever part you have played and move on.

Don't let your passion for accuracy and perfection get in the way of your passionate relationships. Try not to be critical—ask for changes without criticizing the other person.

Get more comfortable with emotions—yours and other people's. If emotional displays frighten you, find out why and do something about it.

To help avoid others' tendency to take advantage of you, try The Magnificent Seven Steps to Setting Boundaries exercise from Taurus (page 48), Developing Self-confidence (page 293) and The Magic of Random Belief (page 309) from Aquarius, and Getting Your Needs Met from Cancer (page 116).

RELATIONSHIPS
(Family and Friends)

VIRGO PARENT

THE TYPICAL VIRGO parent encourages children to ask questions and will explain the reasons for requests that he or she makes to them. He or she supports practical activities during free time and can adapt to almost any practical demand but may get upset by dirt and untidiness and may also find it hard to express affection. However, Virgos will do anything to help their children. They tend to worry about their children's health.

COACH'S TIP

Do not let accusations of selfishness induce you to have more children than you can handle.

Accept that it is important to express physical affection toward children, so put daily hugs on your "to-do" list until this activity becomes second nature to you.

Let your child teach you how to let go, relax, and play—you may find your creativity level rising as a result.

Try not to expect too much of either yourself as a parent or your children.

Allow your children to teach you how to have some fun.
Alternatively, have a look at the Do You Have Enough Fun?
exercise in Capricorn (page 268).

VIRGO CHILD

THE VIRGO CHILD is industrious, so you can bet that a lot is going to be achieved when they're around. This is a child who can make play look like work, and vice versa, so you may not be sure exactly what the state of play is! This hardly matters, for the Virgo child is usually content with, and fully absorbed by, the task at hand, whether it's straightening up the bedroom or playing chess. Scientific and methodical, the Virgo child is likely to be drawn to more involved projects such as cataloging their CD collection or planting a garden. And those plants will flourish, for Virgo is a great nurturer and a perfectionist who doesn't know the meaning of the word "failure."

Along with this quest for excellence comes a penchant for making sure that everything is just so, so the Virgo child's best intentions may often be misinterpreted. It isn't that this child doesn't want to eat vegetables; it's just that they have to be the tastiest vegetables around. (A nervous stomach may also be part of this child's makeup.) Forever tidy, the Virgo child will have a neat room, and they'll also straighten up the rest of the house, arranging things as they see fit.

BRINGING UP VIRGO—COACH'S INSIGHT

YOUNG VIRGO AIMS to please, so as long as they know what is required, you can expect a relatively easy ride. There may be a few problems when they become aware of the opposite sex, as Virgoans often find close sexual relationships very difficult. Some of this stems from a lack of self-confidence, which can be averted with plenty of genuine praise and encouragement. You may need to convince your Virgo teen that they are attractive—many see themselves as absolutely hideous—in order to help the course of true love run smoothly. No teasing, as this may cause your Virgo to withdraw completely and remain single.

Teach Virgo how to use his or her imagination through the use of fairy tales, myths, and make-believe—give your youngster the resources to cope with those moments of loneliness that afflict us all. Show Virgo that imagination is useful. You might like to talk about the great strides that have been made by people who really think outside the box.

Kindly but firmly coach your Virgoan youngster to refrain from criticizing or judging others—we all need to practice a little tolerance when living and working with others.

VIRGO AND FRIENDS

VIRGOS ARE DRAWN to friends who are tidy, clean, and intelligent, with a broad range of interests. They are attracted to people who radiate calmness and who are not prone to great displays of emotion.

Virgoans love theater and pageantry, which allows them to vent their cleverly masked emotions. They also adore fine art, have discerning taste, and are a wealth of information on many subjects.

Like their fellow earth signs, Taurus and Capricorn, Virgoans are loyal to their friends and will be extremely kind, considerate, and helpful.

FRIENDS, BE AWARE

MOST VIRGOS FIND it impossible to admit mistakes but are more than ready to point out others' failings. You will, therefore, occasionally need to soften Virgo's harsh, supercritical remarks with laughter in order to avoid being hurt.

COACH'S TIP

Virgo needs to avoid friends who are worriers, as this will reduce the virgin to a nervous wreck.

You also need to extend your social circle beyond your partner, if you have one, and coworkers. Make sure that work doesn't prevent you from having a social life.

If you are looking to meet new people, try offering your services to those in need. That way you will satisfy your desire to serve and be practical, in addition to meeting inter-esting people in a relaxed setting. However, remember that you cannot fix other people—they have to make their own mistakes. Offer advice only when asked and do not take it personally if your advice is not acted upon.

Try to offer sincere compliments, as many people really appreciate them. Given time, seeing people's good points will become second nature, making "connecting" with them so much easier.

Finally, build some "me" time into your life. We all need periods of seclusion to reflect, recharge our batteries, and sort things out.

HEALTH

YOU are highly goal-oriented; few things will deter you from fin-ishing what you've started. You are able to concentrate, no matter what the distractions. Be sure the things you devote yourself to are worthy of your hard work. If you find you are tripping yourself up consistently, have a look at the Avoiding Self-sabotage exercise in Taurus (page 70). You may also get so involved in detail that you miss the long view of things. Step back every so often and reassess your assumptions. See if you can delegate some of your work. This is often hard for Virgo, but you will free up lots of time, as well as relieve some daily pressure. Just because you are able to stand a great deal of tension, doesn't mean you ought to live with it.

When stress strikes, Virgo feels a need to be in control of its overall physical environment. You'll want to withdraw into yourself to brainstorm, weigh the options, and plot your course (Virgo is nothing if not analytical.) A worrier sign, like Cancer, Virgo can often chew on problems too long and too much. Unlike Cancerians, however, who rely on intuition, earth sign Virgo prefers to rely on logic and practical solutions. You'll go to extreme lengths to be thorough, investing considerable time in studying your problem, and leaving no stone unturned. You can, however, overanalyze and end up completely immobilized because no answer seems 100 percent right. Both Virgo and Gemini are ruled by Mercury, and therefore highly communicative and intelligent. Gemini will ask questions of people around them to get an empirical feel of the situation and to assemble their plan of action. Virgo prefers to rely on documented studies and facts. Virgo is more pragmatic than Gemini but less flexible.

STRESS BUSTING FOR VIRGO

YOUR VERY BEST course of action for dealing with tension is to thoroughly clear it out. Get your physical environment under control and you'll feel enormously better. Organizing is immensely therapeutic for you, for your environment is always an accurate reflection of your inner state of mind. Throw out anything you no longer need, reorganize your possessions, and get new boxes to store things in. You need to feel productive, and you like being physical as you think. Just imagining your organized living and working space will make you breathe easier.

Virgo rules the lower stomach and intestines, and this is where you feel the most tension when you are anxious. As a result, you will find digestion difficult when under stress, so eat lightly. Unlike Cancer, who will crave childhood foods, you will want to eat more leafy green vegetables and fruits, and may even decide to be a vegetarian for a while. A diet light in fats, which are hard for your body to break down, would be best when you are tense.

Keep a journal; write your thoughts down on paper. Like Gemini, you can use your distress to create a moving literary piece. Pour your emotions and tension onto the page, write it all out of your system—you'll feel much better.

Using your hands (another part of the body that Mercury rules) in a variety of hobbies will relax and soothe you. While you work, you'll be able to think more clearly.

Chess, quiz games, and crossword or jigsaw puzzles may appeal to you too, since Virgo is a sign that enjoys mental challenges. Try board games such as Scrabble, Scruples (moral or ethical battles fascinate you), or complex card games like bridge to distract you. Finally, your sign rules small animals, and most Virgos make loving pet owners. If you have a pet, play with it. This could be the time to adopt a new puppy or kitten. If you don't have room for a pet, why not go to an animal sanctuary and offer to help out for a while?

As a Virgo, you are the sole mutable sign of the four earth signs, and therefore the most able to weather change. So relax, sure in the knowledge that whatever life throws at you, you will cope admirably.

FITNESS

VIRGO RULES THE spleen, abdominal organs, duodenum, colon, nails, and small intestine. Your metabolism is high.

As mentioned above, Virgo's lower stomach (intestinal tract) is the first part of his or her body to feel stress. Before you head for the medicine chest, try making changes in your lifestyle that can prevent these attacks. Meditation and an exercise program that emphasizes total body relaxation and proper alignment will appeal to your perfectionist tendencies, while combating their inevitable physical effects.

Learn to delegate work and responsibilities that get in the way of your leading a healthy and fulfilling life. You need to be healthy to perform at your best, so let go of the perfectionist tendencies if you can, or at least consciously police them. Remember to allow for the fact that people will always do things on their own schedule, not yours.

Although you have a high metabolism and rarely put on weight, you need to be careful about your diet. Of all the signs, you tend to eat the most fresh fruit and vegetables—hardly surprising, since Virgo rules the autumn harvest. Many Virgos are vegetarian. Just be sure you are getting a wide variety of all the right foods to be sure you are not lacking iron, or any other nutrient, in your diet.

A word of caution for those Virgoans on a diet: Don't dump your diet just because of one transgression. Be compassionate with yourself, congratulate yourself on progress made, and pick up where you left off. Keep a food diary, or draw up a chart of your progress at the gym to help you see how much improvement you've made. Remember that one of your best qualities is endurance. Since Virgos need all the de-stressing they can get, add some easy, pleasant exercises like biking or walking to your routine, just for the fun of it.

Most importantly, distract yourself now and then. Virgo worries far too much. You run the risk of going a little overboard and getting somewhat compulsive.

Tools for Making a Difference

As the hardworking Virgo can attain most goals that they aim for, one of Virgo's challenges is to choose which goals are worthy of your effort. Many of my Virgoan clients come to me, having climbed to the greatest heights, only to find that they have conquered the wrong summit. This can lead Virgoans to self-sabotage without knowing why. If you are prone to self-sabotage, see the Avoiding Self-sabotage exercise in Taurus (page 70).

Virgoans can also find themselves embracing someone else's values and ethics without ever knowing why. They may end up living a deeply unfulfilling life, due to outmoded concepts of what is right and wrong. Try the Define Your Values exercise in Aries (page 20) and try the following one.

EXERCISE TWO

Developing Awareness

BE HONEST with yourself when carrying out this exercise, carry it out on a regular basis, and expect your answers to change as you do. Ask yourself the following questions:

- ◆ What are my ten top priorities in life? Why?
- ◆ Am I doing or have I done what is most important to me? If not, why not?
- ◆ Do I enjoy life? What do I enjoy? What do I not enjoy? How can I make my life more enjoyable?
- ◆ What do I feel about my relationship with my partner? How important is it to me? What do like about it? What do I dislike about it? What do I want to change?
- ◆ In what ways does my relationship with my lover resemble that of my parents? What parts of my behavior in this relationship do I like? Dislike? Do I want to change any part of my behavior? If so, what and how? Can I expect cooperation?
- ◆ Who is my best friend? What do I see in this person? What do I give my best friend and what do I receive from him/her? Am I satisfied with this friendship? If not, what needs improving?
- ◆ How often do I relax? Is it often enough? Do I need to make any lifestyle changes? If so, what and how?

Learning to appreciate your own worth will help to restore the balance in your life, as will learning when to step back and allow others to succeed or fail on their own merits.

Hang around with your opposite sign, Pisces. From Pisces you will learn how to let go and go with the flow, giving imagination a chance to develop. In this way, you will become far more tolerant of imperfections, especially your own.

Virgo must also learn to prioritize, for all tasks and activities are not of equal merit. This becomes easier once you know what your ethics and values are, Virgo, and commit to building your life around them.

You must also learn not to become so obsessed with detail that you fail to see the big picture.

SPIRITUALITY

AS YOU STRIVE for spiritual perfection, you encounter the lesson of acceptance. From self-acceptance you move to tolerance for others. When you realize that the only hope for humanity lies in each one of us developing our unique strengths and talents, you will find it easier to fine-tune your own spiritual path.

You are also here to grasp the connection between mind and body, for no other sign is better equipped to do so, and to help others apply the connection in their own lives. Virgo's challenge is to bring matters under the control of mind and to do so in a positive way.

The evolved Virgo is capable of great vision and incredible intuition. As a sun in Virgo, you are likely to weigh up different spiritual beliefs until you find one that appeals to your eminently practical side.

CHAPTER 7

LIBRA

September 23–22 October 22

THE SEVENTH SIGN OF THE ZODIAC IS CONCERNED WITH:

- ◆ PARTNERSHIPS, CLOSE RELATIONSHIPS, ROMANCE
- ◆ IDEAS, OPINIONS, RATIONAL THOUGHTS, IDEAS FOR THE GOOD OF HUMANITY
- ◆ POLITICS, DIPLOMACY, TACT, SELF-CONTROL
- ◆ REFINEMENT, SOPHISTICATION, GOOD TASTE, GOOD MANNERS, PERSONAL APPEARANCE
- ◆ MUSIC, HARMONY
- ◆ SELF-CONTROL, BALANCE

RULED by the planet Venus and symbolized by the scales of justice, Libra is concerned with evaluating, making choices, weighing up the evidence, and maintaining balance. Librans can see all the many sides of an argument or issue. And in the interests of fair play, Librans don't really like making a final decision until every last bit of the data has been collected and scrutinized. Everything and everyone is open to analysis. Unfortunately, Libra knows that there's always one more key piece of information, which could be gathered, if only enough time were given. . . . This can lead to an attack of paralysis of analysis in which Libra finds itself unable to make a decision of any sort because it cannot stop weighing options and desperately seeking more data.

Librans are sociable individuals and sensitive to what's going on around them, unless there are other influences in their natal chart

militating against this. Libra's sense of inner harmony is closely
related to (and affected by) what's going on around them. Dishar-
mony, arguments, and disputes going on in the immediate environment disturb Libra's sense of equilibrium. Librans can find
themselves taking on a peacemaker role or backing down from an
argument, in order to attain a sense of inner harmony.

Social interaction with other people is vital to Libra. The Libran
social life centers on Libra's fascination with ideas, attitudes, opinions, and beliefs. Other people act as reflective mirrors through
which Librans can learn more about their own ideas and thoughts.
Librans generally discover what they think about a particular matter or situation after listening fully to what other people think and
have to say on the matter. As the cardinal air sign of the zodiac,
Libra is here to translate ideas into action.

Due to Libra's need to be in full possession of all the facts before
making a move, I frequently find myself coaching Libran clients on
decision making. The following are some of the exercises I use.

EXERCISE ONE

What Commitments Do You Have?

ONE of the first steps you can take to balance your life is to identify all those commitments that you are trying to juggle. For many
of you, there will be more than one hundred.

Write down all the needs and commitments you are trying to
juggle, for example, career, social obligations, religious commitments, relaxing, and having fun, PTA, second jobs, volunteer
work—you get the idea.

Next, work out which of these you really need to keep doing. Get
rid of the rest. We're talking streamlining here.

Group them into related areas, for example, family, work, and
self. You should be able to place everything into one of these categories.

Each day, before you even think about scheduling the "must-
dos," write down one thing in each of the three categories that you

will do on that day. Make sure that you do those things—this will begin to make you focus on these areas of your life.

In addition to this, take thirty minutes, once a week, to see how you are getting on with balancing your life. Is there one area that is being consistently neglected? If so, take immediate action to remedy this. This is a great time for deciding what are the major things in the three areas that you wish to accomplish during the coming week. You can also, should you wish, do this on a month-to-month basis, deciding what you want to accomplish each week.

By devoting time to this exercise, you will find that your life becomes more balanced and that your happiness and self-esteem is not totally dependent on one area of your life. This exercise also enables you to balance left-brain goals—i.e., the goals of getting things done, with lists and logic, with right-brain goals that involve intuition, creativity, and relationships.

EXERCISE TWO

How Balanced Are You?

Would you consider yourself to be more preoccupied with structure or spontaneity, work or relationships? Are you more concerned with achieving or what others think of you? By carrying out this exercise, you will begin to get an idea of how balanced you are.

Now answer the following questions, making a note of which ones you find it difficult to answer:

A

◆ What is the most recent salary rise or promotion you have had at work?

◆ Name one area in which your talent exceeds that of your colleagues.

◆ Name two goals that you want to accomplish over the next year.

- What are your main challenges at work?
- Do you have a five-year plan for your career?

B

- What are the last three books you read that did not relate to work?
- Name one parenting or relating talent that you have.
- What are your main challenges within your relationships?
- When did you last do something creative, for example, writing poetry or painting?
- Do you have a five-year plan for your marriage?

C

- What was your most important accomplishment last week?
- What was the last thing that really excited you?
- What is your favorite time-management system?
- Do you routinely make "to-do" lists?
- Are you analytical?

D

- What did you do this week that was completely spontaneous?
- When did you last feel totally relaxed?
- When was the last time you let go and howled with laughter?
- When did you last have an in-depth discussion about a topic unrelated to work?
- When was the last time you felt deeply moved by something, for example, the sheer joy of being alive?

E

- Name your latest possession.
- If money were no object, what would you like to buy?
- When did you last pick up the phone or use E-mail?
- Whom do you feel envious of?
- Name your three newest useful business contacts.

F

- ✦ Name two people whom you would like as friends because they seem interesting.
- ✦ Name two people who've opened up to you lately.
- ✦ Think of your best friend. What is his or her greatest need?
- ✦ What is the latest thing you have done to gain privacy or time to yourself?
- ✦ When was the last time you had an interesting conversation with a stranger?

Okay, so which did you find easier?

If you found the questions in A easier to answer than those in B, you are more concerned with work and career than family and personal growth.

Finding Cs easier to answer than Ds suggests a tendency toward rigidity and structure at the expense of spontaneity and vice versa.

Easier Es suggests that you may be highly achievement-oriented. If you find the Fs easier to answer, you may need to beware of allowing peer pressure to hold you back.

By doing this exercise, you have begun to identify the areas you will need to work on if you are to create within yourself the qualities of discipline and flexibility, structure and spontaneity. Developing an attitude that allows us to balance the logical left brain with the creative and intuitive right brain enables us to have the best of both worlds.

STRENGTHS TO FOCUS ON

- ▶ Cooperativeness
- ▶ Great companion
- ▶ Artistic
- ▶ Refined
- ▶ Excellent negotiator or mediator
- ▶ Strong beliefs and clear vision, once arrived at
- ▶ Sincerity
- ▶ Charmer
- ▶ Communicativeness
- ▶ Courteous and appreciative of others
- ▶ Leadership qualities

- **Acts on a basis of reason**
- **Loving and romantic**
- **A sense of fair play**

To help you accentuate these positives, see the S.M.A.R.T.est Goals for Aries exercise on page 3.

WEAKNESSES THAT CAN TRIP YOU UP

- **Paralysis of analysis**
- **Fear of making the wrong decision**
- **Tendency to vacillate**
- **Leading people on**
- **Appearing indolent**
- **Mood swings**
- **Gullibility**
- **Can enter into an unsuitable relationship too quickly**
- **Not always able to be objective about yourself or your situation, can attract complications**
- **Going overboard to ensure that everyone else is happy, while ignoring your own needs and happiness**

So how do you turn these so-called negative traits into powerful tools for personal growth? For help with this, visit the Love Your Weaknesses exercise in Aries (page 6).

COACH'S TIP

If you, as many Librans tend to, measure your worth by the wishes of others, you will always feel unstable. By working with a coach—or alone, if you have the self-discipline and motivation—to uncover your deeper values and by basing every decision on honoring those values, you will keep your self-esteem strong and your decisions will become easier to make, while reflecting a more balanced perspective.

Look at any decisions that you are having trouble making. Does one course of action lead to satisfying more of your values than another? If so, take the course of action that enables you to get more of your needs met and values honored. To help with uncovering your core values, look at the Define Your Values exercise in Aries (page 20).

A further way of dealing with indecision is to make a list of the pros and cons of taking a particular course of action. Then make a decision and stick with it.

LIBRA MAN

Unless there are influences in his personal birth chart that are stronger than that of sun in Libra, a typical Libra man will exhibit most of the following personality and behavior traits:

◆ **Excellent financial abilities**
◆ **Generous when it comes to giving advice and an illuminating companion**
◆ **Generous with his money and loves to spend his cash on items that will bring him happiness**
◆ **Adores fine art and melodic music**
◆ **Is determined to amass as much data relating to a situation or course of action as possible so that he can come to a balanced decision**
◆ **Needs inner and outer harmony and balance**
◆ **Can change his mind often**
◆ **Is usually trustworthy and has a strong sense of justice**
◆ **Is a master in the art of romance and is always, always interested in the opposite (or same) sex**
◆ **Dresses to impress—whatever the occasion, Libra will turn up dressed appropriately**

Libra is blessed with a graceful and athletic body. He is usually handsome with a fine bone structure and perfectly balanced features. He has a beautiful speaking voice and superb taste in clothes.

Like Leo man, Libra likes to check his appearance in any reflective surface that he happens to pass. Physically, Libra woman tends to be slim but curvy, with large eyes, flared nostrils, and a generous, well-shaped mouth with even teeth.

LIBRA WOMAN

**In addition to the personality and behavior traits
exhibited by the Libra male, Libra woman is:**

- **Very aware of her looks and will use them to get
  what she wants**
- **Is charm personified and makes a superb teammate**
- **Excels at partnership but can ignore her own needs**
- **Needs a loving partnership; not self-sufficient**
- **Invests in the highest quality clothes, scents, and
  accessories**
- **Expresses her opinions with tact and diplomacy**
- **Has outstanding powers of analysis**

THE HIDDEN (OR NOT-SO-HIDDEN) LIBRA

LIBRANS HATE TO be alone, although they mask this behind a calm, collected exterior. They can also be very moody, as they swing from one type of behavior to its opposite, always trying to attain that perfect balance.

Take my client Mike, for example, a sales rep who came to me because he was stressed out and overwhelmed. It didn't take long to find out why—a naturally gregarious man, he always left his office door open for colleagues to stop by and have a chat. And chat they certainly did, leaving him with no time to do his work, other than at home, which was putting his marriage under severe strain.

One of the first exercises we did was to get him to record exactly what he did with his time and how much control he had over it. We then came up with a very simple strategy to enable him to gain more control over more of his time. I got him to partition his working days into blocks of time when he needed to focus on his work and blocks of time when he was free to talk. He then needed to educate his colleagues, teaching them when he was approachable and when he was strictly off-limits. In this way, he was able to enjoy socializing with his colleagues while being able to comfortably hit his sales targets. He was amazed to find that his relationships with his colleagues were greatly improved by establishing boundaries.

Libra likes

▶ Pleasing surroundings
▶ A good, detailed argument
▶ Being loved and appreciated
▶ Being admired
▶ Being taken care of
▶ Credit cards
▶ Very small animals
▶ Attending to details
▶ Having people around
▶ Being of service
▶ Sensible, tailored clothes
▶ Muted, subtle colors and textures

Libra dislikes

▶ Loud arguments, harsh and abrasive people
▶ Confusion
▶ Ugly places
▶ Sloppiness
▶ Being pressured to make a decision
▶ Criticism of their interests or loves
▶ Being told to effect change

Possible Problem Areas for Libra, and Solutions

All sun signs have unique personality traits. When these traits are suppressed, problems will arise. However, with a combination of astrology and coaching, we can examine the problem and assess the proper solution based on sun sign characteristics. As a Libran, you may see things below that really strike home. Try the solution; you are likely to be amazed at the results.

Problem: Finding yourself frequently trapped in situations that have no depth and little value to you or the other person.

SOLUTION: Try not to pretend that you have feelings that you
do not have. Then find a way to back gracefully
out of a superficial relationship. Look before you
leap in the future, Libra.

PROBLEM: You find that you do not really like yourself and/or
are beating yourself up over not being able to
please another.

SOLUTION: If you learn how to put yourself first without
harming others, then you will be able to please
someone else.

PROBLEM: The situations that make you ill at ease are only
mildly irritating to another.

SOLUTION: Try to cultivate inner security through spiritual
strength and awareness.

PROBLEM: Feeling as if you are worthless and, therefore,
allowing others to take advantage of you. At times
you suddenly feel put upon and snap, which can
lead to others seeing you as frustrating, awkward,
and unpredictable.

SOLUTION: Develop your feelings of self-worth by expressing
the positive in your nature. Finding ways to affirm
your own value as an individual while keeping
strong personal boundaries allows you to create life
on your own terms, while sharing love and care
with those who know you.

CAREER/BUSINESS

BALANCING business and pleasure is among your foremost challenges, because you tend to be extremely hardworking. Many Librans find they can fall into a pattern of working in intense bursts, followed by periods of rest and consolidation to recharge those Libra batteries.

Libra will look at all sides of an issue, then make a careful and deliberate decision once they're sure it's the right one. The sense of justice and fair play attached to those born under this sign is remarkable. They are the diplomats of the business world. Librans enjoy the leader's role and will work hard to be worthy of the privilege. If Libra leads from a position of strength, he or she can become exceptionally influential.

Librans crave exchange of ideas, and if all this takes place in a social situation, even better. Librans are the networkers of the zodiac. The mediator in Libra likes bringing people together, but the scales also enjoy having a partner at their side. There are very few Libran solo-preneurs! Librans are very aware that they produce their best work with skilled collaborators, who have those strengths that the scales lack, so they are highly motivated to keep their partnerships sailing along smoothly.

If there's one thing the scales could use, it's some resolve when it comes to making tough decisions. That swinging back and forth can't go on forever. When it comes to crisis management, however, the scales can spring into amazing action, even if it's a place they'd rather not be.

Harmony is vitally important to Librans. These charmers enjoy beautiful surroundings that are pleasing to all. The Libra office is likely to be beautiful, with fresh-cut flowers and a seating arrangement that places all guests on an equal footing. Of all the signs, Librans are likely to be the most interested in feng shui, and they'll move their furniture around until the placement feels just right. Libra's office is a testament to efficiency and aesthetic excellence. Your office will be immaculate, no dust or grime to throw you off balance. Muted colors and silence (or soft melodious music) abound.

Libra Career Guide

Librans are well suited to work as diplomats, judges, public-relations consultants, counselors, psychologists (no Freudian slips here!), and artists. If you are a typical Libra, both money and an excellent quality of life will be of great importance to you. Here are some further occupations that a Libra might consider:

Academic advisor	HR manager	Notary
Agent	Hairdresser	Painter
Appraiser	Headhunter	Peacemaker
Architect	Host	Personal Manager
Art dealer	Interior decorator	Poet
Beautician	Landscaper	Politician
Business associate	Lawyer	Referee or umpire
Collaborator	Mediator	Sculptor
Designer	Model	Writer
Engraver	Musician	
Graphic artist	Negotiator	

LIBRA BOSS

DESPITE YOUR LOW-KEY diplomatic exterior, Libra likes to be in charge. Being self-employed is often a goal for ambitious Libras. The slightly bossy side to Libra is rarely apparent—your ruler Venus seems to keep this part of you under wraps. You've found that charm works better anyway.

The Libran boss is a persuasive talker who can effortlessly motivate a roomful of colleagues. Librans have an enviable knack of getting others to carry out those tasks that they don't want to do themselves.

Firm but fair, your employees know precisely where they stand with you, as you set standards by which all must abide. You are a masterful strategist who looks at all the facts behind an issue before coming to a decision. You will also take note of everyone's opinions and are seen to value others' input. A skilled communicator, you like to address employee concerns before any situation becomes intolerable. People naturally trust you to come up with a sane and sensible solution to any dilemma. The solution may well be a creative or unusual one.

Librans will go out of their way to smooth even the most minor bump in their business dealings; no problem is too small to receive Libra's attention. With your careful consideration of every issue and your natural sensitivity to the feelings of others, you are a born mediator. You have your finger firmly on the pulse when it comes to business, as people naturally confide in you.

Your sense of honor and loyalty is obvious to all who work with you, as is your dislike of strident, aggressive, or overemotional people. Drama queens and self-publicists need not apply to join your harmonious and effective team.

COACH'S TIP

Beware that your natural tendency to ignore the uglier side of life does not cause you to have a blind spot when it comes to unsatisfactory employees. Rather than let an unpleasant individual upset team dynamics, tackle the issue early on and accept that a firm stand is sometimes needed to restore harmony.

EXERCISE THREE

Decision Making for Libra Bosses

What do you do when everything is important? How do you truly involve several people in decision making and have them go away knowing that their contribution was valued? You need to prioritize, and that's a challenging task when all the choices seem equally important.

This exercise will help you to prioritize all these "A" choices and also harvest the riches of others' ideas and judgments. It's empowerment in practical action. You'll find that even when someone else's top priority isn't the final decision, they are willing to commit themselves because they know that they really were involved and had an equal opportunity to influence the result. A fair as well as a wise decision is the likely outcome.

Brainstorm all the options, choices, possible decisions, and solutions. Get creative here. If your list doesn't contain some off-the-wall ideas, you're probably filtering out your own creative ideas. Now isn't the time to evaluate the ideas, just list them.

If you have more than twenty ideas, you could cluster them into groups and give each group of ideas a name.

Pause. Allow yourself time to look at the list and see if any more ideas come to mind.

If you're doing this with other people, ask if anyone needs clarification about what any item means—what it is not, whether it's a good idea, and how, in detail, it would work.

Number each idea or cluster: 1, 2, 3, 4, 5. . . . Then give out the chart below. (I've given you ten items in this example.)

1 1 1 1 1 1 1 1 1   (Your company idea 1 with ideas 2–10)
2 3 4 5 6 7 8 9 10

2 2 2 2 2 2 2 2   (Your company idea 2 with ideas 3–10 and so on)
3 4 5 6 7 8 9 10

3 3 3 3 3 3 3
4 5 6 7 8 9 10

4 4 4 4 4 4
5 6 7 8 9 10

5 5 5 5 5
6 7 8 9 10

6 6 6 6
7 8 9 10

7 7 7
8 9 10

8 8
9 10

9
10

Total number of times circled:
1   2   3   4   5   6   7   8   9   10

Now it's time to make some decisions. The Paired Comparison Chart asks you to think about just two ideas at a time. Consider items 1 and 2. Which would you choose? Which do you think would work best, be best, have the greatest impact? Circle that number. Then forget about all the other choices and consider items 1 and 3 again. Circle your choice. Now do the same for 1 and 4, 1 and 5, and so on until you (and each of the others involved) have completed the chart.

Time to Total: Count how many times you (and others) have circled a "1." Do this for each number or choice.

The numbers with the highest scores are your top priorities. You'll probably find that you've narrowed your range of decisions to just a few on the original list. Talk about them, get creative again. Use the chart again to narrow the choices even more.

This exercise will help you focus, decide, and move forward with your decisions. When it's used with a group of people, it enrolls everyone in the final choice, whatever their differing opinions and perspectives at the start.

You'll know you've made a great decision—one that comes from both your logical, analytical left brain and also from your creative, imaginative right brain. As an added bonus you'll have the help and commitment you need from others in implementing your decision.

LIBRA EMPLOYEE

LIBRA RARELY REMAINS in a subordinate position for long, requiring status and advancement to stay around. All the skills and traits listed under the Libra Boss heading apply also to the Libra employee. The only difference between Libra boss and Libra employee is the level of task to which the diplomatic Libran applies its thorough intellect.

Librans are often far smarter than their superiors, and one of their first actions on joining a company will be to undertake a concerted campaign to take themselves to the top. Libra will immediately know which corporate executives are the real power players in an organization and will effortlessly form alliances with them. Librans also get themselves powerful sponsors and mentors. For a useful exercise on this subject, see Create a Political Map of Your

Organization, on page 17 of the Aries chapter.

TOP TEN POLITICAL STRATEGIES

IN TODAY'S COMPETITIVE corporate jungle, skills and experience are not enough; you need to master the subtle art of company politicking.

1. Socialize effectively within your company. Make sure that people like you and feel that they know you. This enhances your chances of being noticed and promoted. If you appear aloof, people tend to reject you.
2. Network, network, network. Both within your company and within your industry. You want to be highly visible and have your ear to the ground when those opportunities appear.
3. Be aware that company politics operate at all levels and that you need to watch your back as well as looking for the next move. Mount your own internal PR and marketing campaign.
4. Maintain control at all times.
5. Always, always set political and career goals. This will affect the degree to which you engage in office politics. It also ensures that you know the outcome that you want from any encounter.
6. Always make sure that you are part of the solution, not the problem. Be seen as having a positive attitude.
7. Sharpen up those negotiating skills—you are going to need them.
8. Communication, communication, and communication. Learn how to communicate effectively with people at all levels in your organization. Take a little time to work out why it is in their interests to give you what you want. Put whatever ideas you want embraced into a language that your listener understands.
9. Create a political map of your organization. Identify the real power players who can ease your progression up the career ladder. Then align with them.
10. Keep your friends close and your enemies closer.

EXERCISE FOUR

Culture Vulture

Company culture has a huge impact on your working life. Every company has a so-called open culture, as well as hidden subcultures, social networks, and alliances. A company's true culture may not be the culture it suggests that it has when recruiting you.

In order to establish your company's true culture, so that you know the climate in which you are operating, try this exercise. Be aware that a company's culture is conveyed both directly and indirectly.

Here are a few questions that you should be asking yourself to establish your company's culture. Ask yourself the following questions:

- ◆ Who gets hired and goes on to excel in your organization? Who gets ahead and why? What sort of people are they?
- ◆ Who are the company heroes? What about the villains? What rules have they broken?
- ◆ What are the company rules—both written and unwritten? How are they enforced?
- ◆ What is the main mode of communication between fellow employees, for example verbal, face-to-face, via E-mail? Is communication style formal or informal. What about swearing?
- ◆ How much emphasis is given to training?
- ◆ What is your company mission statement? Is it taken seriously?
- ◆ How does your company see itself in terms of PR and marketing? What kind of events does it endorse or sponsor?
- ◆ Do people work long hours or from nine to five? Do they work through lunch?
- ◆ What do people gossip about—those who succeed or those who fail?
- ◆ Does your organization value diversity or homogeneity? Does it like creative, independent mavericks or yes people?

◆ Does your company expect you to socialize with your colleagues? What kind of events does it hold and when?

Once you have established your company's culture, you can see how well you fit into it. Is there a close fit or do you need to do some work on yourself? Do you want to embrace your current company's culture and adapt to thrive in it, or, would you prefer to move to a company with a more suitable culture for you?

Libra is one of the most diplomatic and empathetic signs of the zodiac. As a result of these characteristics, Librans perform superbly at interviews. This means that Libra could very easily find him or herself being offered an unsuitable job and taking it. After all, Librans hate to upset people, don't they?

If you want to say good-bye to that sinking feeling you get when you know you've just landed yourself the job from Hell, try the Career-U-Like exercise in Taurus (page 53).

FINANCES AND WEALTH

IT should come as no surprise that Librans like things to be in balance—and that includes their checkbooks.

Librans thoroughly appreciate money and what it can buy: the best that life has to offer. Fortunately, there is usually enough cash around to keep the scales in the style to which they've become accustomed, as Libra is a sign that unfailingly chooses the path to peak prosperity. The scales also like to be romanced, so prospective partners are well advised to keep that platinum card handy.

Making the financial decisions is something that the scales would rather not do, as they consider it a bit tedious. Those born under this sign are attractive and charismatic and, as a result, are accustomed to having things come to them easily. This could make for a poor work ethic if it were not for the fact that Libra balances periods of indolence with periods of explosive, focused activity.

The scales will pay the bills on time in one of two ways: by sheer luck or with the aid of a responsible partner. Face it, it's much more fun to be at the symphony. Short on cash? A Libran will charm a pal into a loan. Librans are unlikely to repay the favor, however, unless the loan is a good risk. If their partner needs a loan, though, they'd part with their last penny.

It's not uncommon for Librans to go overboard on one exceptional item, be it a work of art or an expensive holiday. If they choose to do so, however, they will have saved up for the splurge. Libra will also be quite prepared to sell that work of art for a healthy profit when the time is right. Try the Nice and Easy Does It Way to $1000 exercise in Gemini (page 85) to help with building up funds, Libra.

If you had your way, Libra, everything would be sold at a fair price. When products or services cost too much, it upsets your equilibrium. You may want to visit the Determine Your Value exercise in Capricorn (page 274) for some fun with this! Should you feel you need to negotiate, the process comes to you as naturally as breathing. Librans are the zodiac's negotiators, with an innate ability for uncovering the motivations of others and for coming up with those creative solutions that make everyone feel like a winner. Your highly analytical talents give you the ability to negotiate for a living, and are the reason that Librans make such legendary union leaders and lawyers.

Because Venus rules Libra, you would profit from investing in precious gems and natural metals, such as diamonds, gold, and Venus-ruled copper. Your love of art and your sophisticated level of taste indicate that you could do well by investing in fine art objects, particularly if you choose to purchase pieces created by as yet unknown artists after you have seen their work and studied current trends. Since Librans are not overly acquisitive as a rule, you will be perfectly happy to sell these treasures when the market is right.

Partnerships tend to be lucky for you, so think about saving and investing jointly with your mate, or in mutual funds, stocks, or bonds with a trusted business partner. Libra is a very generous sign and enjoys the luxuries of life. Seeing friends is vital to Libra's well-being, so entertainment is where Librans tend to spend the most money. You might do well to take advantage of this tendency, Libra, and look at investing in happening entertainment crazes and venues.

COACH'S TIP

> Looking or feeling shabby can have a negative effect on your
> morale. You need to look good in order to feel good and per-
> form effectively. It may not be such a bad idea to invest in a
> few well-designed pieces of clothing so you can "dress for
> success" while you are going for the gold.

LOVE, ROMANCE, AND SEX LIFE

LIBRA, as befits the sign of the scales, reveres balance and harmony above all. If this can be achieved with a partner, even better, for Libra rules the house of partnerships and revels in things
that come in twos. The scales are sociable and shine in social situations, where their gift of communication is an attraction to
many. Librans also want to be liked, even loved, by those who cross
their path, and it can be very hard to resist the scales when they
are at their most charming and magnetic. It's not unusual for
Librans to possess an easy grace and sense of style, and they move
languidly through a room. Behind that pretty façade is a smart,
often smoldering soul who knows how to get what they want and
would love nothing more than to do so fairly and justly. When the
scales find the partner they've been searching for, it could be a
match made in heaven.

COMPATIBILITY

LIBRANS CAN GET along with most people, though are best when
pairing with fellow air signs or the fire signs Leo and Sagittarius.
Sometimes an earth sign may provide some much needed grounding, and a match with Cancer can produce some blissful moments.

WHAT LIBRA NEEDS

THE PARTNER WHO can encourage Libra to be honest, open,
trusting, and free is on the right track. The scales crave someone

who can give them feedback and support, and affirm that they are a treasure to behold. Wooing them with gifts can be the right stimulant. Some long talks, along with a lesson in give and take, can also work wonders. Anyone who can bring Librans to an open state, who can get them to think less and feel more, will be rewarded with a grateful and passionate lover.

The Libra lover is a harmonious soul who adores love, beauty, and the romance dance. A lover who can take this pleasure principle and make it seductively mental is bound to be at the top of Libra's wish list. Blissfully partnered Libras exude a sex appeal that is off the scale.

THE END OF THE AFFAIR

WHEN LIBRA IS rejected, he or she initially feels extremely demoralized; however, Libra will quickly take the action needed to bounce back from disappointment. Libra will do their utmost to make their loved one fall for them again. Should this fail, Libra will deal with rejection by searching out another true love.

If Libra chooses to end a relationship, the break will be as orderly and dignified as possible. Libra is most likely to reject a partner who is too demanding on the emotional front.

RELATIONSHIPS
(Family and Friends)

LIBRA PARENT

A TYPICAL LIBRA parent will go out of their way to be just and fair with their children. The Libran parent is usually permissive with their children, with a tendency to spoil them. Libra will show his or her children a great deal of affection and will take much pride in their child's appearance and behavior. Libra will also ensure that his or her child receives the best possible education.

LIBRA CHILD

MOST LIBRAN CHILDREN are stunningly beautiful, with a gift for getting their own way. Add to this a penchant for keeping things neat and tidy, and a high degree of intelligence, and you have a child made in heaven! Natural born charmers, these kindhearted youngsters can wheedle just about anything out of instantly smitten adults. The Libran child likes to move at his or her own pace and dislikes being hurried. Libra also hates being forced to decide between two things.

Libran children expect to be treated fairly and will willingly obey rules if they seem to be fair and reasonable. Libran children are unlikely to go through a rebellious teenage phase if treated fairly. The Libran teenager is far more likely to be a romantic than a bully.

BRINGING UP LIBRA—COACH'S INSIGHT

MOST YOUNG LIBRANS grasp, at an early age, how to argue their case with total conviction. They have a natural talent for making their needs and wants known in a way that makes it natural for a parent to respond positively. Parents need to be aware that if they give in to Libran demands all the time, they risk creating a spoiled monster. However, to refuse too often may cause young Libra to become hurt and resentful. Those parents blessed with a Libran child need to be aware of the need for balance when responding to Libra's demands, perhaps taking the opportunity to teach negotiating and prioritizing skills.

A harmonious environment and fair treatment are absolute musts for your Libran child—as are privacy, affection, and plenty of attention. While Librans have a need to spend some time pursuing solitary activities, they also need company. It is through close contact with others that Librans learn who they are.

Young Libra needs to be given direction, gently and firmly, early on in life. If, in addition to telling young Libra what to do and when to do it, you can give them a sound and logical reason for doing things, so much the better. Be aware that a reluctance to obey instructions on the part of young Libra can simply mean that great consideration is being given to the matter in hand. Librans are, for the most part, self-disciplined, so they do not need a strict disciplinarian approach.

As mentioned earlier, young Librans seem to know more about absolutely everything than anyone else around. This can be irritating, especially when they are a third of your age and completely right. Parents need to take a pragmatic and optimistic view of this tendency, giving young Libra plenty of mind food and a few lessons on wearing your knowledge lightly.

Libra and Friends

Librans tend to be highly social individuals who are always on the go. The only time that they will cease from tirelessly making their friends happy is when they need to recuperate and recharge their batteries. For social Libra, life revolves around keeping in touch and connecting with others.

On the plus side, Librans are loving and loyal friends who are unlikely to embarrass anyone with emotional outbursts. A Libran friend is honest, has your best interests at heart, and will be scrupulously honest with you.

On the minus side, Libra can try the patience of a friend with their indecisiveness. Try the decision-making Heads You Win, Tails You Win exercise given toward the end of this chapter, Libra (page 216). Librans can also be jealous of a friend who is better looking than they are, and need to work on their confidence and self-worth.

Libra, look for friends who are prepared to give you what you need. The wrong friendship or relationship can be even lonelier than being alone. Begin to take charge of yourself and your relationships. You can start to do this by asking yourself the following questions:

1. What are the top priorities in my life right now?
2. What do I want and need in a partner? See the Getting Your Needs Met exercise in Cancer (page 116) for help with this.
3. What do I want from and need in a friend?
4. What am I prepared to give in a relationship?

5. What is unacceptable to me in a relationship? See The Magnificent Seven Steps to Setting Boundaries exercise in Taurus (page 48) for help with this.
6. What do I want to accomplish during the next three months in this relationship?
7. What do I want to change about my life during the next month, three months, six months?

Do this exercise on a regular basis, as the answers to the questions will change with time.

FRIENDS, BE AWARE

BE AWARE THAT Libra can slip into a depression; however, this can be lifted by a genuine compliment. Tip for lonely Librans: Write down all the great things about yourself. If possible, get friends and family to do the same. Put these compliments on Post-it notes and stick them up in prominent places. Look at them whenever you're feeling blue.

Remember not to leave your Libra friends alone for too long—Librans get lonely very easily. If you can't get to see your Libra friends, make sure you take the time to connect with them in other ways.

HEALTH

IN times of stress, Librans have to get out and see friends—the more the better. Libra is not a loner. A cardinal sign, Libra does not have a problem accepting change—it just wants to be sure its decision is the right one. As an air sign, you like to poll people around you for an opinion. By taking a consensus, you are able to define your own feelings more sharply. Libras are not the dizzy social butterflies they may appear to be on the surface. Highly intelligent, Libra rarely lets emotion get in the way of the analytical process. Libra is continually taking in new information and reprocessing it, trying, as the scale tips and dips, to find their center.

Librans rely most heavily on their mates and business partners. You need partners to be the sounding boards for your ideas. If your significant other isn't in the mood to listen to all the details of what is bothering you, you can fall into a deep depression.

Venus-ruled Libra does best in soothing, beautiful surroundings. Take your laptop out into the garden to work or bring a bouquet of fresh flowers to your desk. Add a few personal touches to your hotel room when on a business trip—all the better to relax you. Making music will restore your soul's harmony, so put on whatever music suits your mood. If you can make your own sweet music, that's even better.

This need for harmony and beauty extends to your appearance too. That's why you always check your appearance in front of a mirror before a big interview or tough presentation. Don't let others put you off doing this—when you look the best you can, you are the best you can be.

You can benefit greatly from a day at a health spa. Search out a place where light foods are prepared for lunch, and sports or other activities are blended with special treatments to boost your looks. If going to a spa isn't possible, plan a relaxing day at home where you are completely pampered by your spouse or lover. Make sure a loving back rub is part of the day's activities. To complete the day's bliss, have a memorable dinner for two in an elegant restaurant with soft lighting, romantic music, and flowers. Venus-ruled signs love to eat out, and Libra wants the restaurant to be extra special.

Luxury-loving Libra also adores beautiful scents, so finding a new perfume will give you an instant lift. Explore those wonderful shops that produce products with intoxicating, heady aromas. Given your temperament, you might enjoy improving your gardening skills— imagine the joy of creating an aesthetically pleasing, heavenly scented garden. You could even enjoying mastering the skill of flower arranging, and what about a trip to a garden show, where you can combine your need to judge with your need for beauty? When it comes to hearing, sensuous Libra excels, so put on whatever music suits your mood. Do you play the guitar, piano, or some other instrument? Superb! Making music will rejuvenate your soul.

Some Libras thoroughly enjoy a good court case, since Libra rules the justice system. Find a really good courtroom drama to read about in a novel, read an autobiography of a famous lawyer, or rent a courtroom drama at the video store. You could even try watching Court TV. Even if it is a silly case, it might take your mind off your own troubles. Better still, see if you can get a seat in the courtroom during a really, juicy libel trial.

FITNESS

LIBRA RULES THE lower back. Your metabolism is low.

Few signs are as well groomed and polished as yours, Libra. The average Libran takes good care of his or her body but does have to combat a sweet tooth. With your love of luxury, sensuality, and flavor, you can work your way through a box of chocolates pretty quickly. Try to indulge yourself in one sensuous, delicious treat a day and make an occasion of it. Otherwise, you will find that both your body size and your craving for treats grows rapidly.

Libra also loves to party, but partying until all hours can rob you of sleep and your looks. Remember that you cannot make up for neglecting your body, you can only repair the damage. So get back home at a reasonable time after most of your nights out. You'll thank yourself when you look in the mirror.

The ultimate partnering sign, Libra does best when it teams up with another person in any exercise program. Tennis (doubles), squash, badminton, sailing, and other sports and activities that require a partner are all perfect for you. Any sport requiring grace, balance, and coordination will also suit you.

Finally, pay attention to the condition of your lower back. Learn calisthenics to strengthen the muscles in this area and drink lots of water and cranberry juice to stay healthy on the inside, too.

COACH'S TIP

While at the gym, tennis court, or wherever, try not to become distracted by your need to socialize. Remember, you're here to exercise! However, should you miss a few sessions, don't swing to the other extreme and overdo it. Aim for moderation in all things, Libra.

TOOLS FOR MAKING A DIFFERENCE

THE LIBRAN TENDENCY to perfectionism can undermine your power base if you apply unrealistic ideals to a situation or person, including yourself. For tips on combating perfectionism, visit the Personality section of Virgo (page 160).

Other areas Librans might like to look at are increasing decision-making abilities and, in support of this, tools to increase motivation and prioritizing abilities. By working on these areas, you will move away from the Libran tendency to miss deadlines.

STEPS TO MOTIVATE YOURSELF

Use your deepest emotions to move and guide you toward your goals, helping you to take the initiative and to persevere in the face of obstacles and setbacks.

If you're finding it hard to motivate yourself, maybe you're not doing what you really want to do. What do you love doing so much that you'd do it for free? What turns you on, inspires you, excites you, and gives you energy?

Clarify your core values. (See the Define Your Values exercise in Aries, page 20). Values are what are really important to us. They are us. They motivate us and are our criteria for knowing if we are doing the right thing. To clarify your values for a given area of your life, for example, career, health and fitness, relationships, make a list of what's important to you about that area. Better yet, get a coach or friend to ask you directly: "What's important about (area)?" Keep asking yourself this, going beyond the point where you appear to have run out of answers—this is when our deepest motivations often surface. Are these values being satisfied in your life now? How might you satisfy them?

Now prioritize your values. What's the most important value on that list? What's the next most important? Values determine how we spend our time, so in practice only the top five values get significant time devoted to their fulfillment.

Check that there are no value conflicts; if there are, resolve them. If you're not achieving your goals, it can be because two values are in conflict. If you find this, for each value, keep asking yourself "What's important about that?" until you reach a higher-level purpose that can satisfy both.

Establish whether your motivation is toward pleasure or away from pain for each value. Ask yourself, "Why is that important?" You may get a "toward pleasure" answer—"Because I love the status it gives me"—or an "away from pain" answer—"Because I'll be a failure if I don't have it." (Beware: Not everything is always as it seems with this exercise. You can get concealed "toward" or "away from" answers. For example, "Because it's better to have it" is a concealed "away from" answer.

This advice should be familiar to anyone who has practiced visualization or other self-help techniques. You tend to get what you focus on, so focus on what you want, not what you don't want. No point focusing on bills piling up—you'll get more of the same. Focus on money rather than the lack of it. "Away from" motivation can be very powerful, and is great for getting you out of trouble, but it is directionless. "Away from" can be any direction and runs out once you get far enough away from what you don't want. "Toward" motivation gives you more direction and gets stronger the closer you get to your goal.

Ensure that your goal is right for you. Does it raise your interest and renew your energy levels when you think about it? Will it be great for every area of your life? If not, do you really want it? Is it really your goal? To make your goal more compelling, try the following exercise.

EXERCISE FIVE

Make Your Goal Compelling

SEE yourself achieving your goal. How will you know when you have achieved it? Notice how you feel in response to this image. If it feels good, make the image big, bright, colorful, and moving, so your good feelings get stronger. Add some sound. Step into the image and notice how good that feels.

Turn those good feelings up even higher—then step back out of it so your goal is ahead of you. This will motivate you to get there.

Make sure that you set your goal for a specific date, and set a date by which you can feasibly achieve it. Ensure that the date set encourages you to stretch yourself to achieve it, but does not cause you to give up. This is very important—if you leave the date unspecified, the goal will always be at some vague time in the future and will never happen.

Now take the next logical step and install the goal in your future time line. Imagine your future stretching out like a line that you can walk along, then take your goal and walk along this imagined line until you get to the date by which you intend to have attained it. Now let go of your image of your goal and let it float down and become part of the time line. Step into your goal and be there at the moment of its achievement. Notice how good that feels. Now step beyond your goal, turn around, and looking back down the past time line, notice the steps you took to get there.

Walk back along the line to now, slowly enough to learn what you need to learn from each step along the way.

This is a powerful exercise and you might want to get a helper to guide you through it.

Ensure that you set yourself smaller, achievable milestone goals on the way to your main goal. If you feel overwhelmed by how much you have to do to achieve a task, break it down into smaller, achievable steps and plan a reward for each step achieved.

Try setting up a motivation anchor. Remember a time when you really wanted something. Anchor that process (by placing the first and second fingers and the thumb together) at the peak of that remembered experience. You've achieved success when this gesture alone can trigger the feeling associated with the experience you're using as your anchor. Use the anchor whenever you need a little boost to get yourself motivated.

COACH'S TIP

> With things you don't feel like doing, focus on the end result. When people want something done but they don't enjoy the process of doing it—paying bills, doing the laundry—they often make it harder for themselves by concentrating on how tedious or hard it will be to do it. Instead, focus on how great it will be when you've done it. Imagine looking forward to getting mail each day because you've paid all your bills on time. Tell yourself how good you'll feel. Then just do it!
>
> Use your heart and gut feelings as a compass to keep you on the track of what you really want.

Where does your time go? Are you investing it where you should be? Try this fun exercise to get a quick snapshot of how your life looks at the moment.

Take the following five things and write them down in a notebook or your journal, in order of how important they are to you, starting with the most important at the top.

- ◆ Work/career
- ◆ Family/relationships
- ◆ Personal-growth time, for example, reading personal development books and attending courses and workshops
- ◆ Time for beliefs (religious or political)
- ◆ Other interests, for example, recreation and entertainment

Now turn the page and write down how much time you spend thinking about and doing each. Be honest with yourself. For work, commuting time should be included.

To do this exercise properly, buy a diary or planner and each day record time spent on each activity.

If you find that your order of priorities is the same as your order of time allocation, you are already making significant progress toward balancing your life. If your two lists differ, then begin taking steps toward bringing them into line.

EXERCISE SEVEN

Heads You Win, Tails You Win

OFTEN we find our progress blocked by an inability to choose between what, initially, appears to be two equally attractive options. This exercise is a short, sharp, effective way of dealing with this dilemma.

Recognize that you have three choices rather than two. They are:

1. Take the first option
2. Take the second option
3. Do nothing

Usually the situation that gave rise to the first two alternatives demands action. If this is so, then option three can be ruled out. If options one and two are truly as good as each other, then just choose one of them—it does not matter which. Flip a coin if you have to.

Usually you will either feel relief at having made the right decision, or you will immediately realize that the option you have selected is not the right one. You can now choose the other.

One of the characteristics that define successful people is their ability to make decisions, rather than wasting time and energy vacillating between too many options. By making decisions and acting upon them, you will achieve infinitely more than by standing still.

SPIRITUALITY

THE sun in Libra sets two important spiritual challenges. While on earth, your challenge as a Libra is to learn how to follow your own advice (trust yourself and listen to that inner voice, Libra) and to pay as much attention to your own development as to others'.

Librans' task, which must be accomplished in solitude, is to become fully effective by unleashing themselves from the worry of caring what others think. Only then can Librans be the charming agents of revolution and social change that their destiny demands of them. Look at Gandhi, who epitomizes the evolved Libran's desire to inspire dramatic social change through the art of gracious conflict. Think about John Lennon campaigning for peace from a huge Venusian bed.

A further spiritual goal for Librans is to learn the meaning of selfless love—how to love without expecting anything in return.

CHAPTER 8

SCORPIO

October 23–November 21

THE EIGHTH SIGN OF THE ZODIAC IS CONCERNED WITH:

- BIRTH, LIFE, DEATH
- SEX, SENSUALITY, PASSION
- PUSHING THE BOUNDARIES OF DISCOVERY, TABOOS, THE OCCULT
- REGENERATION, TRANSFORMATION, METAMORPHOSIS
- FINANCE, INVESTMENTS, WILLS, INHERITANCE
- HIDDEN MATTERS, SECRETS, COLLECTIVE UNCONSCIOUS, DEFENSE SYSTEMS
- SOCIAL REVOLUTION, REFORMATION, CHANGE

SCORPIO is the deepest of all the signs and is represented by the scorpion, a creature that prefers to live in the dark and is liable to react with a sharp sting when disturbed. The intense emotions of this sign are toughened by Mars, given an obsessive quality by Pluto, and channeled into a rigid mold by the fixed quality.

Scorpio, the eighth sign of the zodiac, should never be taken lightly. Those born under this sign have a deep, driving desire and unstoppable determination to learn about others. This is not a sign that indulges in small talk—these folks will zero in on the essential questions, gleaning the secrets that lie hidden. If you desire privacy or want to hide behind a mask, avoid the scorpion. The curiosity of Scorpios is immeasurable, which may be why they are such adept investigators. These folks love to probe and know how to get to the bottom of things. The fact that they have a keen intuition certainly helps.

Scorpio is associated with beginnings and endings, and Scorpios are unafraid of either; they also inhabit a world which is black and white and has little use for gray. Those born under this sign have an instinctive sense of what is right and what is wrong, and though this may go against conventional morality, it nevertheless provides a powerful motivation.

Scorpios aim to be in ultimate control of their destiny. It is life on the scorpion's terms, too, since these folks vigorously promote their own agenda (they make great executives) and see to it that things go forward. Others may find this overbearing (it can be) and even self-destructive, but that's the scorpion. Scorpios have amazing regenerative powers; they just keep on going, since they are stubborn, resourceful, and determined to succeed (in keeping with the fixed quality of this sign). Scorpios work as hard as they do so that they can some day sit back and feel satisfied with themselves. This is a sign that believes in pleasure deferred and can have a tendency to live in the future. Scorpios are intense, passionate, and filled with desire. They're also complex and secretive, so don't question them too closely, otherwise they'll disappear from view.

Planets Mars and Pluto rule Scorpio. This particular planetary combination makes for people who are motivated, penetrating, and aware. Scorpions don't miss much, since they are highly attuned to the vibrations of others. They are intuitive, probing, and very focused on knowing who's who and what's what. This is a sign that excels at reading the motivations of others and can manipulate with a vengeance. Talking of vengeance, Scorpions can lose their temper (and even become vengeful) when someone gets in their way, so it's best to give them plenty of room. Remember, they're unafraid, and a loss today is considered by Scorpions an opportunity for victory tomorrow.

Scorpio's element is water. As opposed to the turbulent seas of the other water signs, for Scorpions, still waters run deep. Those born under this sign are as emotional as Pisces and Cancer but are far less likely to show it. The Scorpio's emotions are repressed, kept under cover. However, you need to be aware that these folks are clever, perceptive, and always on the ball. They can take an insignificant matter and turn it into a huge slight, in a similar manner to their Cancerian brethren. Beware the Scorpion who feels betrayed! These folks can turn vindictive in no time flat. Luckily, once Scorpions catch their breath, they will return to their usual determined and loyal (albeit strong-willed) ways. Those born under the sign of the scorpion aren't above some subtle manipulation to get what they want, but they'd much rather take a scientific, even mystical, path. Their power and passion serve them well, as long as they don't deteriorate into self-indulgence or compulsion.

Scorpios adore competition in both work and play. They will indulge in any sport or activity that will test their mettle. They also demand a worthy adversary, since it makes the game that much more fun.

Red and black are the colors associated with this sign—and the anarchist flag. No wonder the Scorpio solution to any problem is complete and total change!

The great strength of the Scorpio-born is in their determination, passion, and motivation. Scorpions don't know the word quit, which is why they usually get the job done. They do, however, have to make sure they are doing the right job in order to avoid disappointment once the goal is attained. This sign's one great weakness is its inflexibility and resistance to change; its strength is its powerful commitment.

STRENGTHS TO FOCUS ON

- Self-criticism
- Unshockability
- Intense concentration
- Understanding of failings
- Dynamic, ambitious
- Probing
- Emotional
- Tenacious, strong self-control
- Intense concentration
- Penetrating, quick and perceptive thinking
- Investigative
- Nonjudgmental

- Sensual
- Concerned
- Excellent judgement
- Magnetic
- Passionately caring
- Protective

For a way to make the most of these positives, see S.M.A.R.T.est Goals for Aries (page 3).

WEAKNESSES THAT CAN TRIP YOU UP

- Self-destructiveness
- Moodiness
- Ruthlessness
- Sadism
- Can be brusque and abrupt
- Suspiciousness
- Jealousy
- Insulting
- Secretiveness
- Possessiveness
- Dangerousness
- Quick-temperedness
- Obstinacy
- Intolerance
- Cunning

So how do you turn these so-called negatives into powerful tools for personal growth, Scorpio? See the Love Your Weaknesses exercise in Aries (page 6).

COACH'S TIP

Take a long hard look at your expectations of people and what you give in return. This can help you to lead a happier life.

EXERCISE ONE

Combating Jealousy

IF YOU are having problems with jealousy, learn to detach and think—your partner or whoever is unlikely to be deliberately trying to provoke you and probably has no idea how you feel, so tell them. Be careful to tell them how they make you feel, in a neutral voice, rather than accusing them of doing something. So, for example, you might say, "When you do . . . I feel . . ." rather than, "You always . . . ," which provokes a defensive reaction.

You might also want to try a little self-hypnosis. Begin by sitting comfortably; adopt the lotus position if you can. Set an alarm clock to go off at the end of the time you have set aside for meditating and take the phone off the hook. The usual time for this particular exercise is about five minutes, though some people meditate longer.

- Look at three objects of your choice and then restrict your attention to one.
- Very slowly, letting the words drone, tell yourself you see, hear, and feel three things:
  - I see a candle, flowers, a book.
  - I hear music, a car going by, a dog barking.
  - I feel warm, relaxed, contented.
- Repeat, but with only two things.
- Repeat again, but this time with only one thing.
- Be quiet for a time.
- Focus on your hands and see which one feels lighter. Let the lighter one come up and touch your face.
- Tell yourself you like yourself and also your lover. Tell yourself this three times. Then twice. Then just once. You can repeat this, substituting "love" for "like."
- Blank your mind, breathe evenly, and remain in this position for as long as you can.

You can use this self-hypnosis program to reduce any negative emotion and replace it with a more positive one. The foundation for all positive feelings is self-love, so work on that and expect it to take some time.

For another exercise to help with combating jealousy, see page 45 in the Taurus chapter.

SCORPIO MAN

Unless there are influences in his birth chart that are stronger than his Scorpio sun sign, the typical Scorpio male will have some or all of the following characteristics:

- Is a quick and perceptive thinker
- Ambitious
- Is intense, exclusive in love
- Dislikes sentimentality
- Is never self-effacing
- Has to maintain his dignity
- Is possessive
- Is intensely loyal to friends and will move mountains to help someone
- Never forgets a kindness or an insult
- Has a strong, self-defined moral code and is most courageous in adversity
- Will give 100 percent honest advice, appraisal, or compliments
- Can be a saint or a sinner and pursues either course with great enthusiasm

SCORPIO WOMAN

In addition to the personality and behavior traits exhibited by the Scorpio male, Scorpio woman is:

- Hard to please; her love and respect are not easily won
- Exacting and hard to live with
- Often becomes hooked on a weaker man
- Dislikes sentimentality

- Is stern in matters of principle, can be hard on children
- Never uses flattery and only smiles when she means it
- Is poised and apparently cool
- Regards flattery and flirting as insulting
- Has many talents, all used with passion
- Is intensely loyal to family and home
- Sets and keeps to her own standards, has a strong personality
- Wants total freedom of action
- Wants to dominate but can accept temporary restriction to win in the end

The Hidden (Or Not-So-Hidden) Scorpio

A PERSON WITH strong scorpionic tendencies is a person who is intractable and impenetrable, so Scorpio usually retains his or her secrets. All Scorpios like to keep their true nature as hidden as possible.

SCORPIO LIKES

- Winning
- Activity
- Mystery, occult, the paranormal
- Secrets
- Home
- Sex
- Being acknowledged

SCORPIO DISLIKES

- Being asked
- Being analyzed
- Too many compliments
- Having to trust a stranger, or being indebted to others
- People who know more than they do

Possible Problem Areas for Scorpio, and Solutions

ALL SUN SIGNS have unique personality traits. When these traits are suppressed, problems will arise. However, with a winning combination of astrology and coaching, we can examine the problem and assess the proper solution based on sun sign characteristics. If, as a Scorpio, you see things below that really strike home, try the solution. You may be amazed at the results.

PROBLEM: You suffer from an inferiority complex, feel self-loathing, and are disdainful of help from others.

SOLUTION: Try to admit that others as well as yourself have weaknesses, and then practice compassion, forgiving those weaknesses until you notice them diminishing. Unbend and accept that you can be helped in your problems.

PROBLEM: Even when you have got everyone to agree with you and give you your own way, you are still not satisfied with the results.

SOLUTION: Perhaps it is only at the point where you have nothing more to want for in a given situation that you realize just what you were really after. Look deeply within before you set your goals.

PROBLEM: Disruptive marital relations or a break-up with a loved one.

SOLUTION: Try not to be scornful of what you perceive as a shortcoming in your partner's personality and soften up your rigid, unbending attitude.

PROBLEM: Peers in your group begin to avoid you, or drift away when you approach.

SOLUTION: If you feel persecuted and put upon, you will express it in conversation. This causes people to be "turned off." Try to change your attitude or be guarded in what you say.

CAREER/BUSINESS

THE strong-willed Scorpio is happy to serve others and can be quite helpful, as long as doing so won't hurt him or her. The energetic, winner-takes-all Scorpion is mighty determined and extremely focused. Scorpios are also obsessive about whatever prize they are aiming for, so don't cross them.

Intense, passionate Scorpios know how to live life to the fullest. They know how to zero in on important tasks and, where the art of the deal is concerned, can go for the kill. Scorpios are straight shooters with lofty and important goals, and are devoted to those who have earned their respect. However, everyone else falls by the wayside—this is a sign that doesn't put up with fools at all, let alone gladly. One of the Scorpion's greatest assets is the ability to effect change, if only by sheer will. It's when this virtue spills over into impatience and intransigence that the trouble begins.

Those born under this sign love to create, solve, and manage—both the good and the bad. They tend to lead by example and have an uncanny ability to divine hard truths. They also like to win. As long as Scorpions can control their aggressive, vindictive, and inflexible tendencies (and the need to control in general), much can be accomplished.

The Scorpio office can be a bit macabre, but that's probably to unsettle guests, as part of a psychological war game! This sign needs to show who is in charge. The Scorpion office will also suggest an air of powerful, quiet confidence and be orderly bordering on minimalist. There will be equipment for increasing the Scorpion's knowledge and ability for shrewd analysis. When it comes to time for lunch, Scorpions will delight in ordering red meat—rare—for everyone.

SCORPIO CAREER GUIDE

DREAM JOBS FOR Scorpions include investigator, ecologist, manager, engineer, navigator, and secret agent. Here are some other occupations that a Scorpio might consider:

Analyst	Funeral director	Psychologist
Biochemist	Healer	Psychic
Career counselor	Hypnotist	investigator
Censor	Insurance agent	Refuse collector
Coroner	Investigator	Religious leader
Criminologist	Lab technician	Researcher
Debt collector	Lawyer	Scientist
Detective	Medium	Security guard
Distiller	Miner	Surgeon
Diver	Pathologist	Tax collector
Doctor	Plumber	Union leader
Excavator	Psychiatrist	

SCORPIO BOSS

THE KNOWING, FIERY energy that Scorpio managers possess can make them powerful and intimidating leaders. Brimming with self-confidence even in the most volatile business environment, and with a strong grip on people's emotions, they can also be very mysterious, making it difficult for others to figure out what is really going through their mind. Often Scorpio managers have placid exteriors and appear to have their emotions completely under control; they have learned to control their emotions early on and can maintain an even keel when faced with complete chaos and destruction.

Scorpio managers can be extremely loyal and protective, if not emotionally close, to employees from whom they can gain some knowledge. If emotionally distant loyalty doesn't appeal to you, you had better consider a different job. Beware of crossing a Scorpio manager—that placid exterior is sure to give way to reveal the Scorpio's stinging nature. When crossed, Scorpio will retaliate and hold grudges as long as necessary. When Scorpio managers don't like someone, they may treat them as if they don't even exist. Another way in which their true nature emerges is when they are pushed beyond their limit in a crisis situation. Those well-bottled emotions pour forth like water from a hydrant.

Do not bother trying to hide your true nature from a Scorpio manager. They always know exactly what is going on. You have nothing to worry about, though, provided you get your work done. The Scorpio boss can be sympathetic and understanding and like to know what makes every employee tick. If a well-balanced Scorpio manager uses this knowledge wisely, the result is motivated and happy employees. A Scorpio manager with a less benevolent heart can use this information to manipulate—they know exactly which buttons to push to make you react. If you are trying to get on the good side of a Scorpio manager, be careful to avoid anything that might be interpreted as secretive or covert—Scorpio managers expect to run their operation with honesty and efficiency. Make sure you have information to offer them and present it openly and with all the facts and figures in place.

Scorpio runs a department or company based on merit—those who underachieve are shown the door with great alacrity. This is also a sign that will sacrifice popularity for getting the job done.

Scorpios have to beware that they don't become embroiled in intrigue, corruption, and compulsive behavior—their need for secrecy and their tendency toward underworld activity can lead them to engage in underhanded dealings and deviant business activities. If you are drawn toward engaging in devious business practices, you may well get away with it, Scorpio—unless what you are doing runs counter to your values known or unknown, and you self-sabotage.

Look at the Define Your Values exercise in Aries (page 20) to uncover your true values. You might also want to visit the Avoiding Self-sabotage exercise in Taurus (page 70).

Scorpio Employee

The scorpion is a dream employee who has the poise and containment of a seasoned professional. Although you remain an enigma to those around you, you display self-motivation, initiative, and focus. You are fully aware of your potential and believe that the choice to succeed or fail lies entirely with you. You are also self-contained, so you do not need the feedback of others to attain your goals. You may, of course, alienate colleagues with your secrecy and occasional dramatic changes of course.

You are extremely calculating in the pursuit of your goals, even to the point of tolerating rude and wrongful behavior from those who sign your paycheck. You consider only the power these people have and whether they can influence your likelihood of success. If you need to stay in their good graces, you will, until you are in a position to dispatch them safely. Scorpions shrewdly weigh the price of every action and coolly submit to those who can take them in the right direction.

Scorpio tends to negotiate by being poker-faced, with the implied threat of annihilating opponents who won't conform. This sign can also mesmerize opponents into surrender. However, both these tactics lead to resentment and foul-ups later on, so Scorpio is best sticking to uncovering opponents' motivators and drivers.

Useful exercises for Scorpios at work are Create a Political Map of Your Organization (page 17) and Culture Vulture (page 202).

FINANCES AND WEALTH

FEW can match your business ability, for you are considered one of the savviest signs, financially speaking. The basis of the Scorpio approach to business is in your need to control everything in your life. Many Scorpions are self-made folk, although a surprising number of them inherit wealth. This is a sign that values money and all that goes with it—money buys Scorpions security, freedom, and, best of all, control. That control means power. Scorpions firmly believe that money equals power and ability to win.

An unshakable conviction that they'll come out on top where finances are concerned helps Scorpios to stay in the game no matter how long or how tough it is. This winning attitude attracts money to them because they focus on money rather than a lack thereof. They're also more than willing to make sacrifices for the grand prize. If there are setbacks, Scorpios will generally suffer them well, thanks to their quiet confidence. When the going is good, though, Scorpions will remember their friends with uncommon generosity and are quick to support favorite charities.

The Scorpion's temperament is well suited to astute management of the bottom line. Scorpios are also disciplined enough to stick to a budget, and their eagle eye ensures that they'll never be short-changed at the bank. If Scorpio borrows, he or she always makes good on a debt and has no time for debtors who default or are slow to pay. Control over the domestic purse strings can lead to tension in a Scorpion's relationship.

In the end, Scorpions far prefer to accumulate money than to spend it. To some, your iron will and determination can seem a little extreme. My Scorpio clients who choose to lead a Spartan life because they want to amass a certain amount of money in a certain amount of time do so without any complaint. However, being a Scorpio isn't all about wearing a hair shirt and swearing off luxury. Scorpio likes to live in a comfortable house, drive a fine car, and wear elegant clothing, that's for sure. Scorpios just don't like to flash their cash, and they hate wasting it, so every purchase is a considered one and only the best will do.

Scorpios feel so much better knowing that most of their money is tucked away in the bank or investment fund, multiplying while they sleep. They like the sense of security and power doing this brings.

Scorpio doesn't feel a need to impress anyone. You value your own opinion above all the rest, Scorpio. If something is merely novel or trendy, that doesn't attract you, but if it's well made and a good investment, that's another story. Scorpio doesn't spend a long time craving something. If you want it, you buy it. End of story.

Your ability not to show emotion or give your game away helps get you what you want. Your intuition also helps you to spot a trend before others, which in turn helps you to accumulate wealth.

LOVE, ROMANCE, AND SEX LIFE

SCORPIO rules the house of sex, and Scorpios are passionate lovers, the most sensually energetic of all the signs. Those mystical and magical creatures born under the sign of Scorpio are quick to channel their raw energy, power, and strength into an exploration of their lover's emotions and sexuality. Their overriding urge in loving is to use their power to penetrate beyond themselves and to lose themselves sexually in their partners in an almost mystical ecstasy, thus discovering the meaning of that union which is greater than individuality, and is a marriage of the spirit as well as of the flesh. The Scorpion is intuitive and wants to get to the bottom of things, so there's no way of keeping secrets from this sexy sign (although they'll surely keep a few from you).

Scorpios are capable of the greatest heights of passionate transport, but debauchery and perversion are always dangers, and Scorpios can become sadistic monsters of sensuality and eroticism. Their feelings are so intense that even when their love is of the highest and most idealistic kind, they are nevertheless frequently protagonists in tragic, even violent, romances.

An alluring resourcefulness and self-confidence is evident in Scorpios, these folks being finely attuned to what's best for them and how to get it. Anyone willing to take on the Scorpion will be engaging a cosmic power with plentiful sexual urges. The good news for the person brave enough to take on this sexual powerhouse? A caring and devoted lover waits. A word of warning, though: Don't cross them, because a hurt Scorpio never forgives and will always exact revenge. For those Scorpions prone to outbursts of rage and jealousy, visit the Roar, Toro, Roar and Letting Go of Jealousy exercises in Taurus (pages 64 and 45).

Scorpios always expect to be in charge in relationships. They also demand great sex, adoration, and plenty of money from a lover—and the absolute best where all three are concerned. Deep down, though, it's sex and the power it brings which are most important for the libidinous Scorpion. Scorpions are possessed of a steely determination and a strong sense of what is best for them, which is why they can turn relationships into a battleground.

Scorpio can have a tendency continually to test the limits of the loyalty of friends and lovers. He or she may alienate and dispense with many people during this process, including those whose support she desperately needs.

Thankfully, the Scorpion often takes into account the needs of their partner. With the right lover, they are giving and try to make his or her life easy—though Scorpio will still keep a watchful eye open for transgressions. Scorpions are often poor at communicating what they need from a relationship, so their partner may find themselves being criticized for, to them, no particular reason. Curb your tendency to react out of all proportion to events, Scorpio. Take a good look at what you expect from people, and what you give in return.

COACH'S TIP

Scorpio woman needs to remove the "bad" label that society has taught her to attach to some of her most basic drives. For example:

- She is very highly sexed, and that's perfectly fine.
- She is determined to win, so she might as well accept this.
- She is extremely ambitious, but not at the expense of a healthy sex life.

Scorpio women also need to find an outlet for their competitiveness and ambitions outside of the relationship.

COMPATIBILITY

YOU'LL TEND TO find the other water signs, Cancer and Pisces, too weak unless a comparison of natal charts indicates otherwise. A Scorpio–Scorpio romance can work if you each understand the other's intensity and passion. A pairing with polar opposite Taurus can work, though there is a danger, because both signs are fixed; neither will back down during an argument. When it comes to arguments, have a look at the 100 Point Guide to Negotiating exercise in Virgo (page 171) to enable you to decide whether the outcome of an argument matters more to you than your relationship, Scorpio. If this is indeed the case, then maybe it's time to move on.

WHAT SCORPIO NEEDS

THE SCORPION THRIVES on challenge: The prospect of someone who can test them and who can make the game fast and fun is almost irresistible, provided they are a prize worth having. Scorpio, of course, wants nothing but the best, so only winners need apply. Scorpions are also eager to find a strong, understanding, and perceptive partner, someone who embraces the many facets of this volcanic lover. In short, someone who won't judge them, who possesses raw personal power themselves, who keeps the game interesting, who has a red-hot sex drive, and who knows how to talk when it's important to the relationship. A lover needs to be able to get Scorpio to embark on the journey of self-revelation that is so important in making a relationship work.

The Scorpio lover is determined, forceful, passionate, and strong, and finishes what they start. This is a powerful, compelling, sensual, and sexual being, and isn't for the fainthearted. Those with guts are bound for glory.

THE END OF THE AFFAIR

IF THE SCORPION has an affair, it is usually for one of two reasons: to advance their career or to help with the attainment of a specific goal, for example, power over someone; or because sexual life within the marriage has gone wrong. Scorpios can attract a new partner with little effort. They can also hold back emotionally, so ending the affair comes easily to them.

If Scorpio is rejected, he or she will become very vengeful, either acting immediately or biding their time—this sign never forgets and rarely forgives.

RELATIONSHIPS
(Family and Friends)

SCORPIO PARENT

THE TYPICAL SCORPIO parent is strict and demands high standards. He or she will keep children busy and will take them out a great deal.

Although the Scorpio parent finds it hard to change views and bridge the generation gap (Scorpio also remains uninfluenced by pundits and opinion makers), he or she loves the children and will remain their friend for life. The Scorpio parent enjoys their children and cares passionately about family life.

Scorpio Child

The Scorpio child is penetrating and intense, something which might lead other kids to misunderstand and avoid them. These youngsters aren't necessarily trying to be nosy; they just have an intense desire to know what's going on. They may also be a little less than subtle in their approach with their schoolmates, but at least they're candid. Motivated as they are to get to the bottom of things, once the Scorpio child gets an objective in mind, well, that's it. Trying to deflect these youngsters from the course they are on is nearly impossible.

An extremely resourceful child, the Scorpio youngster will do well on a fact-finding mission, whether it's looking for a good movie to see or seizing the best deal on the latest CD. This child's mind is also geared toward scientific and investigative pursuits, so encourage them to watch the Discovery Channel or buy them a chemistry set. As they can be quite mysterious as well, it will be hard to tell exactly what the Scorpio child is feeling, something which may, again, make it hard for this kid to attract friends. The Scorpio child will usually have one intense friendship. This child can be a bit jealous of others, making for some friction at school. Even so, those kids who do bring the Scorpio child into their circle will grow to appreciate their passionate and all-knowing friend.

Bringing Up Scorpio—Coach's Insight

Scorpio children are usually active, quick to learn, and highly intelligent. They have a passionate curiosity that demands to be satisfied, so investigating anything forbidden is a challenge which this youngster must be dissuaded from rising to.

Scorpionic children need a private place and opportunities to be left undisturbed. This is a basic requirement for them to feel secure.

Scorpio children must be taught to understand the rights and needs of others, so that they can learn to forgive the hurts and mishaps of everyday life.

SCORPIO AND FRIENDS

SCORPIO HAS ONLY a few friends, to whom they are intensely loyal and from whom they expect 100 percent loyalty.

The Scorpion has a fantastic memory and adores telling jokes. Scorpios are generous to a fault, hospitable, and extremely good at giving reliable advice. They can also be trusted to be unshockable and discreet.

FRIENDS, BE AWARE

IF YOU WANT to keep parts of yourself hidden, don't have a Scorpio for a friend. This sign has an almost psychic insight into the thoughts and motives of others.

Scorpio expects friends to make most of the effort in the relationship and rarely drops in on friends without a fixed purpose in mind—this sign can be a bit of a user and may dump friends who are no longer useful. Scorpio does, however, expect friends to call on them—if the Scorpion is out, that's the friend's misfortune; they'll just have to call again.

HEALTH

YOUR sign is the most intense in the zodiac. Change is hard for Scorpio, the fixed water sign, to accept. You are very determined and driven by goals, but while persistence is your forte, flexibility is not. You must learn that not all events are controllable; sometimes all we can control is our reaction to them. As your water element makes you feel the impact of events deeply, you must learn not to take set-backs personally.

Among your talents is a sharp and shrewd intuition, which will help you navigate through turbulent waters and deal with change that is not chosen by you. You have great self-belief and "know" that things will turn out all right for you. At times, facts may not gel with certain hunches you have and it will be hard for you to trust the hunches. Do it. Many Scorpios are psychic or even prophetic, "feeling" events around them that are soon to happen. Try the Decision making: Cultivating Your Inner Voice exercise from the Aries (page 10) to help with this, Scorpio.

STRESS BUSTING FOR SCORPIO

YOUR SIGN, MORE than any other, has occasionally to take time out to be alone. Your Pluto ruler can sometimes make you compulsive about your work. You may need to let up a little, particularly if you're neglecting your other needs. Try to take time out by the sea, listen to a recording of waves, or just visualize a watery scene, as water is truly vital to water signs, and it will be easier to recover your sense of purpose near water.

Meditation and prayer are good for Scorpio, because Scorpio is a deeply spiritual sign, and often has an understanding and interest in religions. Because their sign rules the house of birth–death cycles, Scorpios are close to life's beginnings and endings.

Slow, deliberate exercise, such as yoga or t'ai chi, would be helpful to you, as would any solitary activity, like running (along the water would be perfect) or lifting weights. Yours is a sign that likes to compete with itself rather than others, always reaching for a personal best.

Quiet games of contemplation and skill are perfect for you too. Play chess or war games (good games of strategy for discreet Scorpio) with a friend who can throw you a challenge. You like mystery novels too. Spy stories where the fate of the world hinges on the actions of one individual will relax you and provide you with a hero you can identify with.

An excellent way for you to slow down is by using personal rituals, something your fixed, water nature responds to. By ritual I don't mean an activity connected to religion but one that you create spontaneously to mark or recognize an event, whether it be happy or sad. Whether you lost a pet, got fired, need to say goodbye to an ex-lover, or want to ask your sweetheart to marry you, make a ritual out of it. Rituals help us communicate with our subconscious and focus our intensity and will. The ritual could be a quick, simple one (writing down your feelings about a broken relationship and then burning what you wrote with all the love letters you had saved) or a bigger one (a funeral for your pet). Rituals can help you relax and become more in sync with your life.

Finally, Scorpio, try not to shut out loved ones. A Scorpio who is feeling troubled is nearly impossible to read, and when stress hits, you will seem a million miles away to your family and friends. While initially you will feel depleted by everyday life, including conversation, those around you will want to help you by giving you their perspective on your plight. Sometimes Scorpios remain isolated within themselves for far too long, as tension makes them throw up barriers in self-protection. But if you aren't getting any input from others, your perspective can become distorted. Remember that fear is only False Evidence Appearing Real. It helps to get evidence from other sources in order to get things into perspective. Recognize that this can happen to you. Your need for physical affection is great when you are stressed, and affection will reaffirm your sense of self-worth, but your lover will hesitate to reach out to you if you shut him or her out. Open up a little and see how things go. Accept and give physical love.

FITNESS

SCORPIO rules the nose, back, legs, ankles, spine, throat, and reproductive organs. Your metabolism is high.

Intense, driven, and often secretive, Scorpio needs an outlet for its powerful emotions more than any other sign, even Cancer or Pisces. You can be obsessive, and have an "all or nothing" determination about whatever you do. So, for example, when Scorpios decide to diet, they can go overboard. This can be harmful if it leads to an eating disorder. Whatever a Scorpio puts their mind to, they usually accomplish.

You'll need to be smart about channeling any pent-up frustrations into healthy, stress-relieving activities. Boxing, long-distance running, or a fast game of racquetball (any strenuous sport is good) could help you use up all that energy and stress before it starts to hurt you. You might also like to discharge anger and pent-up frustrations by doing the Roar, Toro, Roar exercise in the Taurus chapter (page 64).

Although your sign is highly competitive, you prefer to be alone when trying to unwind. Scorpio usually does not like to work out in teams or groups and prefers to compete with itself and its own personal best. Try the Stairmaster, weight lifting (Mars governs iron), or gymnastics. Slow jogging or yoga asanas and meditation also provides great ways for you to unwind. Of course, the fact that exercise is good for your sex life should be a big motivating factor for any hot-blooded Scorpio!

A Scorpio without physical affection will soon feel sad or lonely. If your sex life is less than ideal, talk things out with your partner, or get some counseling. If you have casual sexual partners, remember to practice safe sex.

You have a rich and varied emotional life, to say the least. Be sure to share your problems with those close to you as soon as they occur (not months later, which is Scorpio's tendency), so that you can let go of feeling frustrated and resentful. Then you can use the freed up energy for more important pursuits, like achieving your goals. Realize that the demands you place on yourself are higher than those anyone else would impose on you, so you can afford to cut yourself some slack. You continually try to pack as much as possible into every day. Take time to look around you every so often so that you can savor all that you've accomplished and all that the universe has to offer. Remember, too, that you can get to be obsessed with things. Try for more balance.

TOOLS FOR MAKING A DIFFERENCE

MANY PEOPLE HAVE trouble attaining their goals; this is not a challenge for Scorpios, however. Your challenge is to decide what you want and to find constructive ways of getting it. For an exercise on knowing what you want and why, see Getting Your Needs Met in Cancer (page 116). In order to excel, Scorpio, you need to manage that anger of yours—you can choose whether to eviscerate your partner when they irritate you or to go for a long walk to unwind. The choice is yours.

EXERCISE TWO

Dealing with Anger

Learn to identify your anger. Use the following as clues:
- ◆ Your body language—if you are leaning forward flashing your eyes and jabbing your fingers, you are probably angry.
- ◆ The language and verbal expressions you use.
- ◆ Other people's reactions—are they reacting angrily, being confrontational? If so, the chances are that they are responding to your anger.
- ◆ What is going on in your life right now? Is it something you think might make you angry?
- ◆ Your stress levels and body tension.

Identify the kind of anger you feel. Is it:
- ◆ Situational (due to environment/events)
- ◆ Interpersonal (due to people/relationships with others)
- ◆ General—i.e., neither situational nor interpersonal

Let's say, for example, that you are feeling enraged about a situation at work. You could begin to deal with your anger by carrying out the following:

- Determine what can help you cope with your anger on the job
- Establish your goals, both long- and short-term
- Define your resources
- Look at your credentials
  Consider your past contributions
- Look at your personal power
  Think about the people you work with
  Consider your connections in your field
- Build up savings that enable you to take a risk and leave your job

Now let's think about what can help you cope with anger in personal situations:

- Having a sense of humor
- Sticking to specifics when discussion begins
- Developing detachment
- Maintaining a positive attitude
- Crying or some other form of releasing pent-up frustration
- Relaxing
- Not becoming threatened or taking another's reactions personally
- Speaking up

If you need to explode, withdraw and do it alone. Explain the reason for your departure.

SPIRITUALITY

ASTROLOGICALLY, a Scorpio is said to be at one of three stages of evolution.

A stage one Scorpio is symbolized by the scorpion and exercises power through emotion and instinct. In this first stage, the scorpion will sting others and then itself in remorse.

A stage two Scorpio is symbolized by the golden eagle and exercises power through the intellect. In the second stage the scorpion will observe the flow of power, both political and sexual. It will then swoop down and seize its victim.

A stage three Scorpio is symbolized by the dove of peace and the phoenix, and exercises power through love. The phoenix represents the scorpion transformed. Gone is the tendency to be judgmental and power-obsessed. In its place there is the capacity for observation without judgment and, therefore, with compassion. This is a scorpion that can teach others to focus on what is hidden and which really matters.

The scorpion is as complex as his or her three symbols imply, and Scorpio's highest task is to achieve self-mastery through self-reform. In this way, Scorpio can eventually transcend his or her lower scorpion existence and attain the higher levels of the eagle or dove. Deep down, the scorpion knows that it is his or her life task to transform. Scorpio always knows how to recycle itself, rising from the ashes of pain and defeat and a life spent relentlessly pursuing extremes.

Achieving power through cooperation and love is the scorpion's major challenge. Achieving this type of power does not come from trying to conform to someone else's expectations but from developing a deep awareness of one's own being and potential. From Taurus, its opposite sign, Scorpio can learn to recognize and value the talents of others, and in this way value his or her talents more realistically. The scorpion must learn to curb his or her misuse of power and arrive at the point where he or she uses power in the service of love.

Some Scorpios adore organized religion. They love the power of ritual and the sense of belonging. Others of you will explore and embrace more unorthodox belief systems in your quest for spiritual answers. Whatever route you take, you will bring fervent idealism to your search.

CHAPTER 9

SAGITTARIUS

November 22–December 21

THE NINTH SIGN OF THE ZODIAC IS CONCERNED WITH:

◆ PHILOSOPHY, RELIGION, IDEALISM, SPIRITUALITY
◆ OPTIMISM, POSITIVE OUTLOOK, FORWARD PLANNING, ASPIRATIONS
◆ WIT, INTELLECT
◆ TRAVEL, FREEDOM OF MOVEMENT, THE OUTDOORS
◆ OPEN-MINDEDNESS
◆ GENEROSITY, PLEASURE, ROMANCE
◆ FLASHES OF INSPIRATION, INTUITION, IMAGINATION

SAGITTARIUS, the ninth sign of the zodiac, takes its nature from the dualism of the centaur and the flying arrow that he releases from his bow. This is a sign associated with long journeys, whether of the mind, body, or spirit, and as far as this archer is concerned, it is more important to travel than to arrive. As it is the planet Jupiter, the ruler of wisdom, which rules Sagittarius, Sagittarian journeys are often idealistic experiments in religion, philosophy or the arts, of which the desire is to elevate the human spirit. Sometimes the journey will be physical, for Sagittarians are truth seekers, and the best way for them to find truth is to hit the road, talk to others, and get some answers. The lesson Sagittarius needs to learn is that, like a moving arrow, truth is difficult to pin down. The Sagittarian archer is a centaur, a creature with the hind quarters of a horse and the torso, head, and arms of a human being. This suggests a complicated nature, combining beast with human, instinct with reason, body with spirit. Sagittarius's deeper purpose is to reconcile these two opposites. This paradox in the sign's nature is difficult for observers to detect, only emerging in the form of sudden and changeable enthusiasms.

Centaurs were the intellectuals of ancient Roman mythology, and Sagittarians are truly their modern-day counterparts. Those born under this sign are clear thinkers and have an innate ability to see the big picture most of the time. Sagittarians tend to expect others to agree with their well-thought-out point of view, and become brutally argumentative with those who don't. That's not to say that these folks are intransigent—archers will listen to what others have to say, in keeping with the mutable quality assigned to this sign, provided that they rate the person as an intellectual equal. Indeed, Sagittarians are enthusiastic consumers of information (and enthusiastic in general), the better to get the answers they need. As with all seekers of the truth, it's a good idea to give Sagittarians lots of room to explore their world. If you try to constrain them, they'll bolt immediately.

Sagittarians are generous and just, much like a noble leader. After all, Jupiter was king of the gods. The Sagittarian-born are usually expansive in their thoughts, as well as in their approach to life. Sagittarians are eternal optimists continually forging forward in their never ending quest for knowledge, understanding, and answers. They are also a lucky bunch, thanks to Jupiter's golden glow. They're quick to take a risk or make a snap decision, feeling both lucky and smart. The flashes of inspiration and imagination that bless this sign help with luck creation. Sagittarians can be quite self-indulgent, since things come so easily to them (thanks to their charming and sociable natures). Smart Saggies, however, will catch themselves in time, the better to continue their good work.

The element associated with Sagittarius is fire. This, combined with the quality of mutability, makes the sign unstable; its plans are often dropped before completion. This sign has a tendency to enjoy the journey more than the arrival. For the Sagittarius-born, life is all about action and adventure (and not always conclusions).

Sagittarians, the zodiac's wanderers, are often very athletic and full of stamina. Archers are keen to make every second count, so their lives are usually full of experiences, which they are more than happy to share with others. The outgoing, enthusiastic archer is one of the zodiac's great teachers, but in his eagerness to convey knowledge can be blunt and tactless, leading to the occasional hurt feeling. More usually, however, his words serve to inspire others and to get things going. Sagittarians are fun-loving, charismatic, and love to socialize—though they prefer an ever changing cast of acquaintances to long lasting deep connections.

The great strength of the Sagittarius-born lies in their optimism and enthusiasm; their weakness is their impracticality.

STRENGTHS TO FOCUS ON

▶ **Optimistic and enthusiastic**
▶ **Sees the best in others**
▶ **Frank, open, and outspoken**
▶ **Spiritual**
▶ **Sensual**
▶ **Enthusiastic**
▶ **Stimulating**
▶ **Inspiring**
▶ **Disarmingly happy, can turn failure into success**
▶ **Happy-go-lucky**
▶ **Honest and fair-minded**
▶ **Holds no grudges**

For help with making the most of these positives, see the S.M.A.R.Test Goals for Aries exercise (page 3).

WEAKNESSES THAT CAN TRIP YOU UP

▶ **Argumentativeness and impatience to be moving**
▶ **Gambling**
▶ **Tendency to be hot-headed**
▶ **Can fail to plan adequately**
▶ **Critical of those who deny their talents**
▶ **Preachiness**

- Disregard for convention
- Denies sadness
- Uncommitted
- Fears responsibility and curtailment of personal freedom
- Blundering and inept
- Indulgent

So how do you change these so-called weaknesses into powerful tools for personal growth? See the Love Your Weaknesses exercise in the Aries chapter (page 6) for help with this.

Sagittarians can get bored very easily. For areas in your life where you cannot turn this tendency into a strength you might want to take look at Define Your Boredom (page 77), An Awareness Exercise for Gemini and Interesting People (pages 90, 91) all in the Gemini chapter.

SAGITTARIUS MAN

Unless there are influences in his birth chart that are stronger than his Sagittarius sun sign, the typical Sagittarius male will have some or all of the following characteristics:

- Always ready to learn
- Has an adventurous spirit
- Needs to flirt
- Attracted to glamour
- Moves quickly though not always gracefully
- Charming
- Can turn failure into success
- Often gesticulates
- Can be tactless, though never deliberately cruel
- Will say exactly what is on his mind
- Is a formidable opponent
- Is trusting and gullible until let down
- Has a superb memory for facts but can misplace everyday objects

▶ Tells very funny jokes, but can blow the punch line
▶ Likes learning and study

SAGITTARIUS WOMAN

In addition to the personality and behavior traits exhibited by the Sagittarian male, Sagittarius woman:

▶ Attracts complications
▶ Can send the wrong signals, sometimes sees friendship as love
▶ Has a steady, open, and honest gaze
▶ Moves purposefully
▶ Is totally honest
▶ Is often unconventional, particularly in relationships
▶ Takes risks and is adaptable in a crisis
▶ Lives by her own clear moral code and is difficult to change
▶ Gets angry if her integrity is questioned
▶ Needs complete freedom of thought and action
▶ Regards others as equals
▶ Can be deceived in romance, though she is sharp in other areas of her life
▶ Is kind though sometimes tactless
▶ Will laugh even though her heart is breaking. The same stoicism applies when she is in physical pain.
▶ Can be cuttingly sarcastic when hurt

THE HIDDEN (OR NOT-SO-HIDDEN) SAGITTARIUS

A PERSON WITH strong Sagittarian tendencies is someone who wants to be free. Any Sagittarian who is held back in life or love or from an opportunity to grow spiritually will be deeply unhappy, although they will hide this well. Like the centaur, Sagittarius will often experience conflicts between mind and body. The Sagittarian purpose is to reconcile these conflicts so that they may teach others.

SAGITTARIUS LIKES

- Sport and outdoor activities
- Socializing
- Practical jokes
- Total freedom
- Traveling
- Challenges
- Taking risks

SAGITTARIUS DISLIKES

- Being tied down
- Making promises or committing themselves
- Administration
- Authority
- People who don't trust them
- Being confined, restricted or prevented from taking any risks.

POSSIBLE PROBLEM AREAS FOR SAGITTARIUS, AND SOLUTIONS

ALL SUN SIGNS have unique personality traits. When these traits are suppressed, problems will arise. However, with a winning combination of astrology and coaching, we can examine the problem and assess the proper solution based on sun sign characteristics. If, as a Sagittarian, you see things below that really strike home, try the solution. You may well be amazed at the results.

PROBLEM: Others have no time for you, as you are apt to have too many balls in the air at any given time.

SOLUTION: Be sure that you can live up to your promises.

PROBLEM: Others cease to confide in you or to take you seriously.

SOLUTION: Try not to exaggerate or make promises that you cannot deliver on.

PROBLEM: Feeling lost and disillusioned.

SOLUTION: Focus on one thing that will satisfy you and work toward whatever goals it involves.

PROBLEM: Getting tired out and not finishing projects that you have in progress.

SOLUTION: Try not to make too many plans and avoid having them scheduled too close together. Learn to pace yourself better.

PROBLEM: You seem anchored in one spot, unable to move forward.

SOLUTION: Try to think more positive thoughts and set some short-term goals that you can reach, then set more. In this way, you will move ahead in your endeavors.

Look at the Define Your Values exercise in Aries (page 20) for help with identifying areas of your life/goals that you want to focus on. Goals that are in alignment with your values are easier to stick to and are achieved more quickly.

CAREER/BUSINESS

SAGITTARIUS needs a challenge and will seek one in even the most dull or routine job. The travel-loving, challenge-seeking, sociable archer is a great person to have on your sales team—they'll probably get the order, hopefully before they unintentionally insult the client! This is a sign that demands intellectual and physical exercise and needs to do several things at once to perform at its best. It is also extremely versatile, so entrepreneurship or working in a chaotic, fast-paced, and flexible environment will appeal. The archer is a good team player who can plot the course ahead with broad brushstrokes and convince everyone around that it's the way to go. This can be a double-edged sword, though, since Sagittarians tend to look at the big picture and neglect important details. An efficient aide-de-camp is essential for the detail-averse archer.

Sagittarians like to have fun and are positively brimming with optimism. This is a sign that backs its hunches and charges forward to join battle with the competition, or indeed anything that gets in the archer's way. Sagittarians are fanatical about what they believe in and, as befits a fire sign, will work doggedly for their causes. If the archer bumps up against a brick wall, he or she will simply correct their approach and start off again. Public service and turn-around situations were made for the archer.

The archer is adept at social situations and insatiably curious. Knowledge is power to those born under this sign, which makes them excellent researchers. What to do with all this information? Put it to work, of course! The archer may choose to have more than one job and will certainly have intellectual pursuits outside work. This is a sign with limitless energy—the only time the archer flags is when he or she gets bored!

The Sagittarius office is often no more than an address. Virtual offices were made for this sign, since the archer would rather be elsewhere.

SAGITTARIUS CAREER GUIDE

SAGITTARIANS ARE WELL suited for a career as a travel agent, explorer, professor, photographer, ambassador, import–export trader, or thrill seeker.

Here are some other occupations that a Sagittarius might consider:

Academic	Forecaster	Minister
Adventurer	Franchisee	Missionary
Advertiser	Guide	Philosopher
Ambassador	Horse trainer	Preacher
Archer	Interpreter	Promoter
Bishop	Jockey	Publisher
Bookseller	Judge	Sportsperson
Broadcaster	Lawyer	Theologian
Clergyman/woman	Lecturer	Translator
College teacher	Librarian	Tutor
Diplomat	Magistrate	
Editor	Marketer	

SAGITTARIUS BOSS

THE SAGITTARIAN MANAGER is fun-loving and fair, yet not a natural candidate for a managerial role. The archer is far more interested in grand visions than in hands-on management. Sagittarius is more of a teacher and motivator. Sagittarians's tendency to run their team as a democracy can be hard for those who need clear directions, and, due to their tremendous optimism and inattention to detail, Sagittarians may have a tendency to expect too much of their coworkers. It is not because they are trying to work people into the ground; it is only that their grand visions get the better of them sometimes. They visualize great results and don't always understand the detailed work that may need to go into the project. Sagittarians can have a tendency to shoot their mouth off and preach to their people. This is fine when they are giving an uplifting and motivating speech; however, employees might find their impractical and even occasionally tactless nature a little hard to swallow. Try some of the communication exercises in Aries (pages 12–14), if this applies to you, Sagittarius. If a Sagittarius praises your work, the praise given will be honest and sincere. However, if they criticize, things can get unpleasant, as they tend to speak first and think later. They can also be rather arrogant, boasting and grinning their way through the worst messes. They are also people who encourage constant changes in the work routine to provide for new growth, optimism, and creativity. When employees show initiative and independence, they will earn the Sagittarian manager's respect. When you need them, Sagittarians will be there for you, and they are quick to offer advice. This is a sign that regards the role of manager as that of coach inspiring their team to greater feats of creativity. If, as an employee, you find yourself in trouble, you can count on their support, provided that you have been seen to act with integrity and to put your all into your work.

SAGITTARIUS EMPLOYEE

A TYPICAL SAGITTARIAN works best when they are allowed to work at their own pace, which is usually fast. You are not a sign that responds well to hands-on management and will routinely challenge and question orders and procedures.

You can have a tendency toward outspokenness, boasting about your achievements, interrupting your boss, and finishing colleagues's sentences for them. You can also have a habit of taking on too much and then letting others down, leading to frustration and resentment. Learn to under-promise, Sagittarius. If you think a job will take four days, offer to do it in five; that way you'll win plenty of fans when you pleasantly surprise everyone by getting your work done before your deadline. I'll admit that you usually achieve more in a day than most of us do in a week, Sagittarius, but you do still have a tendency to take on too much.

The archer will often focus only on those parts of his or her work that engage the intellect, thus gaining a reputation for taking a casual approach to work. However, when problems arise that require rapid solutions, people rely on you to provide valuable insights. You are usually an excellent judge of character and your hunches are often so accurate that they border on the uncanny.

The Sagittarian employee does not come cheap. He or she is more interested in immediate gratification than long-term incentives and deferred bonus potential. To help you get what you're worth now, have a look at the Determine Your Value (page 274) and Mining "Hidden Gold" Opportunities (page 276) exercises in Capricorn.

Negotiating is not a Sagittarius forte—you are too blunt and competitive. You love battle too much for the concept of win–win to hold much appeal for you. You can become so obsessed with your ideal solution that you forget to consider its feasibility. However, if you can't teach the art of negotiating to a colleague, have a look at the Preparing for Negotiation exercise in Aries (page 25) and The 100 Point Guide to Negotiating in Virgo (page 171).

The only real barrier to Sagittarius's success is a—sometimes excessive—fear of losing their independence if they get too successful.

FINANCES AND WEALTH

SAGITTARIANS love to spend. Due to their tendencies both to demand what is rightfully theirs and to live in the present, they usually have plenty of money with which to do it. Sagittarius is also considered the luckiest sign of the zodiac. This is in no small part due to the fact that optimistic Sagittarians are very good at making their own luck. The archer loves to plan ahead and can usually transform even the most negative situation. This is an enthusiastic sign that travels through life at high speed, forever looking for the opportunity of a lifetime and having great fun on the way.

Sagittarians love money and what it will buy—mainly fun and freedom. Money will give the archer the ability to choose how they spend their time, and that's a powerful motivator for him. Sagittarians rarely worry about money either, since they take the view that worrying won't make them any richer. Sagittarians firmly believe that one day their ship will come in, a feeling that feeds their gambling and risk-taking spirit.

The archer is generous to a fault and is eager to spread the wealth around. Sagittarians also love to lend, especially to friends, and the borrower will often find that these loans are turned into gifts. Lending money to Sag is dicey, as they're likely to forget to pay it back. They are seriously at risk of overspending, as the minutiae of money management bores them to tears—they'd much rather be cutting the next big deal. In short, they are well advised to hire an accountant.

The optimistic archer can have trouble believing that there will ever be a time when they are stretched financially. However, it is advisable to build up a financial reserve just in case. Sagittarius often has a tendency to gamble, but if he keeps his lust for striking it rich under control, he has nothing to fear. Only gamble with what you can afford to lose, Sagittarius. Your biggest financial downfall lies in being overly confident that you can spend today because tomorrow something will show up to improve your economic situation. Most of the time it does—it's the other times you need to plan for! Your unshakable optimism is the reason for your greatest successes and biggest failures. Beware of overestimating the value of future prospects and beware of your tendency to bank on a miracle.

For useful exercises on finances, see Building Up a Rainy-Day Fund in Aries (page 28) and The Nice and Easy Does It Way to $1000 in Gemini (page 85).

LOVE, ROMANCE, AND SEX LIFE

SAGITTARIANS are truth seekers, focused intensely on learning about their lover and exploring them more deeply. Those born under this sign are intuitive, and as a result have a good sense of what and whom they want. In fact, the archer wants to explore everything deeply, so conversations in bed can run the gamut from religion to politics, and which position is most comfortable. These dynamic, freewheeling individuals are highly social. They are also extremely flirtatious and freedom loving, and this can be a heady aphrodisiac to many.

A relationship with the archer will be active and spirited, as Sagittarius adores both the mental and physical pleasures of love. Traveling to far-off lands, whether in reality or as a bedroom fantasy, is likely for those who pair up with the centaur. Sagittarius makes for an enthusiastic and loyal lover, but the Sagittarian's partner must be careful not to make the mistake of becoming boring or possessive. If so, they'll be unceremoniously dumped (minor rifts, though, are willingly patched up in bed).

COMPATIBILITY

OTHER FIRE SIGNS and air signs are compatible with Sagittarius. Polar opposite Gemini makes a great mate.

WHAT SAGITTARIUS NEEDS

THE ARCHER NEEDS a loyal and stimulating friend who is undemanding emotionally and independent. Sagittarius also prizes a lover who understands and embraces the value of time alone. Mental stimulation can be as exciting as the sexual kind for Sagittarians, though the centaur does need plenty of sexual activity. If conversation is honest and open, things will continue to develop and grow. An equal in the bedroom is also a powerful pull.

THE END OF THE AFFAIR

IF A PARTNER is demanding or possessive, the centaur will rapidly ride off into the sunset. Sagittarians are exceedingly sociable and crave stimulation, so are prone to having the odd casual affair if the relationship becomes stale.

COACH'S TIP

Have a look in the sections on Love, Romance, and Sex Life in Gemini and Aries for information on combating boredom in a relationship. You may want to read the Gemini section in its entirety, as this is a sign which, like yours, suffers from a tendency to get exceedingly bored and wary of deep emotional commitments. You are two of the zodiac's free spirits. It might also be advisable to warn partners who are seeking intense relationships that this isn't your idea of romantic bliss—if it isn't. Look at the Choosing an Available Partner exercise in the Taurus chapter (page 57) to avoid mismatched levels of commitment.

RELATIONSHIPS
(Family and Friends)

SAGITTARIUS PARENT

THE TYPICAL SAGITTARIAN parent has very clear moral standards and will always answer questions honestly. The archer also has complete faith in his or her offspring and can have a tendency to expect too much from them intellectually.

The archer is always eager to take his or her children traveling, play with them, or talk to them. This is a very involved parent who is committed to providing a stimulating environment for their children to thrive in. Sagittarius thoroughly enjoys parenting and is great fun as a parent. He or she takes parental responsibilities seriously and is eager to give children all the tools necessary to take on and enjoy the outside world. This is not a parent who encourages dependency; the centaur expects his or her children to leave home when they are grown up.

SAGITTARIUS CHILD

THE SAGITTARIUS CHILD is an eternal optimist and true live wire who will attract and entertain many friends. He or she believes in equality even at this tender age, so friends are likely to be an extremely diverse bunch, all the better to feed this child's imagination. The Sagittarius child has an inquiring, flexible mind and will have no trouble grasping diverse subjects.

A free-spirited youngster, this kid loves to travel and explore. He or she is likely to want to go on school trips, particularly those that involve action, exploration, and adventure. This energy and enthusiasm makes the Sagittarius child a natural at sport. Sagittarian children are talkative, and their candor could get them into trouble—particularly if they start challenging adults or blurting out overheard adult gossip. However, the sunny archer's happy disposition means that they are unlikely to be in the doghouse for long.

BRINGING UP SAGITTARIUS—COACH'S INSIGHT

MOST SAGITTARIANS LOVE learning and hate being held back by what they see as needless rules, so they need to be given a logical, reasoned explanation as to why they should obey parental or societal strictures. The Sagittarian child is extremely bright and will lose no time in uncovering and questioning or making fun of adult hypocrisy—the best thing you can do with this child is to be totally honest.

Sagittarius must be given and allowed to take every opportunity for socializing, exploring, and learning to prevent boredom and frustration setting in.

As Sagittarius is a sign that is uncomfortable with intense, possessive love, this is a child that needs love in the form of encouragement and demonstrations of pleasure in their achievements.

In addition to being taught that some rules have to be obeyed for very good reason, young Sag needs to be taught how to handle money from an early age. Given that this is a very libidinous sign, a thorough grounding in the facts of life would be wise as well.

SAGITTARIUS AND FRIENDS

SAGITTARIANS TEND TO prefer friends who are open-minded, ready for adventure, and trusting. They are friendly, gregarious people who will collect friends from all walks of life, provided that they meet the centaur's personal standards. They themselves make loyal friends who speak their minds (they can be brutally honest) and who will respond to any request for help. Sagittarius is a sign that has a special bond with animals, so don't be surprised if your Sagittarian comes with assorted wildlife—as my husband found to his dismay.

FRIENDS, BE AWARE

SAGITTARIUS IS LIKELY to have a maximum of one or two close friends—everyone else will have the status of acquaintance. The archer will also block people who try to get too close too quickly. Sagittarius will be the one to set the pace in any dance of friendship.

The centaur may be a little eccentric and may also find it difficult to keep a secret.

Truth or Dare: Telling It Like It Is

YOUR tendency to be brutally honest can serve to kick-start your relationships and ambitions or kill them stone dead. While I'm not advocating deceit, there are more palatable ways of telling it like it is. I know that you feel it's important to tell the truth—you feel uncomfortable around disingenuous people—but there are ways of doing this without alienating others. This exercise will help you become better at telling the truth without hurting others.

First, get a friend or lover to draw up a range of questions asking for your opinion on political, personal, and sexual issues. Questions might range from "Does my behind look big in this?" to "Do you think hunting should be banned?"

Make up different answers to each question, ranging from sincere and sensitive to blunt and brutal, so that you get a sense of the different ways in which you can answer each question honestly.

Which mode of response is the most effective in terms of getting your message across?

Ask your friend or lover whether they agree with your conclusions and what their emotional responses are to the ways in which you answered each question.

What have you learned from this?

What will you do differently as a result of carrying out this exercise?

HEALTH

AN EASYGOING and tolerant sign, you rarely get stressed or irritated by life events. As a mutable sign, you deal with change exceptionally well, adjusting your course as soon as alarm bells begin to go off. You're intuitive and usually pick up warning signals before incurring too much damage. Your only real problem may be a tendency to be overoptimistic, not allowing for delays or plain old bad luck. You also like to move ahead quickly and get extremely bored with details. This combination can occasionally trip you up, since you can miss something important or judge a situation incorrectly. To help combat this, I suggest that you surround yourself with detail/analytical air types (Gemini, Aquarius, or Libra) or hire an earth sign (Virgo, Taurus, or Capricorn) assistant to balance you. The fire in your nature makes you enthusiastic, energetic, and creative in thinking up new plans and ideas.

STRESS BUSTING FOR SAGITTARIUS

WHEN STRESS BEGINS to get to you, do something physical, preferably outside. Being outdoors regularly is good for you, as Sagittarius is not a sign known to sit still happily or stay cooped up inside for too long. Many Sagittarians enjoy going for a good long walk, preferably with a four-legged companion. Walking usually enables the archer to clear away mental clutter and allows creativity to surface. This unity of mind and body is highly regarded and maintained by Sagittarius. Since your sign is symbolized by the centaur, you might enjoy horseback riding. Games of agility, such as fencing or archery, could also appeal.

Sagittarius rules large animals, so perhaps visit a wildlife sanctuary or safari park. If it's human company that you seek, hang out with positive spirits like yourself. Choose a Leo, Aries, Gemini, Aquarius, or Libra. The water signs are likely to be too emotional for you, and the earth signs too serious (earth puts out fire).

Like your opposite sign, Gemini, you thoroughly enjoy books, so to help you unwind, why not go to the nearest bookstore or library? Books that deal with philosophy and mysticism are likely to appeal, as are books on travel, different cultures, and heroic exploits.

As a sign that is engaged in a perpetual search for truth and meaning, you might relish talking to religious people, scholars, or philosophers—anyone whose take on life fires your imagination. Sagittarius is a give-and-take sign that is not threatened by others' differing views. Highly cerebral, you like the process of debate and will relish the challenge of converting another to your point of view. Through exposing yourself to unfamiliar points of view, you may be able to come up with creative solutions to whatever is causing your tension. Failing that, the process of learning something new always relaxes the centaur.

Finally, think about getting away for a short break if you can spare the time. Sometimes it is necessary to get away to see one's problems with objectivity.

FITNESS

SAGITTARIUS rules the pelvis, hips, ileac arteries, sciatic nerve, femur, thighs, gluteus muscles, and sacrum. Your metabolism is high.

Lucky Sagittarius! You are active and often excel at one or more sports. More Olympic champions are Sagittarius than any other sign. You've got a lot going for you: strength, natural rhythm, speed, and confidence that you'll win. Outgoing and social, you enjoy being with friends when you exercise and like a little friendly rivalry to engage your active mind.

Curious and dynamic, you'll give most sports a try and, as a result, your body is probably the envy of your friends. Sagittarius intuitively feels the link between body and mind and regularly seeks ways to strengthen both. Sports that require physical activity and focus are the sports of choice for you, Sagittarius.

You can have a tendency to overindulge in rich foods and drink, particularly when bored and frustrated. Fortunately, Sagittarius is usually so active that weight gain does not tend to be a problem. If it is, the archer will usually manage to shed excess weight through sheer determination once they have decided to do so.

Just before you get too complacent, Sagittarius, watch that boredom and ill discipline don't get in the way of developing that fine physique. If you feel bored, try a new outdoor sport (forget exercising indoors, it's too confined) to get out of a rut.

TOOLS FOR MAKING A DIFFERENCE

SAMENESS BORES SAGITTARIANS. You continually search for greener pastures, often failing to appreciate the treasures you have close to home. Try listing ten things you feel grateful for. Do this each and every morning in order to combat your tendency to institute change for change's sake.

You can also find yourself dissatisfied as you continually rearrange and redo things in your search for solutions. You can be so blinded by your vision of how life should be that you lose your sense of self. You need to keep your critical faculties in place, Sagittarius—what is "blatantly obvious" to you is not always correct.

You can grow impatient when the pace of life fails to keep up with your ideals and expectations. You may also become judgmental of those whose beliefs are different from your own, but if you direct your zeal toward developing tolerance, you can escape the traps of self-righteousness.

While boredom is not usually a problem—you're interested in everything—committing to one course of action often is. Your constant need for stimulation can lead you to neglect projects that seem more of an obligation than fun. As you let these projects pile up, you can feel an overwhelming urge to cut and run, leaving chaos behind you. Watch that your wanderlust isn't born out of an urge to duck responsibility. If you really want to attain your life's goals, you're going to have to learn to rein in and discipline that restless mind of yours. You could make a start by seeing a boring project through to the bitter end.

A great challenge for you is to understand the needs and emotions of both yourself and those closest to you. You have a tendency immediately to move away from feelings of self-doubt and anger, which means that you can find yourself failing to learn the lessons that life offers you. You need to bite the bullet and become a little more self-analytical if you are to realize your potential and create a life that really works for you. While you are able to read the feelings of a group with ease (and often champion group causes), you are less adept at understanding or reading those closest to you. In order to have an easier time dealing with your own feelings and those of others, you need to become more adept at two-way communication. Take a look at the listening exercises for Aries to help with reading others (page 12–14), and The Magnificent Seven Steps to Setting Boundaries exercise in Taurus (page 48) to help you with telling others what you need from them.

As a sign that is goal- and action-oriented and shuns self-analysis, you can have a tendency to self-sabotage. For an exercise to help combat this see Avoiding Self-sabotage in Taurus (page 70). By doing this exercise, you will be making use of both your analytical and intuitive faculties. As a Sagittarius you are often happiest when acting impulsively, so be careful that you don't allow your rational brain to inhibit this process—just because you can't articulate the process that leads you to a particular decision doesn't mean that it's the wrong one. By all means, use your intellect to filter your intuitive decisions, but don't become too heavily reliant upon it. If you need to reconnect with your inner voice, have a look at the Heads You Win, Tails You Win in Libra and Cultivating Your Inner Voice in Aries (pages 216 and 10), and the Intuition Workout exercise from Cancer (page 113).

Your greatest resource—your limitless energy—is also your greatest challenge. To harness this fund of power you need to learn how to control it. By control, I mean using self-discipline to focus and direct your mind and actions toward attaining those worthwhile goals that you are constantly seeking. Worthwhile goals are those that are in keeping with your values and ethics. By focusing on goals that are attainable (you do need to inject a dose of realism into your quests) and value-led you will find that you have a stronger self-instilled sense of mission.

When you have developed a powerful sense of who you are and what you stand for, you will be in a position to form intimate relationships with others without losing your independence or identity.

SPIRITUALITY

EXPANSIVE Jupiter can cause you to dissipate your energies through overindulgence if you allow restlessness and boredom to take hold. However, you do have the courage and strength to identify these imbalances and overcome them, going on to be the visionary that others admire and follow. With your continuing quest for perfection and, therefore, your tendency to try out alternative lifestyles, you can show the rest of humanity that there is an alternative to being locked into unproductive and unfulfilling stereotypes. To do this, you need to adopt your chosen lifestyle for long enough to be seen to make it work, then you will be credible. You need to lose your tendency to assume that having a little knowledge of a subject (and a creative mind) makes you an expert.

You really don't care what others think, so you are an ideal person to introduce new ideas to the rest of humanity. You are also blessed with an ability to take great spiritual truths and translate them into a practical, pragmatic pattern for living that all can understand. For you, liberty and power are inextricably linked, and you hate the thought of using power to limit human potential. You despise power without wisdom. The pursuit of enlightenment drives you forward, and you're willing to look for the truth that underpins various belief systems to get there. You are likely to pull out common threads from various belief systems in order to create one that seems right for you. You know that truth will set you free. While material abundance may initially appear to you to symbolize power, once your actions and thoughts are harmonized with your highest needs, you will have a sense of the abundance of life. Like your opposite sign, Gemini, you will sample a vast array of spiritual beliefs until you find one that you can commit to wholeheartedly. The difference between you and your opposite number, though, is that you will delve very deeply.

CHAPTER 10

CAPRICORN

December 22–January 19

THE TENTH SIGN OF THE ZODIAC IS CONCERNED WITH:

- PRACTICALITY, REALISM
- HIGH STATUS, ACCOMPLISHMENT, REPUTATION, MONEY, WEALTH, SUCCESS
- PLANNING, DETERMINATION, PERSISTENCE, DIFFICULTIES, PROBLEMS
- LONG-TERM PROJECTS, DISCIPLINE, AUTHORITY, PATERNALISM
- GOOD QUALITY, SENSITIVITY TO BEAUTY
- LOYALTY, WISDOM

THE Capricorn sun is located in the element of earth—and earth is a world of concrete reality, sensory perception, and roots built on physical sensations. The sun in earth feels most comfortable when surrounded with the world of the five senses. Whatever cannot be touched, heard, smelled, seen, or tasted is either denied or made as concrete and tangible as possible.

The sun in earth is very concerned with physical security and lives each moment in the present. Those who are born with Capricorn as their sun sign do not as a rule live in the dead past or the unborn future. The here and now is what matters most to the sea goat. Your search for physical security can give you a reputation for being conservative, practical, and on occasion a little dull, can't it?

Capricorn is best known for self-control, caution, and dependability. The sure-footed mountain goat energy of Capricorn makes its world more secure by building structures and form. The Capricorn goat works its way slowly but surely to the top of the mountain. That may not sound too sexy or exciting to some folks, but I like the way you slowly, carefully work your way up the mountain. I also admire the way that Capricorns build their lives on solid foundations. Each achievement is consolidated before you move on to the next.

Capricorn is a cardinal sign. The lesson for cardinal signs is how to put their resources to best use. In your case, Capricorn, those resources represent practical skills: material, financial, and social resources that can be used to further an ambition.

The planet Saturn rules Capricorn. In mythology, Saturn was the unpleasant, ruthless father of the twelve Olympian gods, who dealt with the rumor that one of his children would one day overthrow him by swallowing all twelve. This myth powerfully demonstrates one of Capricorn's more negative characteristics: a tendency to allow inner fears to dominate decisions. As a Capricorn, it would be helpful for you to keep in mind the story of Saturn and remember not to stifle all your best creations out of fear.

In astrology, Saturn's lighter face is the archetypal energy of the wise old man (and/or wise old woman). The wise old man earned his wisdom and insight the hard way, through all the varied experiences and trials encountered during a long life. As the wise old man of the zodiac, Capricorn helps you define yourself through what's called the process of limitation or, more accurately, the process of elimination. Capricorn teaches us that we often best define who we are by first determining who we are not.

What really makes Capricorns overjoyed is being able to shape (i.e., organize) the world around them for their own sense of comfort and safety. Capricorn is concerned with authority and would prefer to be the sole author of its life and surroundings. The sea goat is one of the most self-directed signs of the zodiac and is usually willing to work long and hard to reach its goals. Capricorn energy is persistent, focused, determined, and willing to wait for just the right opportunity. While sea goats live primarily in the present, they will also have a one-, three-, and five-year plan up their sleeve.

One practical suggestion for enhancing your communication skills: Not everyone, at all times, appreciates your wise old man suggestions on how to get organized (even, and especially, when we know you're right). When we share our problems, feelings, or emotions with you, it's not usually a signal to chime in with a blueprint for solving our problem for us. Most of the time, we just want you to listen and sympathize a little. Try a little empathy, Capricorn; it will smooth your route to success.

For exercises on listening and communication see the Aries chapter (pages 12–14).

STRENGTHS TO FOCUS ON

- Good organizing skills
- Hardworking, ambitious
- Scrupulousness
- Cautiousness and realism
- Takes calculated risks
- Fearlessness
- Is an admiring spectator, reserved
- Concern
- Conventionality
- Gives sound advice, diplomatic
- Respects authority
- Loyal to tradition
- Has high yet realistic standards

For help with making the most of these positives, see the S.M.A.R.T.est Goals for Aries exercise (page 3).

WEAKNESSES THAT CAN TRIP YOU UP

- Egotism
- Allows inner fears to dominate decisions
- Tendency to believe your way is the only way of doing things
- Unforgivingness
- A slave driver
- Overcritical, negative, perfectionist, snobbish
- Fatalism

> ◗ **Pessimism**
> ◗ **Notorious for bad moods**
> ◗ **Status seeking**
> ◗ **Not always able to be objective about yourself or your situation**

So how do you turn these so-called negative traits into powerful tools for personal growth? Have a look at the Love Your Weaknesses exercise in Aries (page 6).

CAPRICORN MAN

Unless there are influences in his birth chart that are stronger than his Capricorn sun sign, the typical Capricorn male will have some or all of the following characteristics:

> ◗ **Appears unapproachable and self-protective**
> ◗ **Is totally reliable with a sensuous outlook on life**
> ◗ **Takes his time to size other people up before letting them get close to him**
> ◗ **Seeks honor and status while shunning publicity and fame**
> ◗ **Has strong opinions**
> ◗ **Is completely without vanity**
> ◗ **Is dignified and formal in manner**
> ◗ **Is usually trustworthy**
> ◗ **Is extremely well-mannered but loves innuendo**
> ◗ **Is conscious of his appearance and is unlikely to display any discomfort in public. The man wearing his jacket in a heat wave is likely to be a Capricorn**
> ◗ **Is impartial, precise, and careful; rises through effort and merit; has a strong sense of history and tradition.**

CAPRICORN WOMAN

In addition to the personality and behavior traits
exhibited by the Capricorn male, Capricorn woman is:

▶ Very self-conscious and cannot bear to be teased
▶ Will dress according to what she wishes to
   achieve that day
▶ Behaves in a very ladylike manner in public
▶ Appears to be completely at ease and placid but
   is often full of inner turmoil
▶ Is totally loyal to those whom she likes
▶ Has an immaculate home, while finding domes-
   ticity extremely dull
▶ Is ambitious for herself and her family
▶ Has little time for friendships
▶ Dislikes laziness and apathy, has a tendency to
   interfere and offend people, can be controlling,
   even to the degree of attempting to play "match-
   maker" with family, friends, and colleagues

THE HIDDEN (OR NOT-SO-HIDDEN) CAPRICORN

A PERSON WITH strong Capricorn tendencies is a person who
worries about security—physical, social, and emotional. I find that
my Capricorn clients really buy into the coaching concept of building a reserve of resources. I always advise my clients to pay themselves first, save a minimum of 10 percent of their earnings—even
if they have to cut back on their spending to do so—and build up
a minimum of three years' living expenses. This removes the need
to make bad decisions out of financial necessity and allows you to
take the odd calculated risk.

Most Capricorns cannot bear to be embarrassed in public, yet
long to let go a little and join in the fun around them. A sense of
duty and a fear of looking ridiculous tend to inhibit Capricorn's
enjoyment of the lighter side of life.

Do You Have Enough Fun?

WHY IS it that as we get older and take on more responsibility, the fun seems to go out of life? We plan, project, estimate, set goals, and find that fun and laughter have passed us by.

Let's take a look at how fun can be introduced into your life. You'll be amazed at how injecting some fun can improve the quality of your life. Answer the following questions:

- ◆ What makes you smile? What gives you pleasure and amusement? Are there little things that would make the day more fun for you if you took a fraction of a second to notice them?
- ◆ How can you do something simple that will bring more fun into your life?
- ◆ What will it cost you to have fun? What are the downsides, financial and timewise? If you have reservations, how could you have great fun at minimal cost?
- ◆ What will you gain by having fun? Will it improve your relationships? Will it reduce stress for you? For others?
- ◆ Will you become more attractive to others, or open up more opportunities, by adding fun?
- ◆ Imagine for a moment that you have had a fun day. What did it include? How do you know that it was fun? Notice changes in your posture, breathing, and center of gravity as you imagine this super fun day. Do you find that your thinking is clearer, your energy levels higher, and your thinking sharper and more positive?
- ◆ Now, think about today. What fun things can you add in or what can you do differently so that when you close your day you will know you have had fun?
- ◆ Imagine that in each day from here on you add a little fun for yourself and others. How does that make you feel? Are you ready to take the risk?
- ◆ Start each day by thinking about fun, having fun, and

doing those things that bring you pleasure. Before you
go to bed at night, say a little prayer of gratitude that
you were able to do these things for yourself and others,
and ask to be able to do a little more.

By taking a calculated risk and adding fun into our day-to-day living, we are able to enjoy life more fully and embrace new challenges.
Our tolerance to stress also rises. We become far more aware of others and ourselves, and find a more balanced way of being generous
and loving. Adding fun can help Capricorns attain their spiritual
goal of understanding the needs and feelings of others.

CAPRICORN LIKES

▶ **Hot, plain food**
▶ **Antiques, history**
▶ **Privacy**
▶ **Sexual love**
▶ **Duties and responsibilities**
▶ **Not being under pressure**
▶ **Quality status symbols**
▶ **Home and family**
▶ **New books**
▶ **Diamonds**
▶ **Gives tasteful and tradition gifts**
▶ **Membership in an exclusive club**

CAPRICORN DISLIKES

▶ **Untidiness**
▶ **Being mocked or teased**
▶ **Overfamiliarity**
▶ **New ideas**
▶ **Surprises**
▶ **Being embarrassed in public**
▶ **Being made to feel useless**
▶ **Loneliness**

Possible Problem Areas for Capricorn, and Solutions

All sun signs have unique personality traits. When these traits are suppressed, problems will arise. However, with a winning combination of astrology and coaching, we can examine the problem and assess the proper solution based on sun sign characteristics. If, as a Capricorn, you see things below that really strike home, try the solution. You may be amazed at the results.

Problem: People taking advantage of you and your good nature.

Solution: Try being more careful with your favors, and putting yourself first for a change. Practice what we in the coaching profession call enlightened selfishness.

Problem: People getting turned off by you.

Solution: Look at whether you have been aggressively defending or pushing causes lately; make wiser choices about when and how much to discuss them.

Problem: Coworkers not liking to work alongside you or share projects.

Solution: Curb your tendency to act like an authority figure when working in tandem with another as an equal.

Problem: Getting tired out and feeling overwhelmed by the projects that you have in progress.

Solution: Try not to make too many plans, and avoid having them scheduled too close together. Learn not to take on too much.

CAREER/BUSINESS

CAPRICORN is usually the workhorse of the zodiac. Practical and conservative, Capricorns thrive on working hard and getting things done. Their patience, determination, and high standards help them persevere where others might give up. Those born under this sign are most comfortable as leaders, since a leadership role gives them a measure of control, which is soothing to them. The goat is superb at rallying the troops in a way that inspires everyone to give their best. As Capricorns also crave independence, they can do just fine in an ivory tower office, directing the battle down below.

The solid, earth sign goat doesn't need a massive entourage in the workplace—a few trusted colleagues are so much better. Capricorns also value image and are likely to insist that coworkers, as well as themselves, look as professional and respectable as possible. The sea goat tends to take a traditional approach toward working practices, which includes dress. Capricorns are highly organized, so being on their team is a study in cool efficiency. It's unlikely that the team will fall apart, since the goat knows how to do the right thing for everyone and is happy to carry a heavy load. Given Capricorn's tendency to carry his or her fair share and more of life's burdens, Capricorns must remember to avoid overexertion if they are to reach the peaks to which they aspire.

The Capricorn office is as solid and predictable as they come, filled with sturdy wooden furniture and regimented reams of files, which will facilitate good, hard work. If they hit the need to travel in the course of their work, goats are most likely to jump into a solid, safe car, with plenty of metal around (just in case). Lunch will be reliable and of good value with no frills—a nearby steak house will convey the right message to both clients and friends.

CAPRICORN CAREER GUIDE

CAPRICORNS ARE WELL suited to become generals, ministers, and computer wizards. Here are some further occupations that a Capricorn might consider:

Account manager	Coach	Official
Administrator	Event planner	Overseer
Ambassador	Executive	Operations
Astronomer	Geologist	manager
Banker	Governor	Physicist
Career counselor	Industrialist	Premier
CEO	Manager	

Commissioner	Mason	Programmer
Dentist	Mayor	Proprietor
Economist	Mentor	Scientist
Engineer	Mountain climber	Statesperson
Estate agent	President	Teacher

CAPRICORN BOSS

CAPRICORNS CAN MAKE strong and successful managers, as management comes naturally to Capricorn. They really aren't happy unless they are at the top. Most goats at the top feel the need for stability and security and so lean heavily on order and authority. To this end, they are quick to dismiss new ideas, as well as neutralize ambitious coworkers who they sense are moving in on their territory. They rarely offer praise, due to their reserved nature, but they are sympathetic listeners. In fact, they will want to hear about everything that is going on. It is important for them to keep their fingers on the pulse of everyone's business in the office. With their eyes firmly fixed on their goals, Capricorns want everyone working hard and can sense when people are slacking off. They are quick to fire off orders and demands to keep everyone from wasting time. This can create problems, as we all need periods of downtime to function at our best. Capricorns must be careful not to confuse number of hours worked with productivity—often the most productive people put in very few hours, they just work very effectively.

Capricorns depend on past experience heavily, resisting deviation from what they have found to be historically true and successful. This can cause them problems in fast-moving, freewheeling, innovative companies where chaos and inventing new rules for conducting business are the order of the day. Avoid fire sign-dominated companies like the plague!

Capricorns tend to believe that honesty, hard work, and order lead to success. If you are trying to relate better to your Capricorn boss, try to understand that beneath that serious and determined exterior is someone who may actually want to cut loose and enjoy some freedom for once. Unfortunately, if their fears get the better of them, Capricorns will go through periods of moodiness when this inner conflict is reaching a peak. Understanding this will help those around them when they feel they cannot tolerate Capricorn's inflexibility and demanding nature any longer.

CAPRICORN EMPLOYEE

CAPRICORN IS LIKELY to embrace and thrive in a large, formal, hierarchical, established corporate enterprise. Capricorns are ideal corporate employees who strive for efficiency and excellence above all else and revere success. While other signs find climbing the corporate ladder somewhat tedious, Capricorn is thrilled to be handed such a clearly defined route to power and prestige. As Capricorns like to specialize and focus, they are unlikely to be found in small start-ups, where generalists are needed.

The reserve and formality of corporate life is much appreciated by Capricorns, who do not fear being lost in a mass of fellow employees. Capricorn is well aware of his or her strengths and weaknesses and knows that a seat on the board is assured. All Capricorn has to do is keep goals firmly in mind, and enjoy the journey to the top.

Bosses dream of the Capricorn employee, a hardworking, dependable, safe pair of hands. Not only do you shoulder immense responsibility with cool composure, but you practically demand it. You act as a safety net without demanding so much as a favor in return! What is the payoff for doing all this? Feeling needed, of course.

Capricorns expect to be well paid for what they do, but they are so conservative in their demands that they often do not earn what they should. Perks and titles do not impress Capricorns either. So how can those Capricorns who are worth their weight in gold, yet ask for raises that barely tip the scales, work out what they're worth? Here are a couple of exercises to help you alleviate this little problem.

EXERCISE TWO

Determine Your Value

WHAT DO you think is a reasonable markup on a product or service? 10 percent? 50 percent? 100 percent?

How about 950 percent? I have a friend who makes the most superb cakes, which she sells at $3.50 a slice. Each cake provides twelve slices and her cost to produce each cake is $4.00. Her profit per cake is therefore 950 percent. How does she pull this off? She does this because she is not only selling a great-tasting cake, she is selling an illusion (someone can pretend to guests that they baked the cake) and she is saving the consumer the time and effort of sourcing the ingredients, baking the cake, etc.

Can you apply this logic to your own circumstances? Try carrying out the following steps:

1. Think about a product or service you are currently selling. (If you are an employee, you are the product.)
   Example: Executive Coaching
2. Determine what you think is a "fair" price based on how much effort you put in, how much it costs you to develop the product or service you offer, and "reasonable market value."
   Example: Setting my fees at $100 an hour, based on a decade's experience, market knowledge, my network of contacts, and considering fees charged by competitors of a similar background.
3. Next, work out as best you can the value of what you're offering to the other party, and the ability to market the premium value. If you come up with any unanswerable questions, write them down. By researching the answers to these questions, you gather the critical information that allows you to set a price based on "value to them" as opposed to "value to you."
   Example: Following up with various clients has shown that their average increase in annual income after our coaching sessions ranges from 30 percent to 300 percent. In addition, numerous "soft benefits" were reported, ranging from increased hap-

piness, well-being, and self-confidence to enhanced relationships and having more fun at work.

4. What percentage of the value you are adding to the other party
do you think will make them want to do business with you?

Example: 25–50 percent of actual increase or 10–15 percent of
projected increase, depending on individual circumstances. In
most cases, this would set my minimum hourly rate at $200
an hour ranging to $1000+ an hour.

Another way of looking at this is shown in the diagram overleaf.
By looking at your current market value, you can work out what you
need to do to increase this value to your customers or employer.
Let's say you are learning a new skill. You probably need to set your
fees at below the normal market rate to make up for your inexperi-
ence as you learn new skills, gain experience, and win the confidence
of clients. As your skills and ability to market them improve, the fee
for your services aligns with the normal market rate—you are now
considered "one of the pros." As you improve even further and build
a reputation, you should now be able to charge a premium for your
fees. This is the added value that you provide. Your "value premium"
consists of your top-notch skills, your ability to execute or implement on time and to high quality, and your increasing reputation
and hence desirability to clients. Ideally, you should be looking to
increase your value premium constantly and consistently. By sketch-
ing this diagram for yourself, and adding figures to the diagram, you
can quantify in cash terms where you are now, and work out what
you need to do to close the gap and then move ahead of the curve.

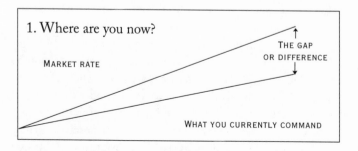

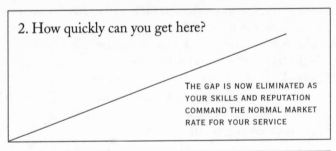

2. How quickly can you get here?

THE GAP IS NOW ELIMINATED AS
YOUR SKILLS AND REPUTATION
COMMAND THE NORMAL MARKET
RATE FOR YOUR SERVICE

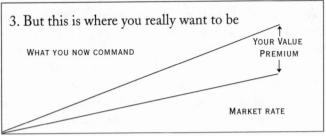

3. But this is where you really want to be

WHAT YOU NOW COMMAND

YOUR VALUE
PREMIUM

MARKET RATE

EXERCISE THREE

Mining "Hidden Gold" Opportunities

SINCE the day a client paid me an exorbitant rate to headhunt personnel for his Internet start-up, I have looked for opportunities to extract the hidden gold in jobs I would not mind doing, but do not particularly want to. If someone is willing to meet my over-the-top (to me) terms, I will do the job on offer graciously and well.

In 1998, one of my clients made more money from one month's work at "hidden gold" money, than they did in the whole of the rest of the year! They did a little business planning and were staggered at the consequences of focusing on this type of work, although they also knew that they didn't actually want to do it themselves. So they took on an additional member of staff. The investment of $25,000 in another salary actually produced additional revenues in excess of $250,000 that year. Try it for yourself by following the instructions given here:

1. Think of something on offer to you that you are not especially interested in doing or having, where you genuinely will not mind how things work out.

   Example: A decent but uninspiring job offer, buying a house or apartment that's "less than perfect," a promotion to a department which is okay but not your first choice, selling something you don't particularly want or need to sell.

2. Given that you don't particularly want to do it or have it anyway, what would make it worthwhile to you? Let your imagination run wild . . .

   Example: A salary of a million dollars, offering a dollar for the house or apartment, you'll take the job if you only have to work one day a week and they give you a raise, etc.

3 Rather than just saying "no" or walking away, go ahead and put in your "hidden gold" offer. While it's possible they'll say no, now and again you will be surprised to discover that the limitations you had put on what is possible were in your mind, not in the world.

Capricorn respects authority and takes work more seriously than the non-Caps at the top of the corporate ladder (if there are any!). Capricorns rarely move companies but work their way steadily up the corporate ladder. You Caps are blessed with the 3 Ps—punctuality, perseverance, and practicality. You are never sidetracked or distracted and will apply your efforts to attaining some definite goal that you set some years ago.

Is there anything a coach can teach Capricorns about goal setting? You could try the S.M.A.R.Test Goals for Aries exercise on page 3. For more on climbing up the corporate ladder, take a look at the Culture Vulture exercise in Libra (page 202). If you're after money, have a go at the Get Rich Working for Someone Else exercise in Cancer (page 111).

FINANCES AND WEALTH

THE goat is exceedingly careful where money is concerned. Disciplined and focused. Capricorns adore routine and thoroughly enjoy the hard work involved in achieving financial success. The goat takes great pride and pleasure in slowly and steadily climbing up the mountain of achievement, pausing every now and again for a look around (to check that no one's too close behind and to take stock of all that's been achieved so far) and then continuing, even higher. Capricorns expect things to be tough, since they tend toward pessimism. In the end, however, this expectation is exactly what will spur them on, because they want to get to the top of that mountain in the hardest way possible. Surmounting incredible odds is a blissful state for sea goats. Being acknowledged is what the goat wants most, and if that can happen with a bulging wallet in hand, fabulous!

Capricorns are among the shrewdest people at making and keeping money—these are the true money mavens of the zodiac. Money gives these folks a feeling of strength and security, and a delicious sense that they have arrived. Having money also means that Capricorns will be able to stay in the game, which is what these hardworking souls want, along with the ability to make even more money. Goats work steadily and methodically toward financial success and generally won't relax until there's plenty of cash on hand. Of all the coaching processes, that of building a financial reserve excites Capricorns the most.

For an exercise on doing this, see Building Up a Rainy-Day Fund in the Aries chapter (page 28).

Managing money comes so easily to Capricorns that they can, if they choose, keep accounts in their head. Knowing the score as well as they do, Caps hate to borrow—or to lend. They also like holding the purse strings, so frustrated family members might have to revolt. A goat combing the sale racks? Never. Though the goat will know who has got a sale and where it is located. The goat will also know exactly how much items cost wholesale and will try to pay as near this price as possible. These folks only shop when absolutely necessary and prefer to pay cash.

While you goats hate to negotiate, you do need to sometimes. You especially dislike spontaneous negotiations and can't bear heated debates. Conspicuous displays of emotion embarrass you. While you will pretend to agree with others during debates, you will quietly go your own way, not deviating from your chosen course. You will grind others down by your intransigence and stubborn resistance. I can think of quite a few Capricorn clients who have completely undermined cultural exchange programs, leaving bewildered consultants in their wake!

For help with negotiation, see Preparing for Negotiation in the Aries chapter (page 25) and The 100 Point Guide to Negotiation in Virgo (page 171).

Cautious by nature, you manage risk very well, Capricorn, and are unlikely to be seduced by get-rich-quick schemes, preferring to grow your finances at a slow but steady rate. You are such a financial whiz that others are likely to approach you to manage their finances. You are forward-thinking, and when you decide on a plan, you stick to it—one of the best ways to build and retain wealth. Power and influence motivate you enormously and your sign is considered the most ambitious of them all. You want to be CEO of a massive corporation and you want the power to be in your hands, not in those of shareholders, colleagues, or consultants. You are certainly not afraid of hard work—the opposite, in fact. You can easily become a workaholic, but as you enjoy every moment at your desk, this is a life that satisfies you. If one subscribes to the theory that living a "balanced life" means doing only what you want to do, then workaholic Capricorns lead supremely balanced lives.

Capricorn tends to make his or her wealth by rising to the top of Fortune 500-type companies or through investing. If you invest, make sure that you do your research thoroughly and consult with reputable industry experts.

LOVE, ROMANCE, AND SEX LIFE

CAPRICORNS are the worker bees of the zodiac. Ambitious and determined, they are willing to do what it takes to get what they want and that includes romance. They are extremely interested in love and are willing to use their stunning organizational abilities to craft a beautiful romance for that special someone. Capricorns are reputed to be the most capable and loyal of lovers. Social status is most important to Capricorn, so it's more than likely that the mating game will involve a healthy dose of glamour and dazzle. The one who wins their heart is likely to be powerful in both the boardroom and the bedroom. You've guessed it. Power is a strong aphrodisiac for the sleek sea goat, and in return their lover will get a most devoted and grateful partner.

Capricorns need to guard against a tendency, similar to the Scorpion's, to use sex to gain power over others or to win a battle. Should this be the case, ask yourself whether the outcome you seek is more important than your relationship. If this is the case, you may want to think about moving on.

Some sea goats can be a little insecure when it comes to love—they assiduously court intimacy yet run in fear from it, opting for a union that is loveless but high in status. If this is you, then look at the exercises for overcoming fear in the Cancer chapter (page 101) and, also, visit the exercises for building confidence and self-esteem in Aquarius (page 293). Going without love, especially for a sign as emotionally intense as yours, is never safe. Guard against a tendency to deny your own needs in a relationship, Capricorn. Visit the Getting Your Needs Met exercise in the Cancer chapter (page 116) for help with this one.

COMPATIBILITY

CAPRICORN GETS ALONG well with fellow earth signs Taurus and Virgo but is unlikely to consider them as perfect candidates for romance. Of the water signs, scary Scorpio can be too intense and ambivalent Pisces makes you want to scream. Cancerians top your wish list because you are both cardinal signs, with a love of tradition and a head for business.

WHAT CAPRICORN NEEDS

THE COMPETITIVE STREAK in the sea goat means that they are attracted to games—particularly those that they can probably win. It's likely that their sights will be fixed on someone classy and sexy, with plenty of money and tales of success to turn heads, including theirs. The right partner is also responsive and has their feet planted firmly on the ground, as does Capricorn. If the sea goat's mate can both chill them out and bring them out, it could be a match made in heaven.

The Capricorn lover sets goals, works hard, and won't be denied. Capricorns are ambitious yet devoted, an intense (often internal) flame waiting to burn for the right person. Those lucky enough to latch on will have a winner in their midst on their side.

THE END OF THE AFFAIR

CAPRICORN IS NOT a sign that indulges in casual affairs and can be slow to notice cracks appearing in a relationship. Once a partnership begins to fail, Capricorn can be slow to take action, out of a sense of loyalty and duty to partner and family. Capricorns tend to dislike divorce. However, once the sea goat has decided that he or she has chosen the wrong mate, the parting will be abrupt and final.

If a partner betrays Capricorn, she or he will do their best to reunite with the partner and keep the family together. If, however, the betrayal continues, the sea goat may turn rather nasty.

RELATIONSHIPS
(Family and Friends)

CAPRICORN PARENT

THE TYPICAL CAPRICORN parent is strict but fair, with a tendency to take parenthood seriously. Balanced against the tendency for strictness is an ability to exhibit tenderness and sensitivity toward offspring.

The Capricorn parent provides the very best for their children but has difficulty with very young children. This difficulty eases as the children get older.

CAPRICORN CHILD

THE CAPRICORN CHILD is that kid who looks and acts like an adult from an early age. Interested in adult matters and entrepreneurial from early on, the Capricorn child has a simple game plan, and that is to be king of the hill and top of the heap. You can bet that this plan will be mapped out in great detail with various staging posts along the way. What can you expect from your Capricorn youngster? Well, for starters, business schemes. It's the Capricorn child who sets up a baby-sitting service and hires employees to provide it for them! Fear not, though; the Capricorn kid is fair, so those other youngsters helping out will be well remunerated. Cautious and responsible, the Capricorn child is not likely to attempt anything that doesn't have a good chance of succeeding.

If you're looking for a child to look after and teach others, Capricorn's your boy (or girl). These kids have a way with their peers and will surely keep everyone in line. However, make sure you don't abuse his or her tendency to take on responsibility. The perfectionist in the Capricorn child ensures that they will work hard for that allowance, too.

BRINGING UP CAPRICORN—COACH'S INSIGHT

YOUNG CAPRICORN IS unlikely to be remotely interested in outdoor pursuits, so in the interests of your young sea goat's health, you need to encourage them to spend time outdoors.

Young Capricorn needs a secure, warm home with a regular routine and appreciative, reliable parents in order to thrive. In spite of their capable maturity, young Capricorns can lose their self-confidence very easily, so no teasing, please.

Young Capricorns need to be taught how to relax and switch off from their responsibilities, otherwise life can become somewhat joyless. They need plenty of reassurance because they are natural worriers. Health, diet, and exercise need to be carefully handled—like true goats, Caps have delicate constitutions, and young Capricorn is not the most resilient of children. Capricorn's constitution improves with age.

CAPRICORN AND FRIENDS

CAPRICORN IS DRAWN toward friends who are well-bred, well-mannered, and not too extroverted. Sea goats are usually kind and very generous toward friends. They will remain loyal to a friend no matter how dire their circumstances—old age and disability are not passports to loneliness if you have a Capricorn friend. They will show total devotion to a friend, which can be unfortunate if they have chosen their friend poorly. This can happen, as Capricorn is not the best judge of character.

FRIENDS, BE AWARE

CAPRICORN CAN BE a little insecure, so friends can expect to have their own loyalty tested severely over the course of time. Capricorns can have an irritating habit of organizing things for a friend—things that in the eyes of the sea goat will be good for that friend but that the friend does not want. Sea goats can also be quite shameless about using friends to further their own ambitions.

HEALTH

CAPRICORNS thoroughly enjoy working, and when faced with stress, their instincts tell them to work harder, longer, and with more focused intensity. Your ruler, Saturn, causes you to take responsibility to heart. You value practical and realistic solutions, and, having a cardinal quality, you like to get on with things. You are most definitely action-oriented. You have a tendency to be so busy tackling one particular area that you lose sight of the bigger picture. Be very sure that what you are working on so intently is worthy of that amazing Capricorn output. One way to do this is to make sure that what you're currently focused on fits in with your core values, and moves you toward the outcome that you seek. To help with setting goals that work for you, see the Define Your Values exercise in the Aries chapter (page 20).

COACH'S TIP

If your spouse, boyfriend, or girlfriend keeps complaining that you're never around anymore, that's a sign to rethink your schedule.

STRESS BUSTING FOR CAPRICORN

CAPRICORN IS AN earth sign, so you are more likely to enjoy taking a breather in the mountains than relaxing on the beach. A day of hiking, mountain climbing, or exploring caves would recharge your batteries and exhilarate you. Play baseball or start a football team with your pals (Capricorn rules teamwork)—just don't get too obsessed with winning.

As a social animal (which is why you eventually rise to the top of your field), you enjoy relaxing over a meal, as long as the restaurant is classy and traditional. One Capricorn client of mine adores relaxing at his country club, with its traditional ambience, oak paneling, and fireplaces. The goat also likes heights, so a restaurant with a view is just right for you, provided that it has a calm atmosphere. Do make sure that you stick to talking about general things—not all lunches have to be business meetings. Sports with a social twist are good too, so you might think about taking up tennis or golf.

Since Capricorn likes history, you can relax in front of the History Channel, check out the Museum of Natural History, or visit the museums of your nearest city. Many Capricorns enjoy browsing around antiques shops. Auctions are another good bet, and even if you don't bid, you'll have fun handling the valuable objects and documents. Don't expect to unwind instantly. It may take weeks of vigorous fun to loosen you up!

Finally, renting a funny movie—either a new release or a golden oldie—could also be good medicine. Other ways to tickle your funny bone would be to check out funny sites on the Web like cartoon Dilbert (www.dilbert.com) or turn on the Comedy Channel on cable. Tell a few jokes to your friends (if you can't remember any good ones, go to a comedy club and steal a few for friends and family). Or try hanging out with a funny, witty friend.

FITNESS

CAPRICORN RULES THE bones, teeth, sacrum, gluteus muscles, thighs, pelvis, hips, iliac arteries, sciatic nerve, femur, and knees. Your metabolism is steady to high.

Capricorns are the most driven people in the zodiac. While I take the view that balance means doing exactly what you want to do, I do find that Capricorns need to beware of pushing themselves too hard and neglecting to eat healthily. Be careful not to undermine your constitution, Capricorn. Perhaps those computer programmers getting their pizzas pushed underneath the door are all sea goats.

In order to function at tip-top efficiency, try to eat a little more healthily, however tight your deadlines are. Plan ahead. If necessary, enlist the help of family members or friends to help you do bigger, more economical shopping expeditions. This will save your time, money, and health. Cook up large portions of healthy, nutritious food and freeze half, or find a healthier, less greasy venue from which to order take-out meals.

Be aware that Capricorns are extremely self-critical and very hard on themselves, especially if they feel that they've been "lazy." They do want to look their best, and feel that maintaining a positive self-image will help in their business life. This is true, but don't use it as an excuse to torture yourself.

COACH'S TIP

Play to your strengths, Capricorn. As an earth sign you will prefer leisurely sports such as golf, rock climbing, hiking, or jogging, where you can set your own rhythm and feel the earth beneath your feet. Stiffness in the joints can be a problem for Capricorn, so build some exercises to develop flexibility and suppleness into your regimen. Yoga would be a good option.

TOOLS FOR MAKING A DIFFERENCE

THE SYMBOL FOR Capricorn, as already mentioned, is a goat. When astrological symbolism arose, there were two kinds of goat: the domesticated animal gloomily chained to its post, and the feisty, randy, wild creature. These refer to the two aspects of the Capricornian nature. If Capricorn feels chained and duty-bound, it has the most amazing capacity for deep gloom. In this situation Capricorn can be good and dutiful though hardly joyful. If Capricorn is free to follow its other path, then the feisty, randy Pan like zest of the wild mountain goat appears.

As the feisty goat can climb any mountain, one of Capricorn's challenges is to choose which mountain to climb. Many of my Capricorn clients come to me having climbed to the greatest heights only to find that they have conquered the wrong summit. This can lead to Capricorns self-sabotaging without knowing why. If you are prone to self-sabotage, see the exercise in Taurus, Avoiding Self-sabotage (page 70).

CLIMBING THE WRONG MOUNTAIN

CLIMBING THE WRONG mountain is precisely what Kate, a feisty Capricorn client of mine, did. Kate was vice president of a prestigious merchant bank. Having worked long hours and made immense personal sacrifices, she was horrified to find that she had chosen the wrong career. She came to me for coaching when she realized that she would need the support of a coach to break free from the golden chains that bound her, and to make sure that the next mountain she climbed was the right one.

To make a long story short, we worked together to find out what Kate really wanted to do—coaching. Kate then applied her Capricorn strength and determination to acquiring the skills needed to build up and run a thriving coaching practice. She managed to combine working long hours as a financier with building up her practice. Many banking colleagues who became aware of her coaching skills subsequently went to Kate as private clients. It took a great deal of determination and stamina to achieve this career shift—typical Capricorn traits.

Capricorns can become out of touch because they are so insular. That characteristic solitude, combined with a fierce work ethic, management capacity, and a hungry ambition can produce extremely successful characters in conventional terms. The problem with this kind of success is that it can leave the sea goat surrounded by yes-men who cannot give the objective feedback that is sometimes required as a reality check. Capricorns can get very out of touch, especially when they inexorably progress along the wrong path while receiving acclaim for doing so. In order to maintain a sense of balance, Capricorn must go out of its way to connect with people who hold differing views from Capricorn's own, and to develop the skills required to cope with opposition.

Capricorns are never satisfied or fulfilled; no amount of money, acclaim, or fame can compensate for the feelings of hunger and lack often left over from childhood. Capricorns seem to be born lonely—hence the need to conform and be accepted. Try letting who you really are shine through, Capricorn—then you will be accepted by people with the same values and with whom you can form a deep connection.

SPIRITUALITY

CAPRICORN'S primary spiritual goal is to understand the needs and feelings of other people. As lovers, Capricorns need to tran-

scend the tendency to provide material security but to leave partners emotionally high and dry (and cold). Visit the listening and
communicating exercises in Aries (pages 13–16) to combat this,
Capricorn.

Capricorn's spiritual quest is to find the right mountain to climb,
but what is the right mountain? A clue to this is given by the fact
that Capricorn begins on the winter solstice, heralding the season
of the redeemer. The days lengthen and become brighter, bringing
joy to all of us. When Capricorn is devoted to something larger
than itself, it creates a structure or society that serves and enriches
the whole of humanity. One has only to listen to Capricorn Martin Luther King's "I have a dream" speech to see this sign at its most
visionary and noble. In the spiritually evolved sea goat, the soul
perfectly understands its purpose in this life.

EXERCISE FOUR

Climb Every Mountain

JUST for today, imagine giving up your career and refocusing your life on your passions. Try answering the following questions to get insights into how this might change your life for the better.

1. If you gave up your career today, what would you want to do with your time over the next month? The next year? (Remember, it's okay if what you would want to do is the same as your former career!)
2. If you weren't trying to get anywhere, what would you want to do with your time?
3. If you decided to make your working decisions based on your highest passions, values, and desires, what would you choose to work on next?

The sea goat flourishes within organized, firmly established religion. Capricorns bring the same serious intensity to their spiritual beliefs as to all the other aspects of their lives—just beware that you don't become too dogmatic, Capricorn.

CHAPTER 11

AQUARIUS

January 20–February 18

THE ELEVENTH SIGN OF THE ZODIAC IS CONCERNED WITH:

- INDEPENDENCE, DETACHMENT
- SCIENTIFIC ANALYSIS, EXPERIMENTATION, GENIUS, ORIGINALITY
- FRIENDSHIP, COURTESY, KINDNESS
- MYSTERY, INTRIGUES, MAGIC
- FAME, RECOGNITION
- POLITICS, HUMANITARIAN ISSUES
- ECCENTRICITY, CREATIVE ARTS
- ELECTRICITY, MAGNETISM, TELECOMMUNICATIONS

AQUARIUS is one of the most enigmatic and interesting signs of the zodiac, an air sign represented by a water carrier, and ruled by two planets with totally incompatible natures: Saturn, which desires order, and Uranus, which tears it down. The combination of these planetary energies is strong and vibrant. The Saturn face of Aquarius believes in authority, which is one reason why Aquarians love to impose their unusual (Uranian) ideas on other people—against their will if necessary. It's Uranus that gives Aquarians their visionary and anarchist spirit. If an idea is new, radical, and rebellious, Aquarians can't wait to embrace it. It is up to them to establish order out of their own chaos, to take control of their unconventional instincts, and define and channel them into something of merit.

Aquarius is symbolized by the water bearer, an image that expresses the ability of this sign to spread new ideas. Aquarius is concerned, sometimes to the point of obsession, with being new, radical, and different. While the Aquarian thought process is inventive and original (many water bearers are near-geniuses), the water bearer can appear awkward, eccentric, and overly obsessed with personal freedom.

Aquarians are happy to bestow their off-the-wall ideas as a gift to humanity. This is a sign that is eager to make the world a better place for one and all, and they are much happier when the rest of the world agrees with them. Those who argue or block Aquarian progress will quickly find out that the water bearer can be impatient, even temperamental, with those who disagree. Yes, these folks can be fixed in their opinions, in keeping with the fixed and Saturnian qualities assigned to their sign.

The element associated with Aquarius is air, which represents the mind and the ability to think. Aquarian ideas may be unusual or even original, but once formed they tend to remain fixed. Fixed air represents fixed opinions. Those born under this sign are altruistic, humane people who are determined to make a difference.

STRENGTHS TO FOCUS ON

- Communicativeness
- Thoughtful and caring
- Cooperative and dependable
- Scientific
- Strong belief in humane reforms
- Independence of thought and action, broad-mindedness
- Intense interest in people
- Loyal friendship
- Inventiveness

For help with accentuating these positives, see S.M.A.R.T.est Goals for Aries (page 3).

WEAKNESSES THAT CAN TRIP YOU UP

▶ Unwillingness to share ideas
▶ Tactlessness and rudeness
▶ Perverse and eccentric individuality
▶ Self-interested
▶ Unwillingness to question beliefs, dogmatic
▶ Uncertainty and lack of confidence
▶ Likes to observe others closely

So how do you turn these so-called negatives into powerful tools for personal growth? Visit the Love Your Weaknesses exercise in Aries (page 6).

AQUARIUS MAN

Unless there are influences in his birth chart that are stronger than his Aquarius sun sign, the typical Aquarius male will have some or all of the following characteristics:

▶ Needs to study others before deciding whether to trust them
▶ Dislikes being observed or interrogated
▶ Needs a partner who is a friend as well as a lover
▶ Hides his feelings
▶ Is very friendly and is a group person
▶ Has a wide range of interests
▶ Is fair-minded with his own strong, personal moral code and values
▶ Is eager to learn and loves to experiment
▶ Does not usually aim to be rich but to develop his ideas and communicate them
▶ Is a truth seeker

AQUARIUS WOMAN

In addition to the personality and behavior traits exhibited by the Aquarian male, Aquarius woman:

▶ **Is unlikely to be swept away by a wave of emotion**

▶ **May be thought cold, which can make it hard for her to form relationships**

▶ **Ignores feminine conventions but always looks stunning**

▶ **Has a wide circle of friends from all walks of life and a wide variety of interests**

▶ **Is concerned about and deeply involved in the community**

▶ **Is a superb mediator**

▶ **Is totally unpredictable**

▶ **Needs a partner who is not possessive**

▶ **Will have a basic lack of self-confidence**

▶ **Can be easygoing nonjudgmental.**

EXERCISE FIVE

Developing Self-confidence

You do not have to believe in written words for them to have a powerful effect. As you read their messages over and over, they will become automatic in your thinking and you will find yourself increasingly responding to them.

When you can, read the following words out loud. They will help you to develop self-confidence. I suggest that you read them first thing in the morning and carry them with you throughout the day.

- ♦ You have incredible willpower
- ♦ You have incredible confidence
- ♦ You are relaxed and confident
- ♦ You have absolute, unshakable confidence in your ability to create the life you desire

If the sentences here don't strike a chord with you, make up some that do.

Auto-suggestion is very effective in building confidence. While most people do not believe what they are saying at first, after a short time they realize that what they are saying is in fact perfectly correct. This then gives them the confidence that they have been seeking. For more on confidence building see the 911 Affirmations exercise in Aries (page 7).

COACH'S TIP

The subconscious is an entity in its own right, similar to the inner child of popular psychology, and so responds much better to being addressed as a separate person. This is why the affirmations begin with the word "You" rather than "I."

The Hidden (Or Not-So-Hidden) Aquarius

A PERSON WITH strong Aquarian tendencies can be extremely uncertain of his or her identity. Aquarians relish being different, which can lead to a life of isolation and frustration. To truly make a difference to humanity, one needs to connect with one's fellow man, which is tricky if one appears too extreme. Aquarius, sometimes called the zodiac's reformer, needs to learn to give and receive unconditional love on an individual basis. In this way, the water bearer will truly connect with and embody the positive qualities of its planetary ruler, Uranus.

Aquarius likes

▶ **Fame or recognition**
▶ **Privacy**
▶ **Magic**
▶ **Dreams**

- Self-analysis
- Change, eccentricity, and surprises
- Credit cards, e-commerce, Internet shopping
- Telling others what needs to be done—and watching them get on with it
- Weird and unconventional friends
- Living within their means
- Philanthropy

AQUARIUS DISLIKES

- Emotion and intimacy
- People who show off
- Being taken for granted
- Being pinned down, pressured
- Being sold to
- Borrowing or lending
- Violence and fighting
- Extravagance
- Self-disclosure

POSSIBLE PROBLEM AREAS FOR AQUARIUS, AND SOLUTIONS

ALL SUN SIGNS have unique personality traits. When these traits are suppressed, problems will arise. However, with a winning combination of astrology and coaching we can examine the problem and assess the proper solution based on sun sign characteristics. If, as an Aquarius, you see things below that really strike home, try the solution. You may be amazed at the results.

PROBLEM: Being left all alone while others enjoy the companionship you long for.

SOLUTION: Learn not to make such a big deal out of being different from others—it can alienate them. A little self-disclosure wouldn't be amiss either. You need to practice a little more compassion and tolerance by accepting people the way they are and not finding too much fault with them.

PROBLEM: You always seem to miss the boat when it comes to love.

SOLUTION: Try being a little less guarded and a little more available emotionally.

PROBLEM: You always seem to miss out on the better jobs or big promotions at work.

SOLUTION: Learn to become a team player; the lone hero approach will get you nowhere.

PROBLEM: You seem to become physically ill more than you should.

SOLUTION: By repressing your emotions, you drive the unrest deep inside, where it can cost you in terms of health. Express your feelings—but do it with tact.

CAREER/BUSINESS

AQUARIUS will tend to like working as part of a group, possibly in a charitable, trade union or nonprofit-making organization, as this is a sign that is powerfully motivated by working for the good of humanity.

The water bearer enjoys plenty of stimulation, variety, and a chance to express their inventiveness and creativity. It is no good expecting the water bearer to fit into a conventional corporate structure.

The mentally quick water bearer will enjoy an intellectual challenge, whether it's dreaming up a totally new way of carrying out a given task or attempting totally to restructure the organization for the good of colleagues and clients. Aquarians are very firm in their beliefs about how best to do the job—they've spent a lot of time considering them—so will be viewed as a renegade or pioneer, depending on your point of view. The Aquarius office is probably Zenlike in character, free from emotional tensions and noise, with the latest communications technology. His or her mode of transportation is likely to be a small, funky, environmentally friendly car and lunch is likely to be taken in an organic restaurant with an eclectic menu.

AQUARIAN CAREER GUIDE

Here are some occupations that an Aquarian might consider:

Academic	Consultant	Navigator
Adventure travel	Electrician	Pilot
guide	Entrepreneur	Radio or TV sta-
Advisor	Extreme sports	tion employee
Affiliate	professional	Science fiction
Airline personnel	Guide	writer
Alternative healer	Inventor	Senator
Astrologer	Humanitarian	Sociologist
Astronaut	Legislator	Technologist
Aviator	Market researcher	
Chancellor	Mechanic	

AQUARIUS BOSS

THE AQUARIUS MANAGER doesn't always fit into the nine-to-five corporate norm. Although not a natural executive—we are talking about the sign of antiestablishment and revolutionary activity here—he or she will carry out the role of boss, using the Aquarian skills of quick thinking and shrewd analysis. While Aquarians do not aspire to join the ranks of higher management (they are too freedom-loving and responsibility-averse), they do make successful managers. Their humanitarian nature allows them to strive for equality for everyone in the organization. They are likely to ask for everyone's opinion when it comes to setting objectives or standards, and to allow subordinates to make the ultimate calls. While they are understanding and sympathetic to staff, they do expect their staff to think independently, inspiring innovation and creativity. Unfortunately, most people like clearly defined guidelines by which to work and find the Aquarian approach to management more than a little daunting.

Aquarians are usually intuitive and extremely intelligent, more than capable of thinking outside the box. They are more likely to be interested in exposing inconsistencies in organizational process than maintaining the status quo. Colleagues will consider the Aquarian manager either a genius or a loose cannon who should be contained at all costs.

The Aquarian manager will expect a day's work for a day's pay, though the pay will be fair. The water bearer will also see to it that those who go the extra mile are well compensated for their efforts. While Aquarians are unshockable, they will not forgive dishonesty or broken promises.

The Aquarius personality may be extremely inconsistent—usually wavering between eccentricity and calm wisdom—and is certainly unique. Aquarians are remarkably adept at seeing the big picture of an organization and know who and what needs to change. Unfortunately, they tend to lack patience with people who do not support their vision, and Aquarius, having devised a new way of doing things, will stubbornly stick to it, whether or not there is evidence for it being right. They can be as inconsistent in their work as they are in their moods—they will go through periods of intense activity followed by complete inertia.

If you work with an Aquarius manager, be sure to think things through before you present any idea or project, and make sure your conversations are interesting—otherwise, Aquarius will switch off.

AQUARIUS EMPLOYEE

THE TYPICAL AQUARIAN employee appears aloof. You do not force your ideas or company on others but gather a wide circle of friends. With your humanitarian and insightful nature, you appeal to your colleagues, and your stunning intellect and fresh-minded approach to doing things usually keeps your employers happy. Your apparent lack of competitive drive tends to ensure that coworkers feel at ease with you. As a sign that appears to others to have no worries about money or future security, you work for the joy of it until boredom kicks in. You are likely to switch jobs or careers a great deal when younger; in later life you will probably settle down with one employer.

You are a worker who regularly explores future possibilities, looking at everything from a broad perspective and combining wide-ranging knowledge with sharp insight to advise superiors about innovative growth opportunities. You tend to focus on humanitarian visions rather than your own needs and will thrive in an environment where you can develop business alliances and products for the common good.

You are tolerant and nonjudgmental of colleagues, occasionally prying into others' lives out of curiosity and as a learning exercise, but never betraying confidences. You do not like to be tied down to schedules, set routines or responsibilities; a freewheeling creative role is best for you. Entrepreneurship would suit you, provided that you can become more comfortable with decision making, leadership, competition, and combat. As a sign that is more stimulated by ideas and invention than making money, you are best teaming up with a forward-thinking fire sign to excel truly as an entrepreneur.

Negotiating savvy is not something that most Aquarians are blessed with. You tend to be uncompromising in your viewpoint and at the same time reluctant to push your point of view on others. You are likely to become interested in uncovering the motivations of others and in so doing find yourself wanting to do what's best for them—even at your own expense. If you really can't avoid negotiating, try the Preparing for Negotiation exercise from the Aries chapter (page 25) and the 100 Point Guide to Negotiating exercise in Virgo (page 171).

FINANCES AND WEALTH

THE water bearer, as mentioned before, is far more motivated by innovation, intellectual pursuits, and saving the world than material gain. When an Aquarian is interested in money, they are more likely to be stimulated by a vision of what money can achieve than by a strong desire to be wealthy.

Uranus-ruled Aquarians can be somewhat erratic in their saving and spending habits, though debt is unlikely to be a problem for this sign, which hates borrowing (or lending, for that matter). Aquarians do not have the approach to budgeting of fellow Saturn-ruled sign Capricorn so a financial advisor or at the very least good accountancy software is a must for you. You might like to try the Building Up A Rainy-Day Fund (page 28), Nice and Easy Does it

Way to $1000 (page 85) and Combating Impulse Spending (page 141) exercises for help with finances.

Your best route to riches is through innovation and new ideas. Patent, copyright, or trademark your ideas, and launch that new product or service, Aquarius. The marketplace is changing as never before and new trends continue to emerge with breathtaking rapidity. Your sign, more than any other, has an innate ability to see into the future and predict what the market will be crying out for, especially in the communications and high-tech industries.

When you do strike it rich, Aquarius, you are likely to spend some of your gains on philanthropic ventures, satisfying your great need to make society a better place for one and all.

COACH'S TIP

Aquarians are fiercely independent, and don't like to be told what to do. This attitude can be great, because it motivates you to become a self-made person. Your willingness to take full responsibility for your choices is admirable. As you like to say, you will have no one to blame but yourself if things go wrong. However, this attitude can be negative too, when a "not-invented-here" policy prevents you from considering new financial advice. No one person has all the answers. Recognize that asking for advice can be the sign of a supremely self-confident person.

LOVE, ROMANCE, AND SEX LIFE

TO Aquarius, love is about caring for all of humanity rather than just one individual, and the water bearer has a deep-seated fear of emotional commitment. The glamorous, aloof Aquarian will guard his or her independence jealously, often preferring to have a long-distance relationship. He or she will attract plenty of admirers due to Aquarius's open, friendly manner. Aquarius desires friendship and a deep mental connection with their loved one. A lover who shares the Aquarian commitment to humanitarian efforts is likely to win the heart of the water bearer, who sees the beauty in shared ideals.

The water bearer has many relationships and will keep looking until he or she finds that perfect one. While in a relationship, Aquarius will be loyal and faithful but will move on if curiosity leads them elsewhere.

Aquarians love to give pleasure and can have a tendency to lose sight of their own needs. The water bearer has to learn that it is okay to have needs—they are not a sign of weakness—and that some needs can only be met through an intimate relationship. See the Getting Your Needs Met exercise in Cancer (page 116) for help with this. Aquarians also tend to hate confrontation, seeking to resolve disputes in a friendly and harmonious way or removing themselves from the scene if this is not possible. While your sense of detachment can serve you well in dealing with anger (you can often channel the energy born of frustration into other endeavors), if you internalize your anger too much, it can be self-destructive and lead to health problems. See the Roar, Toro, Roar exercise in Taurus (page 64) for some help in dealing with anger.

It is worth noting here that anger, when expressed constructively, can have a powerfully positive effect on a relationship or situation. If you feel uncomfortable expressing anger, try the following exercise.

EXERCISE SIX

The Positive Face of Your Anger

1. List the times when anger has been useful to you, for example, as a signal that you need to change jobs.
2. List the times when anger has been harmful to you, for example, it makes it easier for colleagues not to take you seriously.
3. Also list those things, situations, and people which make you angry. Divide them into two columns: those situations that you can control and those situations that you cannot.

4. Where you can do something about the situation, do it.
5. Where the situation is out of your control, leave your goal of wanting to change it behind. Either withdraw or learn how to control your response to your situation.

The Aquarian is happiest with a lover who can leave behind traditional gender and other stereotypes and who can make intimacy safe for them. Aquarius fears intimacy and rejection, so a lover who can gently lead them down the path of self-disclosure is necessary. If a lover can break through the barriers imposed by the water bearer's tendency to intellectualize and overanalyze what should be felt, they will tap into a torrent of emotion waiting to be released. Analytical Aquarius will approach love cautiously, methodically, and deliberately. Every move will be analyzed and made with perfect precision. Aquarius can even decide on a persona to adopt each day—believe me, the water bearer can play myriad roles. The greatest challenge in love for the water bearer is the emotional and empathetic aspects of love. Without them, love is incomplete, so those born under this sign must learn to cope with intimacy in order to experience love in all its glory.

Here are some questions that I typically ask clients who are wary of intimacy to consider:
- ◆ What is intimacy? Do you have it in your relationships? Do you want to have it?
- ◆ If you want intimacy yet lack it in your relationships, what are you prepared to do to get it?

You might also want to look at some of the tactics that you use to keep others at a distance. Are they helping or hindering you as you journey through life? Be aware of when you hold back from physical contact and of the fact that you have a choice—you can touch or you can continue to withhold contact. Which are you going to do and why?

When you are thinking about forming a deeper, more intimate connection with someone, try this exercise.

EXERCISE SEVEN

Overcoming the Fear of Intimacy

LISTEN to the thoughts that flit in and out of your consciousness as you think about intimacy. You also might like to try saying to yourself, "I fear . . ." and see what words your subconscious uses to finish the sentence. Are these fears rational? Can you overcome them? How? Do you want to?

COMPATIBILITY

NONJUDGMENTAL AQUARIUS can get along with anyone. Aquarians are particularly attracted to polar opposite Leo, to Aries (though the relationship might not last), and to Libra.

WHAT AQUARIUS NEEDS

AQUARIANS FIRMLY BELIEVE that their way is the only way so will go for a lover who has similar qualities and values to them. A sociable being with a social conscience is a must, as are flexibility and open-mindedness. A lover who exhibits warmth and understanding can fill a key void in Aquarius's life, and if they also embrace the beauty of space and connectedness, the relationship could go very far.

THE END OF THE AFFAIR

AQUARIANS TEND TO devote themselves to one partner at a time and will only stray when curiosity leads them elsewhere.

The water bearer likes to dominate any relationship—as a way of keeping those scary emotions in check—and will not tolerate possessiveness. As Aquarians hate both confrontation and divorce, they will tend to manipulate subtly an unwanted partner into being the one to end the relationship.

RELATIONSHIPS
(Family and Friends)

AQUARIUS PARENT

The typical Aquarian parent tends to treat his or her offspring as a friend, or miniature adult, and will encourage independence from day one. He or she will not concentrate on discipline and will be prepared to discuss even adult problems, as long as this is done in a rational rather than an emotional manner. This is not a parent who can help with the turmoil of emotions experienced through having one's first broken heart.

The Aquarian parent will aim to provide the very best modern education for their children.

AQUARIUS CHILD

THE AQUARIUS CHILD is always independent and free-spirited. The only predictable things about Aquarius is that he or she will always do the unexpected—and is likely to have a love of gadgets and gizmos. This youngster is likely to be surfing the net and investigating the DVD player from day one. If you can't program your VCR, ask Aquarius.

This youngster will have plenty of books around, as well as the latest technology and is likely to be adept at multitasking. Don't be surprised to see them writing an essay while watching football, as this may just be when their thinking is clearest.

The Aquarian child can appear to be slightly aloof, though in reality they are merely lost in thought or observation. This is really a child who loves the company of friends. Finally, the Aquarius child has a rebellious streak that is incompatible with stringent rules. Discipline them at your peril!

BRINGING UP AQUARIUS—COACH'S INSIGHT

YOUNG AQUARIUS HAS an inquiring and analytical mind and is always on the go. He needs plenty of space and the freedom and opportunity to discover and invent new things.

He or she needs a peaceful and harmonious environment, as this child is extremely sensitive to underlying emotional undercurrents. Aquarians do not like to be smothered but do need to be shown love, especially in the form of respect, appreciation, and friendship. You'll need to listen too.

Aquarius is less confident than he or she may appear, so plenty of understanding and encouragement are needed. He or she needs to be taught how to think logically, as their lightning-fast thoughts can get jumbled up. Aquarius sometimes needs to be taught powerful techniques for enhancing memory, as this sign is not always great at retaining information.

AQUARIUS AND FRIENDS

AQUARIUS GATHERS MANY friends but few close confidants. He or she will tend to view all relationships as platonic and will choose a friend who is Aquarian in outlook and temperament.

Aquarians will not pass judgment on their friends, other than to expect them to be consistent in their behavior, standards, and ethics. The water bearer will work hard at any friendship and will prove to be a great source of intellectual stimulation and sound advice.

Friends Be Aware

AQUARIUS SHOWS LITTLE give-and-take when it comes to sharing problems—friends will be expected to sort out their own messes and the water bearer's too. He or she will take over a friendship, slowly but surely putting the friend under obligation—this is the water bearer's way of asserting control of the situation.

Aquarius will show great interest in a friend's ideas, often adopting the more appealing ones as their own.

HEALTH

THOUGH you rarely appear stressed, you feel stress, just as everyone else does—you are just better at covering it up. With your objective approach to life, you may, however, be less prone to stress than most, but even you get overwhelmed sometimes. You're not always aware of when you are feeling stressed because you tend to block out feelings as much as possible.

When you are feeling "wired" you will find it easier, as an air sign, to switch off in the company of some laid-back, entertaining friends. A fixed sign that tends to get its head down and plough through projects without a break, you need to think about scheduling some downtime in order to recharge your batteries, Aquarius.

Stress Busting for Aquarius

WHEN YOU ARE feeling stressed out, you can find close relationships claustrophobic and smothering, so you need to get away from loved ones for a while. However, you do need to be aware of their feelings and explain why you are withdrawing rather than leaving a lover feeling that they've done something wrong.

You could also look at doing some pro bono work to unwind, perhaps joining a special-interest group that tackles the issues that concern you, or how about playing with some new technology—now, that is bound to turn you on!

FITNESS

AQUARIUS RULES THE eyes, circulation, lungs, breath, tibia, fibula, ankles, Achilles tendon, and calves. Your metabolism is high.

As a sign that tends to live in its head, you need to remember that there is a mind–body connection and that your physical health underpins your mental health. You have few, if any, major health risks but do need to break away from a tendency to be sedentary. Sitting in front of a computer all day piles on the pounds if you do not make a determined attempt to build periods of exercise into your day.

You tend to concentrate hard on what you're doing, and you can become so immersed that you forget to eat balanced meals. Like your fellow Saturn-ruled sign, Capricorn, you may forget to plan meals and just grab junk food when you're feeling hungry. Try to plan ahead, Aquarius, and either buy plenty of exotic foods to try, or team up with a group of buddies and take turns cooking meals. You can freeze any leftovers to help combat your tendency to live off take-out. While we're on the subject of sharing and socializing, how about getting together with a group of friends and hiring a personal trainer for a couple of sessions a week? Remember to build plenty of variety into any fitness regime, as routine drives you crazy.

As an innovator, you are likely to be up to date with the latest diet and fitness crazes. Just use your common sense and don't try anything that seems dangerous or ludicrous.

TOOLS FOR MAKING A DIFFERENCE

WHEN THE WATER bearer becomes aware of all of his or her needs and accepts that some of these can only be satisfied though deep connections with others, he or she will be in a far, far better position to change the world for the better. See the Getting Your Needs Met exercise from the Cancer chapter (page 116) to help you with this, Aquarius. You might also want to look at the exercise for developing empathy and communication skills in the Aries chapter (page 15). With an imaginative mind and a concern for others, Aquarius is a natural leader, provided that he or she gains self-confidence and becomes comfortable with expressing who they are.

In order to take your place in the world, Aquarius, you need to learn how to feel—people respond to warmth rather than intellectual concepts. You need to learn how to let go and go with the flow every so often; there are some things that we cannot control and there is no point trying. Learn to trust yourself, and others, by taking risks—you might enjoy it.

SPIRITUALITY

AQUARIAN revolutionaries are unlikely to stick to organized religion. You are likely to insist on finding your own path, one that honors "the family of man."

Your spiritual goal is to learn how to develop true self-confidence. For help with combating fear, see the Fear Zapper exercise in the Cancer chapter (page 101). From your opposite sign, Leo, you can learn how to make choices that are right for you, rather than holding to some unrealistic ideal. Making right choices comes naturally from knowing what your true values are—like how you want to live your life and what are your standards and what is your internal belief system. We all live according to our values, whether we know what they are or not. It is far better to uncover them now rather than have them trip us up later. It is all too easy to find yourself living a life that feels wrong for you or constantly self-sabotaging. If your goals are in alignment with your true values, you will always be pleased when you attain them. Life really isn't meant to be hard. Try the Define Your Values exercise in the Aries chapter (page 20). By making choices that are right for you, you will develop the emotional self-confidence to make the world a better place for the rest of humanity.

To help put you in the frame of mind for making for some radical changes, you might want to try this exercise.

The Magic of Random Belief

CHOOSE any belief that you feel will move you further forward, for example, you might choose to believe that you are great at managing money. Now run through your life to date, finding evidence that this is indeed the case. You will find some. We all find evidence to back up whatever belief we hold, so we might as well hold beliefs that propel us forward rather than hold us back.

How does embracing this new belief make you feel—more confident, more empowered, more successful, more ready to trust yourself and take risks?

Try this for other beliefs that you want to enhance, work with, investigate, or change. You might also want to experiment with beliefs that are opposed to the ones that you currently hold, to see whether you gain an enhanced understanding of or empathy with people holding those beliefs.

As a sign that has the power, communication skills, and inventiveness to change the world, you need to learn to tune into the inner voice that will guide you on your quest to make the world a better place rather than relying too heavily on group consensus. Only by knowing what you truly feel to be right, can you speak from the heart and communicate your vision to the rest of humanity. Anything less will be sterile and academic.

CHAPTER 12

PISCES

February 19–March 20

THE 12TH SIGN OF THE ZODIAC IS CONCERNED WITH:

- COMPASSION, SYMPATHY, LOVE, ALTRUISM
- DREAMS, THE PSYCHIC, PRECOGNITION, THE SIXTH SENSE
- ILLUSIONS, MAGIC, FILM, FANTASY, MAKE-BELIEVE
- ART, DRAMA, MUSIC, POETRY, PROSE, DANCE
- UNUSUAL TALENTS, MEMORY, WISDOM, VERSATILITY
- SENSITIVITY, INTUITION, HUMOR, SATIRE
- SECRETS, FULFILLMENT OF LIFE, ETERNITY

PISCES is the twelfth and final sign of the zodiac and as such brings together many of the characteristics of the eleven that have come before it. Pisceans, however, tend to keep most of these qualities well hidden, as they tend to be spiritual beings and very focused on their inner journey. They also place great weight on what they are feeling, as they are as content to live in the subterranean depths of their subconsciousness as a fish is to inhabit the depths of the ocean.

Pisces is the unworldliest of all the signs of the zodiac. Its two ruling planets, Jupiter and Neptune, rule religion and mysticism respectively, which is hardly a combination guaranteed to produce material or earthly success. Pisces is the sign most likely to withdraw from the external world into the realms of the imagination.

Emotional, sensitive, and vulnerable, Pisceans lack the hard outer shell of fellow water signs Cancer and Scorpio. Their defense against the world has, therefore, to be camouflage. Pisces is a master of disguise, blending into any group or situation by subtly masking his or her real feelings. Pisceans are true social chameleons, appearing to be part of whatever is going on but in reality drifting off into a private world of fantasy and illusion. Pisceans can use this ability to become part of the scenery to manipulate others. An ability to hide true feelings and assume a different persona means that Pisceans can excel as stars of stage and screen, politicians, and even members of the clergy—in short, anywhere where performance and ritual are involved.

Pisceans are blessed with exceptional imaginations and have the intuitive and psychic capabilities of fellow water sign Scorpio. They have to guard against picking up the psychic and emotional vibes given off by others. Those Pisceans that learn to develop practical skills are likely to use these for the benefit of others—a tendency to be too self-sacrificing can lead to Pisces being exploited.

Pisces's weakness in handling the real world can lead to chronic indecision. Pisceans have a habit of dismissing most worldly matters as unimportant and tend to fail by default. Chronic indecision can also be caused by the Piscean tendency to fall into a deep depression if they feel they aren't being heard.

Pisces is represented by a pair of fish, a symbol that prompts others to suggest that these people "go with the flow" and "don't make waves." Both of these labels are true, since Pisceans are fluid and easygoing, in keeping with the mutable quality assigned to this sign. The fact that the two fish of the Pisces glyph are swimming in opposite directions illustrates the dual nature of Pisceans, who alternate between reality and illusion.

STRENGTHS TO FOCUS ON

- Helpfulness, love, and caring
- Romantic
- Trusting
- Hospitable

- Creativity
- Mystical
- Gentle and kind
- Compassionate and understanding of others
- Vivid imagination

For help with making the most of these assets, see the S.M.A.R.T.est Goals for Aries exercise (page 3).

WEAKNESSES THAT CAN TRIP YOU UP

- Self-pitying and depressive
- Gullible and naive
- Escapist
- Shy
- Temperamental
- Dependent
- Sensationalist
- Jealous
- Can lose touch with reality
- Can become too emotionally involved with the problems of others
- Tends to blame self for everything

So how do you turn these negatives into powerful tools for personal growth? See the Love Your Weaknesses exercise in the Aries chapter (page 6).

COACH'S TIP

You have a marked tendency toward pessimism, Pisces, which leads to procrastination and lethargy. At times like this, Pisceans are well-served by taking some time out to center themselves and reconnect with their inner voice. Many Pisceans also immerse themselves in the arts and other creative pursuits in order to regain their sense of equilibrium, and they are usually talented in these areas.

PISCES MAN

Unless there are influences in his birth chart that are stronger than his Pisces sun sign, the typical Piscean male will have some or all of the following characteristics. The typical Pisces man

▶ Often goes out of his way to avoid rivalry or competition
▶ Is fatalistic
▶ Has few prejudices
▶ Is very romantic
▶ Is not ambitious for fame, status, or fortune, but will make the most of any good opportunities that come his way
▶ Is perceptive
▶ Has few material needs and doesn't mind restriction but needs his dreams
▶ Is rarely jealous, but easily hurt
▶ Tends to hide his true personality and feelings
▶ Talks slowly and is knowledgeable on many subjects

PISCES WOMAN

In addition to the personality and behavior traits exhibited by the Piscean male, Pisces woman is:

▶ Is loving, kind, and tender
▶ Needs a supportive and romantic partner
▶ Is extremely attractive to men arounding their protective instinct
▶ Has an air of mystery
▶ Is very approachable
▶ Has great charm
▶ Does not try to dominate others, including her partner, in any way
▶ Often appears vague and dreamy yet is surprisingly capable

- Reaches out to the vulnerable and the needy
- Is financially astute
- Masks her emotional vulnerability with humor or a veneer of sophistication
- Needs to be in a relationship

THE HIDDEN (OR NOT-SO-HIDDEN) PISCES

A PERSON WITH strong Piscean tendencies can soar to the top or plummet to the depths, depending on the life choices they make. This duality is symbolized by the two fish. To ensure that they rise to the top, Pisceans need to find peace and harmony, and work that will help them achieve this—acting or charity work are possibilities. Pisces is blessed with many talents that may be used to develop his or her character.

The Piscean needs to turn mystical vision into reality in order to avoid being caught up in a world of illusion and failure.

PISCES LIKES

- Being loved and romanced
- Freedom to move at his or her own pace
- Privacy
- Colorful food, especially seafood, artistically presented
- Personalized gifts wrapped in imaginative paper
- New books
- Diamonds
- Mystical settings
- Romantic places, particularly those near water
- People who need their understanding, charity, and compassion
- Background music and poetry
- Fluid, flowing, sensual clothing

PISCES DISLIKES

- Dirty, ugly places
- Loud, bright, crowded places that assault the senses
- Being told to get a grip or to "pull yourself together"
- People knowing too much about him or her
- Authorities

POSSIBLE PROBLEM AREAS FOR PISCES, AND SOLUTIONS

ALL SUN SIGNS have unique personality traits. When these traits are suppressed, problems will arise. However, with a winning combination of astrology and coaching, we can examine the problem and assess the proper solution based on sun sign characteristics. If, as a Pisces, you see things below that really strike home, try the solution. You may be amazed at the results.

PROBLEM: You find yourself being walked on or over in all manner of ways.

SOLUTION: You need to become more assertive and to articulate your requests in a nonemotional way. (Try looking at the Magnificent Seven Steps to Setting Boundaries exercise in Taurus, page 48).

PROBLEM: Never seeming to have enough money.

SOLUTION: Accept that money is important and that you need to develop a healthy relationship with it. Learn to budget.

PROBLEM: Feeling despondent and isolated.

SOLUTION: Have the courage to tell others how you are feeling and get their perspective on your situation.

PROBLEM: Causing others to be quarrelsome or to walk out on you all together.

SOLUTION: Try to be less manipulative and don't force others to meet your ideals. Accept that you cannot change others and from that position of acceptance choose whether you still want to be with them. Lighten up a little and learn to live and let live.

CAREER/BUSINESS

PISCES enjoys work that allows for freedom of expression, which usually means working alone or in an autonomous position. The emotional, dreamy Piscean has to walk a tricky tightrope as he or she balances a need for accomplishment with a desire to let imagination run free. Typically, Pisces needs work where he or she has plenty of outlets for human understanding or creative imagination. Consumed with their psychic perceptions and visits to higher planes, Pisceans tend to feel things more intensely than most, a quality that is aided by their sharp intuition. The Piscean can feel overwhelmed with information and sensory perceptions, but he or she can often appear to pull out of thin air a way of helping humanity and the universe. The Achilles heel of Pisceans may be their tendency to dally in a dream state much too long. A reality check every now and again can be helpful.

The typical Piscean does not aspire to hold an executive position and can only tolerate being part of a team if there is an opportunity for frequent changes and adaptations, as befits this sign's mutable nature.

The Pisces office is likely to be soothing and must feel comfortable. It will be large and the accommodation and furnishings will be colorful and selected for their flexibility. When the Piscean goes for a spin, a chauffeur is a must, since Pisceans would much rather dream than drive. Business luncheons are likely to be held at a seafood restaurant, near running water, and which serves organic food and wine.

PISCES CAREER GUIDE

Here are some occupations a Pisces might consider:

Advertising producer	Counselor	Poet
Actor	Criminal justice personnel	Religious leader
Art critic	Curator	Scrap dealer
Bar person	Dancer	Secret agent
Brewer	Designer	Shoe repairer
Charity worker	Illusionist	Shoemaker
Chemist	Illustrator	Social worker
Clergyman/woman	Musician	Spiritualist
Conductor	Painter	Window dresser
Costume designer	Photographer	Wine waiter
		Writer

PISCES BOSS

THE PISCEAN IS more likely to be found as a director than as a boss. Pisceans as a rule are not by nature great leaders—they are too inconsistent in temperament and better suited to a creative or conceptual role. However, that rarest of breeds, a successful Piscean boss, regards their work as a calling rather than a career. Even the toughest Piscean boss will be a strong believer in mysticism, albeit a secret one. The Piscean boss will serve people rather than accumulating power and will be a shrewd judge of character, always using his or her gifts to make the correct move. He or she will never refuse help to an employee in need.

Some Piscean bosses, however, may not be able to convince themselves that there is honor or any form of higher purpose in running a company. These fish sit behind their desks with a glum expression on their face, depressed, lazy, and useless. Beneath their surface lies uncertainty and an unwillingness to make decisions.

Despite their lack of leadership ability, Pisceans are usually well liked in the office. Their employees are generally loyal and sympathetic to this understanding and humanistic, if absentminded, boss. Pisceans are, however, very aware of their failings and tend to value those conventional employees who can cover Pisces's back and allow the fish's creative ideas to fly.

Pisces is hopeless at saying no, and therefore not very accomplished at negotiating, so beware of appealing to them directly. They will feel pressurized and taken advantage of. They may even resort to duplicity, causing resentment all around. The way to get the most out of your Piscean boss is to solve your own problems and come up with ways of turning their visions into a workable reality.

PISCES EMPLOYEE

THE PISCEAN CAN swing between two extremes as an employee. A happy Piscean who works in an attractive environment where he or she can be creative and serve humanity will be an extremely loyal worker. He or she will work with focus and efficiency on those activities that truly inspire. Although nobody knows how you operate and your timekeeping leaves a lot to be desired, Pisces, you will always manage to get the job done. As an added bonus, no employee understands their employer better than you, or contributes more to the creative vision of your company.

An unhappy or frustrated Pisces will become depressed, lazy, and totally useless—and certainly won't stick around to discuss the potential for improvement. See the Career-U-Like exercise in the Taurus chapter (page 53) to help you decide what type of company you would thrive in.

The Piscean employee is never open about their career goals—sometimes they don't even know themselves. The Define Your Values exercise in the Aries chapter (page 20) can help with this. If you know what values underpin your decisions, it is easier to set attainable goals and to avoid aimlessness and self-sabotage.

You are undemanding as an employee, expecting little in terms of material reward. In order to avoid being exploited, I would recommend that you steel yourself to do the Determine Your Value and Mining "Hidden Gold" Opportunities exercises (pages 274 and 276) from the Capricorn chapter.

FINANCES AND WEALTH

ALTHOUGH Pisceans can seem more than a little vague and unworldly, they are surprisingly good with money. Pisces does not feel compelled to make money for its own sake but for the sake of his or her dreams. The self-sacrificing and compassionate fish often feels compelled to achieve financial success for the greater good. Fortunately, Pisces is a sign that often attracts a sizable inheritance or affluent partner. Failing that, most Pisceans are blessed with gifts that can easily lead to a fortune of their own. The fish has a healthy appreciation of money and is well aware of its higher, spiritual value. Once wealthy, Pisces is in an even greater position to help those less fortunate.

You swim away from rules and restrictions, and will often opt for self-employment in a creative field. *Fortune* magazine reported that more millionaires are Pisces than any other sign. How can this be? Thank ruler Neptune, which gives you the uncanny ability to detect deficiency in anything, including the marketplace.

Pisceans have what can only be described as a relationship of extremes with their money—one day ultra-cautious, the next day ultra-generous, spending on extravagant gifts for everyone. The compassionate and caring fish cannot say no when someone asks them for a loan and, as they are not attuned to the flow of money in and out of their bank account, they'll never remember where their money went.

Your generosity makes others think, erroneously, that you don't have a self-preserving bone in your body. Are they ever wrong! Pisces's survival instincts are legendary. You are tenacious and very determined. Your powers of persuasion and empathy permit you to see the concerns of others and negotiate accordingly. You have the winning edge.

LOVE, ROMANCE, AND SEX LIFE

TO Pisces, there is no difference between love, affection, and romance, and the romantic, eager-to-please fish needs all three. An unloved Pisces is a very unhappy person for whom the world seems gray. Loves revitalizes Pisces, and the fish needs to be assured frequently of a partner's unswerving love and devotion. The dreamy Piscean—who frequently appears to be helpless, delicate, and vulnerable—copes extremely well with life's challenges, no matter how tough, with a devoted lover at their side.

Selfless, loving Pisceans will immerse themselves in a relationship, becoming so emotionally involved that they can fail to realize when a partner is treating them shabbily. The emotions of the fish run deep and can be erotic if their lover knows how to release them.

Pisces makes a wonderful mate, provided that he or she feels loved enough. However, the fish often fails to attract the supportive partner that they need. Pisceans must learn to love and value themselves before others can.

COACH'S TIP

List all the things that you feel are great about yourself. List all your accomplishments too.

Get a friend, a colleague and, if you have one, a lover to list all your accomplishments and the things that are great about yourself.

Place these lists in a prominent place and look at them on a daily basis until you realize how great and worthy of love you are.

COMPATIBILITY

Other water signs might appear to be an obvious choice for you, but Scorpio may overpower you and Cancer may be too clingy. Earth sign Capricorn is often too grounded for you, but Taurus can make a great partner, as can mutable Gemini.

WHAT PISCES NEEDS

The fish needs a partner who can draw them out and propel them toward taking action while treating them sensibly. They need to be encouraged to engage and communicate as opposed to retreating into a dream world. Pisceans also need comfort and reassurance, that level of security that enables them to feel okay about themselves and that helps them to relax and trust. The ideal partner will value their dreams, protect them from harsh criticism, and will not take advantage of them.

THE END OF THE AFFAIR

A PISCEAN CAN drift into a second relationship without even noticing, or may get different needs satisfied by different partners—this is a sign, which can compartmentalize romance(s) easily.

Many Pisces drift from affair to affair, hoping to dispel the self-doubt that can only be quelled (and then only for a short time) by repeated assurances that the fish is indeed lovable.

Pisceans can also drift out of a relationship for no apparent reason, still loving the partner (as a friend) but no longer being in love with them. Even the fish may not know the reason for the breakup.

The worst possible rejection for a Piscean is to be abandoned by a lover who no longer cares for them—ending a relationship with a Piscean requires steely resolve. Pisces will continue to cling, unable to accept that the relationship is over and convinced that if they reform in some way everything will be fine. An ex-partner of a Piscean may have to take extreme measures to extricate themselves from the emotional mess that a hurt Pisces can create.

RELATIONSHIPS
(Family and Friends)

PISCEAN PARENT

THE TYPICAL PISCEAN parent can easily accommodate all the fantasies of childhood and will allow a child plenty of imaginative freedom. They are too laid back and fluid to be strict disciplinarians and will probably be quite undisciplined when it comes to parenting. They will have a very personal and unusual set of rules to which children must adhere.

Pisces is an empathetic listener where children are concerned and is adept at understanding them. He or she will encourage personal development and is a warm and loving parent. Pisceans love children and connect with them on a deep level.

The Piscean parent rarely uses harsh words—usually the reverse, in fact—and may be guilty of spoiling their children.

Pisces Child

THE PISCES CHILD often lives in its own imaginary world, one filled with adventure and imaginary foes and friends. This youngster has a different way of relating to the outside world from the rest of us and often feels perplexed and misunderstood—surely everyone must feel as they do? For this reason, the Pisces child is likely to require more of your attention than children born under other signs.

Artistic and musical by nature, the Pisces child will love to create things that make others happy. If this activity can be carried out in the comforting company of a loving parent, all the better. This is a child who needs to belong to someone (or several someones). Compassionate Pisces often offers his or her fellows a shoulder to cry on. That said, these are very emotional kids, so they may be doing a fair bit of crying of their own. It's part of that caring and sympathetic nature of theirs, a sensibility that allows them to feel others' pain deeply. Piscean children must beware of feeling others' pain too deeply.

An introverted dreamer by nature, young Pisces can attract the unwelcome attentions of the school bully, so parents will need to be especially vigilant and teach tactics for dealing with bullying. Dreamy young fish can also have a tendency to procrastinate and drift off into a fantasy world—lessons in punctuality and getting things done cannot come a day too soon for this infant.

BRINGING UP PISCES—COACH'S INSIGHT

AT SCHOOL, YOUNG Pisces will tend to avoid the limelight and leadership, so be careful not to force him or her to embrace either. However, Pisces will be a source of wonderful ideas for play and adventure, in which he or she will be happy for others to take the lead.

Caring parents need to teach young Pisces the difference between fantasy and reality without destroying his or her rich inner life.

Emotional connections to others are essential for young Pisceans. They are far less attached to places or things, unless we are talking about living things such as animals and plants.

A Piscean child needs to be taught to stand on his or her own two feet and believe in himself or herself, as this sign can have feelings of low self-esteem and self-worth. Clinging to young Pisceans does them no good at all.

Piscean children will absorb information like sponges and convert it into rich fantasy.

Pisces needs to be taught some home truths about human nature and some clear rules of engagement to avoid being deceived when dealing with others. This can be achieved without destroying Piscean compassion and caring and may even enhance it.

Pisces also needs to be taught some simple routines and ground rules to avoid the small fry dominating the household with their changing desires.

PISCES AND FRIENDS

PISCES IS DRAWN toward friends who are useful and reassuring. In return they will give unprejudiced understanding and loyalty to their friends. Pisceans are emotionally attached to their friends and fail to notice if they are being used.

Pisces people tend to be warm, caring, and good-humored friends. They will greet you with genuine delight even if there are long periods of time between meetings.

Pisceans will always think up something interesting to do and are sufficiently in tune with people to make any social event go perfectly.

FRIENDS, BE AWARE

Pisceans can be a little confusing, which can lead to difficulties in making arrangements.

Pisces can appear to be a little self-absorbed and uninterested in you. This is due to the sign's tendency to drift off into a dream world. Normality is usually soon resumed.

Pisces does not find it easy to conform; friends with conservative outlooks will find this a trial.

Pisceans need a hero or heroine to emulate. If this is you, brace yourself for a rough ride if the fish expect you to demonstrate talents that you haven't got.

COACH'S TIP

Pisces needs to discriminate between commitment and attachment.

Commitment is when you accept a person for who they are and choose to support and be with them.

Attachment is holding onto the person because you need them and expect them to love you and care for you in your way, rather than in their natural way of expressing love.

Attachment leads to disappointment in love and is best avoided. The immature and clinging type of Piscean may mistake attachment for love and end up feeling very unhappy and unfulfilled.

HEALTH

STRESS BUSTING FOR PISCES

WHEN PISCES IS feeling the strain, he or she will withdraw from the world. The natural reaction of this sign to stress is to want to hide and hope that everyone will go away. Unfortunately for you, Pisces, you absorb others' emotions like a sponge and that includes their stress. You really need to let go of your cares like dropping a heavy backpack from your back. In fact, one stress buster that works a treat for my Piscean clients is to fill a bath with hot water, add some pink food dye (one that won't dye you or the bath) and add some rose petals. Imagine yourself placing your worries in a heavy rucksack and carrying it to the edge of the bath. Imagine the backpack slipping from your shoulders as you slowly lower yourself into the warm womb of the bath. Wallow in the bath, feeling the love of the universe recharging and refreshing you.

You are the only mutable sign of the water signs, and therefore the most flexible. Your very flexibility can give you problems when it comes to making that final decision. In order to curb your tendency to see both, or more, sides to every story, decide on an amount of time that you will devote to the decision-making process, and then set a deadline for action. Look at the decision-making exercises in the Libra chapter (page 198) and in Aries (page 10) for help with this.

Creative visualization is one of the most positive ways to deal with change, and Pisces is more adept at this than most signs. Give yourself private time every day to indulge in visualizing—and make it a playful process rather than work. Some might accuse you of escapism, but retreating into your inner world is often the best way to combat stress. Just beware of using alcohol and drugs as an escape route. Your ruler, Neptune, also rules alcohol and drugs, but that doesn't mean that you have to take them.

Pisceans can also work with their dreams to alleviate stress or shed light on difficult decisions. Make sure that your bed is nice and comfortable in order to ensure a good night's rest, Pisces.

Pisceans seem to have trouble saying no to people. When you feel drained by people's incessant demands, take private time to go to a place near water. Relax on the beach, go to a spa, or meditate by a stream to center yourself. If you can't get away, take plenty of showers or jacuzzis. Pisceans regain their sense of self by water.

Many Pisces love the movies (Neptune rules film and photography), so go to the movies for a quick pick-me-up. You might also want to unwind by taking pictures or making movies. Poetry also relaxes you. So does music, which is also ruled by Neptune, so listen to music, play it, or just dance the night away—if you can do this with an attentive lover, so much the better.

Talking of dancing, Pisces rules the feet, so treat yourself to a new pair of shoes, a pedicure or a barefoot wander through the sand.

When tense, Pisces usually does not like to cook, so head for a restaurant. Choose one that will fire your imagination and transport you to an exotic location. Try Indian, Thai, Vietnamese, or other Asian cuisine (Pisces rules the Orient), and be sure the restaurant has great ambiance. A highly visual sign, you will be affected by the environment as much as the food. If the restaurant is softly lit, even dark, and plays ethnic music, so much the better.

When you are going through a hard time, mix with people who are as sympathetic as you are. That means a fellow water sign (Cancer, Scorpio) or a serene earth sign (Taurus, Capricorn, or even Virgo, if the latter isn't too critical of you). What you need most is for someone to give you the support and confidence for you to help yourself. Biting realism will only hurt your feelings, adding to your anxiety.

Pisces is highly spiritual. Find peace in prayer and meditation either alone or on a retreat. Alternatively, go and do some volunteer work. Focusing on the plight of others usually allows you to forget your own troubles.

FITNESS

PISCES RULES THE lymphatic system, glandular system, tarsus bones, metatarsus bones, toes, feet, and gastro-intestinal system. Your metabolism is low.

Pisceans live so fully in the realm of the imagination that they often forget that they have a physical body to care for. Never very energetic physically, Pisceans must pay attention to the negative emotions that they harbor, for these have a profoundly negative effect on health. Pisces needs to find effective ways to release tension in order to thrive, and must take on board the interrelatedness of mind, body, and spirit. If any of these are diseased, the Piscean will suffer more than most.

Pisceans are very sensual, so whatever you do has to feel good— you aren't a sign who will exercise for exercise's sake. Try swimming, diving, or other water sports. If you do land-based exercises such as aerobics, make sure that you have plenty of music to distract you. You may want to get some glamorous sports gear, to help you feel good about exercise.

Dancing is an effective form of exercise and stress relief appropriate to Pisces, which rules dance. As Pisces rules the Orient, you might also want to try t'ai chi. Also, don't forget to give yourself a treat after exercising—a refreshing shower or sensual massage, perhaps.

COACH'S TIP

Use your strengths, Pisces. You are very adept at visualization, so motivate yourself to get fit by visualizing how much better life will feel when you're super-fit. If you need to lose weight, which you may do because you love the feel of food in your mouth, give yourself a goal you can visualize. Put up on the fridge a "before" photo of the way you look now, or a photo of someone whose physique you admire.

Tools for Making a Difference

PISCEANS HAVE GREAT intuitive and psychic powers that are often dimmed by a tendency not to trust themselves and to be too reliant on others. You are a person who should trust your inner voice, Pisces, for it is usually accurate. To gain more confidence in your hunches, try the Intuition Workout exercise in Cancer (page 113). You could also try affirming "I believe in me" fifteen times on getting up and going to bed for twenty-one successive days.

Pisceans do not thrive on challenge and change, yet allow themselves to be swept along by the murky undercurrents of the subconscious. In order to save themselves from depression and lethargy, they must learn to form links to the outside world rather than fearing ridicule and rejection. They must learn to share their hunches and fears with others in order to gain support and a fresh perspective—from this will come a greater sense of being able to shape their own destiny.

The Piscean also needs to find friends and lovers who will believe in and help Pisces to act on their dreams.

Pisceans must develop a better sense of humor (see the Do You Have Enough Fun? exercise in Capricorn [page 268] for this) and to learn how to open up to intimates and tell them what kind of relationship you need. In this way you can develop trust.

Experiencing Rejection in a Low-Risk Setting

HERE is a simple exercise to help you get comfortable with risking and dealing with rejection. For this exercise I am going to ask you to experience rejection in a nonthreatening and fun environment.

I want you to go out on the street and ask fifty people a question that they are bound to reject (Note: Make sure you have an answer ready if they accept). For instance, "Can I persuade you to donate $1,000 to (choose your favorite charity here)?" Make sure you persist until you have a yes/no reply. You could try, "Will you sponsor me $100 to become a successful actor?" You can build this up, starting with a nonpersonal question/rejection, followed by personal but silly questions/rejections, followed by direct personal questions/ rejections in order to develop your ability to take risks and face rejection.

Pisceans have two powerful choices in life: They can choose self-realization or self-denial, to swim forward or to drift backward. In order to keep moving onward and upward, you must counteract apathy by having clearly defined, realistic long- and short-term goals. You must then persist in reaching them.

In order to avoid escapism, Pisceans need to engage with the outside world, either by establishing a routine or by having supportive friends. They also need to develop a healthy degree of self-care. Doing what feels good is not selfish—you need to look after yourself before you can attempt to look after others.

SPIRITUALITY

PISCEANS allow themselves to be drained by many professional and personal situations. They need to protect themselves by developing boundaries and developing the Virgoan traits of analysis, mental detachment, clear goal setting, and rational thought. In this way they can take the positive route through life and stick to it. Pisceans can help themselves develop more persistence by engaging in tasks that enhance their belief in their ability to perform and deliver.

Pisces's spiritual goal is to find an outlet for its psychic, healing, and artistic powers so that it may find peace through serving others. The Piscean needs to find those who will value what he or she has to offer and who will ensure that the dreamy Piscean brings their talents to bear on the physical world rather than living in a state of reverie.

Pisceans want to see the whole picture, which can make focusing a challenge. They can become overwhelmed by the level of detail they pick up, leading to obsession instead of rational decision. Pisceans need to develop the Virgoan traits of attention to detail and practicality in order to manifest their dreams.

With your ability to tap into higher spiritual realms and the collective unconscious, Pisces, you can, at your best, bring the wonders of the spiritual realm to earth, possibly through films or music. At your worst and most disconnected from higher consciousness, you drift aimlessly, your vision clouded by mental fog. Negative energies from others or too much self-sacrifice can cut you off from the connectedness that you need to feel comfortable and thrive, so do take care to establish boundaries. Once you are connected to a higher power, you feel supported and sure of yourself as you go with the flow.

CHAPTER 13

HOW TO HAVE YOUR
BEST YEAR EVER

TWO QUESTIONS:

1. MADE ANY NEW YEAR'S RESOLUTIONS THIS YEAR?
2. WANT TO KEEP THEM?

WE often think of New Year's as the time to start anew and make those famous resolutions. We force ourselves to start fresh on January 1 and know, in our hearts, that we are just setting ourselves up for failure. Could there really be a worse date for embarking on a course of restraint and radical overhauls than immediately after we've got used to lazing around and overindulging?

Immediately after any long break, I can guarantee my telephone will be ringing nonstop with people who want to start fresh, to change everything about their lives. I always give them a week's breathing period and, guess what, most of them slip back into normality with practiced ease. A long break during which we totally unwind, followed by the sinking feeling of returning to normality and responsibility, causes most of us to feel deeply unhappy. This does not mean that we are really unhappy or that major changes need to be made; we are merely experiencing resistance to change. This syndrome is at its worst at New Year's, when everything takes a while to get going again and boredom thrives. You are practically guaranteed to think your life needs a radical makeover when really it's fine.

Far better to choose a date that works for you to begin to design and live the life you want. You may choose to do this:

- After New Year's—having ridden the wave of New Year's resolutions
- When you've hit bottom—no place to go but up
- At the spring equinox—the burgeoning of new life, plants, animals, ideas
- Today—the beginning of the rest of your life
- Whenever an old door shuts—it's time to open a new one
- At the new moon—a time for expansion and growth
- Whenever you realize you've made a mistake
- Best of all, your birthday—the start of your own personal annual cycle

For most of us, our birthday is much, much more significant than the new year. It is that special day on which we were brought into this glorious world. It is a day on which we should give ourselves a pat on the back, celebrate our accomplishments, buy ourselves something really special, treat ourselves like the special person that we are, and generally celebrate our birthday with as much ceremony as possible. A birthday is a day for rejoicing, and for many of us a natural time for reflection. On our birthdays we will often reflect upon how far we've come and the ways things have turned out. We may feel that we've accomplished all that we wanted to and that our lives are going according to plan. We may feel supremely fortunate and that we've had many lucky breaks. Alternatively, we may feel extremely dissatisfied with our lives—that we've not lived up to our potential—particularly as we reach our thirties.

If this is the case, our birthday becomes a natural date on which to start to take control of our future. We can't rewrite the past, but we can still create a bright and glorious future. We can choose how we will live. Real success in life is about balance, about choosing priorities and then following a plan to focus on the things that are most important to us. Here are some actions you can take to create a great new year.

1. Accept that there are some resolutions that you are not going to stick to this year and don't waste time on these. If you continually have to struggle and force yourself to do something, you are paying a high price for progress. Relax and let go. Tackle this particular resolution when the time is right (usually when you're more motivated).
2. Take time to decide what you really want this year. What would make it a great year, a fantastic year, for you? Dream and scheme, and then dream bigger. And write it down, just for the fun of it. Create a vision for the future that pulls you forward—a bright future that you can't wait to create and enjoy.
3. Decide what sort of person you want to be and what you want your life to be about. To help with this part of the exercise, do the Define Your Values exercise in Aries (page 20), if you haven't already done so.

Now I'm going to introduce a process that will help you to set goals that flow naturally from your values and wants:

1. Take some time to identify what matters most to you. Write a list of words that express these things (love, money, happiness, freedom, etc.).
2. Now, make a list of the various roles you play in your life (for example, wife, author, columnist, speaker, coach, daughter, etc.).
3. Go back through these two lists, and draw a ring around the most important values and roles—aim for around seven (for example, freedom, happiness, author, coach, love, daughter, and wife).
4. Choose one of the values or roles on your shortlist to be your primary focus for the year. This doesn't mean that you won't spend a lot of time on the others, just that you will spend extra time on this one.

5. For each of the values and roles on your shortlist, make a list of what you would want in this area if you could just wave a magic wand and make it so. When you have finished, go back through your lists and ask yourself, "What would be even better than that?"

6. Now choose one or more wants from each list and turn it into a goal for the year. For example,
   Role: wife
   Want: to spend more quality time with my husband
   Goal for 200X: to take at least two romantic vacations a year. Not to take my laptop on vacation with me

7. Choose your top ten goals for 200X, prioritized in the order of their importance.

8. Now—draw up a plan to achieve these goals. Break each goal down into mini goals to help you stay motivated.

9. Take action—start to achieve these mini goals.

10. Keep a diary—tick off each goal as you achieve it. This builds positive feedback and momentum.

As you look through your list of goals, make up some beliefs (make believe = make beliefs) that will support you in their achievement. Remember, you can make a belief real in your life by acting as if it is true and by focusing on any evidence you can find, no matter how small, that it is operating in your life or in the world.

Here are some of my favorite and most supportive "make believes":

- I create what I want in my life.
- Creating what I want in my life will be easy and fun
- The more fun I have going for what I want, the more effective I will be in getting what I want
- My destiny is revealed to me in my most heartfelt desires
- I am enough
- I am complete—there is nothing I need to be, do, or have

Feel free to adapt these "make beliefs" to make them work for you.

Good luck and welcome to a bright new future!

Measure Your Progress

A further reason why the resolutions we make in January are broken by March is that we just don't bother to measure our progress.

Imagine running a marathon with no watch. How would you know when to speed up and when to conserve your energy? You could try to gauge your performance against the other runners, but you would never really know how you were doing, only if you were doing better or worse than them. If they were terrible, your being better might cause you to become arrogant and complacent. If they were absolutely wonderful, your being worse might cause you to give up, when in truth, you have everything it takes to complete the course. The fact is, if you don't keep score as you go, you don't have any yardstick against which to gauge your performance. If you don't have a marker to measure performance against, you don't have any way of knowing when it's time to change your strategy and do something different.

In coaching, we teach a simple and obvious success formula:

1. Know your outcome (goal)
2. Notice where you are in relation to your goal
3. Adjust your behavior accordingly

It is in step two, being able to determine at any time whether you are on track to reaching your goals, that creating a meaningful marker for success becomes so useful.

Let's take two examples.

If you are running a marathon, what yardstick might be useful to measure your performance? Many successful runners create ideal times for each segment of the race. If you want to run your marathon in under two hours, you know you have to average no more than four minutes and forty seconds per mile. At any point during the race you know whether you need to speed up or can afford to conserve your energy in pursuit of your goal.

When I coach salespeople, I encourage them to create a personal scorecard to measure their performance. In a field like consultancy, where it can take twelve months or more to complete one major sale, this becomes absolutely essential. Here's a sample "yardstick" from my days as an executive search consultant:

- Dial the phone—one point
- Get through to the person I want to speak with—two points
- Keep them on the phone for more than a minute—three points
- Get through my entire pitch—four points
- Send out a job description and application form (assignment brief)—five points
- Get further leads to contact—six points

In the example above, I decided to set a personal target of seventy points a day. Instead of waiting until I had found someone who wanted to receive an assignment brief to get any sense of progress, I was able to track my performance every step of the way.

Now it's your turn. This week, experiment with creating a yardstick by which you can measure your own ongoing progress in pursuit of your goals. Here's how you do it.

1. What are the key stepping-stones on the way to your goal? These can take the form of "mini goals."
   Example: quitting smoking
   Possible mini goals: cutting down to one pack a day, cutting down to 19 cigarettes a day, 18, 17, etc.
2. What is the relative value or optimal sequence of steps that you feel will keep you motivated and on track?
   Example one: optimal sequence: one pack a day, less than a pack a day, fifteen a day, ten a day, five a day, one a day, none (success!)
   Example two: relative value: buy a pack without smoking it all—one point, put a cigarette out before I finish it—two points, put a cigarette in my mouth without lighting it—three points, get a craving and ignore or redirect it—four points, go an hour without thinking about it—five points

3. Last, but by no means least, create a chart, journal, or computer file in which to track your progress.

Great job! You've finished the book and come to the realization that coaching is an ongoing program and that to keep up the progress you have already made, you need to stay with it. You can keep using the tools in this book to enable you to work on whichever areas of your life you need to concentrate on to stay fulfilled and balanced. By balanced I mean equally fulfilled in each area of your life rather than allocating equal amounts of time and effort to each area.

THE WHEEL OF LIFE

TO help get my point across I'm going to introduce you to one of the concepts we use in coaching, which is called The Wheel of Life.

The Wheel of Life has two purposes.

1. It helps you to look at which areas of your life may be causing you difficulty, where you may be experiencing stress.
2. It offers the opportunity of looking at how you can make the ride smoother (less bumpy), so that life gets easier.

To create your own Wheel of Life, I want you to draw a circle with eight spokes running from the center to the perimeter, dividing the wheel into eight equal segments. Assign one of the following labels to each spoke:

- Physical environment
- Health
- Finances
- Friends and family
- Work
- Partner/Relationships
- Fun/Recreation
- Spirituality/Personal development

Now imagine that each spoke is scaled between 0 and 10, where 0 (at the center) is lousy and 10 (at the outer rim) is perfection. What I would like you to do is to rank the level of each spoke, in terms of how personally fulfilled, contented, happy, and satisfied you feel with your life, by marking a point at each spoke at the position that represents what feels right for you.

Join the points together with straight lines, as shown in the diagram below. This new shape graphically represents your current Wheel of Life.

So what does your Wheel of Life look like?

◆ What is the overall balance of the shape?
◆ How in balance is each area with the others?
◆ Are there any imbalances that concern you?
◆ What goals might you need to have, what action would you want to take, to encourage your wheel to become bigger and smoother?

The best way to work with this exercise, on an ongoing basis, is to repeat it on a weekly basis to see how each area averages out. If there are frequent fluctuations in a particular segment, it may indicate that there are problems that you are not dealing with in that area of your life. Your overall objective is to get the shape of your life to match that of the perfectly balanced Wheel itself—your ideal shape would be an octagon perfectly aligned with the spokes of the Wheel.

If you score highly in areas, make sure that you don't become complacent. Continue to set goals for yourself in that area, continue to develop new skills, and remember to record, and congratulate yourself on, your achievements. Should you run into problems in a particular area, begin to work on them immediately. Remember not to let a high scoring area lose points by becoming complacent. The aim is too keep your score in all areas as high as possible.

When you review your Wheel of Life at the end of each week, spend a few minutes listing the actions that you have taken toward accomplishing your goals. Remind yourself of which goals you have set yourself for each category. If you find that your score is slipping in any section, set yourself some specific tasks, for the following week, to rectify this.

One of the most exciting aspects of the exercise is that you will find that improvements in one area of your life will improve other areas. You get more results than you initially expected for your efforts—a great motivator.

THE WHEEL OF LIFE

An Example

THE WHEEL OF LIFE is explained in the following diagram, which provides a template and three examples. As earlier, the Wheel is divided into the following eight segments:

1. Physical environment
2. Health
3. Finances
4. Friends and family
5. Work
6. Partner/Relationships
7. Fun/Recreation
8. Spirituality/Personal development

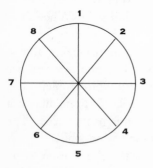

The first circle is a blank template. It is there to be filled in with your view of your life as it currently is experienced, ranked against each of the eight qualities. The wheel can be hand-drawn or rendered using a computer graphics application. The latter option gives great flexibility in modifying the Wheel as things move on due to your efforts and increasing ability to harmonize all elements of your experience—it is a great way to measure progress. Many clients find it useful to use colors to add vibrancy and personal meaning to the Wheel.

The second circle represents the Wheel as it may be for some of you now. It is clear that some areas are emphasized at the expense of others. This person is very focused on work, to the exclusion of much else. Their finances are strong, but there is a negative effect on their health, family, and relationships and other important areas of their lives. This could be an entrepreneur focused on building a business or a corporate high flyer, or simply a quintessential workaholic. There is a clear danger of burn/stress out in this unbalanced lifestyle, but the strong financial situation will at least finance private health care or a coffin of the highest quality.

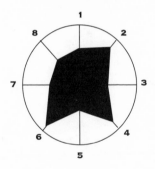

The third circle shows a more harmonious balance, with work still important but not emphasized at the expense of the other qualities. Finances are still very strong, and health and quality of life has improved noticeably. Work of course does not necessarily mean paid work. If finances are strong, traditional employment may be unnecessary, but work refers to the way time is spent in creative or other enterprises that keep the mind fresh and vital, providing the social interactions and sense of meaning and purpose that most of us require.

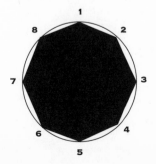

The fourth circle shows an ideal balance, harmonizing all elements of the wheel and creating a perfect Octagon, Maslow's self-actualized individual.

Some of the goals that you set yourself will seem an uphill battle. That's fine, trust in the coaching process, and yourself, and you will attain them. The coaching process covered in this book can be summed up in the acronym GROW.

GOALS: The goals you set yourself
REALITY: Your current situation. You may need to revise your goals in the light of this
OPTIONS: What options are open to you for attaining your goals?
WILL: What action will you take to attain your goals?

And with that formula in mind, let me wish you every success with your star sign life coaching program. I hope that the techniques contained in this book become an invaluable part of your everyday life.

RESOURCES

If you wish to take your interest in astrology further, contact:

UNITED STATES
American Federation of Astrologers
PO Box 22040
Tempe, AZ 85285-2040
Tel: (888) 301-7630
Web site: www.astrologers.com

Association for Astrological Networking
8306 Wilshire Blvd.
Suite 537
Beverley Hills, CA 90211
Web site: www.afan.org

The American Council of Vedic Astrology
PO Box 2149
Sedona, AZ 86339
Tel: (928) 282-6595
E-mail: acva@sedona.net

National Council for Geocosmic Research
PO Box 38866
Los Angeles, CA 90038
Tel: (818) 705-1678
Web site: www.geocosmic.org
Oregon Astrological Association
PO Box 6771
Portland, OR 97228

Tel: (503) 246-3714
Web site: www.oregonastrology.com

Washington State Astrological Association
PO Box 5386
Seattle, WA 98145
Web site:
    www.washingtonastrologers.com

San Diego Astrological Society
5521 Ruffin Road
San Diego, CA 92123
Tel: (888) 405-6825
Web site: www.sandiegoastrology.com

The Astrological Society of Connecticut
PO Box 290346
Wethersfield, CT 06129
Tel: (860) 568-8617

CANADA

Astrology Toronto Inc.
4 Caracas Road
Toronto, Ontario
Canada M2K 1A9
Tel: (416) 930-9287
Web site: www.astrology-toronto-
    inc.com

Astrology Montreal
6 Harwood Avenue
Roxboro, Quebec
Canada H8Y 2W2
Tel: (514) 684-7164
Web site:
  www.astrologymontreal.com

The Frazer Valley Astrological Guild
PO Box 833
Fort Langley, British Columbia
Canada V1M 2S2
Tel: (604) 888-9579´
Web site: www.astrologyguild.com

Edmonton Astrological Society
66-07-92 B Avenue
Edmonton, Alberta
Canada T6B OV8
E-mail: cmcra@compusmart.ab.ca

Vancouver Society of Astrologers
#8 1786 Esquimalt Avenue
West Vancouver, British Columbia
Canada V7V 1R8
Tel: (604) 926-9027
E-mail: warwickdiana@hotmail.com

For those of you interested in coach
training, contact:

International Coach Federation
www.coachfederation.org
The largest international professional
  coach organization

Coach University
www.coachu.com

Coachville
www.thomasleonard.com
(for online and telephone-based coach
  training and referrals)

Cosmic Coaching
(The author's personal site)
www.cosmiccoaching.com
E-mail: info@cosmiccoaching.com

RECOMMENDED READING

ASTROLOGY

Arroyo, Stephen. *Astrology, Karma and Transformation*. California: CRCS
   Publications, 1978.
Birkbeck, Lyn. *Do It Yourself Astrology*. Shaftesbury, England: Element Books,
   1996.
Birkbeck, Lyn. *Do It Yourself Lifeplan Astrology*. Shaftesbury, England:
   Element Books, 2000.
Birkbeck, Lyn. *Do It Yourself Relationship Astrology*. Shaftesbury,
   England: Element Books, 1999.
Cope, Lloyd. *Your Stars Are Numbered*. Shaftesbury, England:
   Element Books, 1999.
Olesky, Rio. *Astrology & Consciousness*. Tempe, Arizona: New Falcon Publica-
   tions, 1995.
Sasportas, Howard. *The Twelve Houses*. London: Thorsons, 1998
Spiller, Jan. *Astrology for the Soul*. New York: Bantam Books, 1997.

COACHING

Bridges, William. *Creating Your Own Company: Learn to Think Like the CEO
   of Your Own Career*. London: Perseus Books, 1998.
Lansberg, Max. *The Tao of Coaching*. London: HarperCollins UK, 1996.
Leonard, Thomas. *The Portable Coach*. New York: Scribner, 1998.
Richardson, Cheryl. *Take Time for Your Life*. New York: Bantam Books, 1998.
Robbins, Anthony. *Unlimited Power*. London: Simon and Schuster, 1988.
Robbins, Anthony. *Awaken the Giant Within*. London: Simon and Schuster, 1992.
Sylver, Marshall. *Passion, Profit and Power*. New York: Simon and Schuster, 1995

INDEX